HAITI
RENEWED

ROBERT I. ROTBERG

Editor

HAITI RENEWED

Political and Economic Prospects

BROOKINGS INSTITUTION PRESS
Washington, D.C.

THE WORLD PEACE FOUNDATION
Cambridge, Massachusetts

Library of Congress Cataloging-in-Publication Data

Haiti renewed: political and economic prospects / Robert I. Rotberg, editor.
    p. cm.
    Includes bibliographical references and index.
    ISBN 0-8157-7586-5
    1. Haiti—Politics and government—1986- 2. Democracy—Haiti.
3. Haiti—Economic policy. I. Rotberg, Robert I.
JL1090.H35 1997
972.9407'3—dc21   97-4623
                                   CIP

9 8 7 6 5 4 3 2 1

The paper used in this publication meets the minimum requirements of the American National Standard for Information Sciences— Permanence of Paper for Printed Library Materials. ANSI Z39.48-1984

Typeset in Times Roman

Composition by Linda Humphrey
Arlington, Virginia

Printed by R. R. Donnelley and Sons Co.
Harrisonburg, Virginia

Contents

Preface: Haiti's Last Best Chance

Robert I. Rotberg

THE ECSTATIC election of charismatic President Jean-Bertrand Aristide in 1990, his American-supported restoration to office in 1994, and the peaceful election in 1995 of President René Préval collectively were harbingers of a radically new and promising era in Haitian political and economic life. For the first time in Haiti's 190-year-old independent tradition, men of and chosen by the majority of Haiti's people had gained power and attained their positions legally and peacefully.

Aristide and Préval are populists, with agendas as leaders that are much more forward looking than those of any of their predecessors, especially the three-decade-long dictatorships of François and Jean-Claude Duvalier and the several military juntas that followed the Duvaliers (and interrupted Aristide's presidency). Préval has the opportunity, rarely afforded to his predecessors, of reconstructing and remolding the Haitian state, raising Haitian living standards, and creating a new political culture of democracy and tolerance. The modern future of his country, and the success of Haiti's last best chance to break its chains of poverty, desperation, and deprivation, depend on the choices that he and his colleagues make during his five-year term of office.

The context of those choices is stark. Haiti remains the poorest and least industrialized nation in the Western Hemisphere. Two-thirds of its 7 million citizens live below the national poverty level. In 1985 its official GNP per capita was a paltry $242; the Dominican Republic, next door on Hispaniola, boasted a per capita GNP in the same year of $1,230. Honduras, the second least-advantaged country in the Americas, had a per capita GNP in 1995 of $600, and Jamaica $1440. In Africa, Haiti's per capita GNP compares with Mozambique's ($100), Malawi's ($322), and Zimbabwe's ($520).[1]

Haiti, at 27,560 square kilometers, is approximately the size of Maryland. It has long been among the most densely populated countries in the world. Since less than 20 percent of Haiti is still arable, densities on arable land are even higher, and have approached Javan levels.[2] In 1995, Haiti counted 2,605 persons per 1,000 hectares. The figure for the Dominican Republic was much smaller—1,617 per 1,000. Cuba's density is 671 per 1,000, Honduras's 505, and Nicaragua's 373. Only Jamaica (2,259) and some of the smaller island nations of the Caribbean have comparable densities.

Seventy percent of Haiti's population is rural and is dependent almost entirely on subsistence or cash cropping. But agriculture contributes only about 30 percent to GDP. Most peasant holdings are small, too, with farms of a hectare being considered large. Only 4 percent of all farms are more than five hectares in size. For such structural reasons, and because of acute soil erosion and farming techniques that are less advanced than any in the Western Hemisphere, Haitian crop yields per arable hectare (rice, maize, and beans for subsistence and coffee, sugar, and sisal for cash) are low. Haiti has been a net importer of food since the 1980s; in the mid-1990s, 10 percent of all Haitians were fed daily by international aid organizations. Simultaneously, rural average per capita incomes have continued to decline through the 1980s and 1990s.

Haiti was once heavily forested. The gathering of fuel wood and the clearing of forested land for crops denuded the hillsides and mountain slopes and has led to severe erosion. Haitian forested land has been reduced from 68,000 acres in the 1970s to 35,000 acres in 1992—or 4 percent of the total land mass. The World Bank estimates that 6,000 hectares of topsoil a year are lost to erosion.[3]

Haiti's population is growing at approximately 2 percent a year, a rate that has been steady for about two decades. That rate is lower than the rate of many of the countries in Central America, but higher than that of Jamaica.[4] Strikingly, however, the rate of contraceptive prevalence is a very low 9 percent, compared to more than 60 percent in Costa Rica and Cuba, 35 percent in Honduras, and 52 percent in the Dominican Republic.[5]

Population growth clearly has been moderated by mortality rates that are higher than in other countries of the Western Hemisphere. Life expectancy is a low 57 years, compared to the Dominican Republic's 70 years, Honduras's 68, and Costa Rica's 76. Infant mortality rates in Haiti exceed 84 per 1,000, down from 500 in 1970. But Haiti's rate is more than double the Dominican Republic's and Honduras's (40 and 41 per 1,000, respectively), and seven times higher than that of Costa Rica and Jamaica (14 per 1000). A 1996 survey by the Institut Haitian pour l'Enfance reported that 13 percent of Haitian children die before age 5, 37 percent from diarrheal diseases and 32 percent from malnutrition.[6]

As these figures hint, Haiti had 1 physician for about each 11,000 persons, more than Malawi's 1 per 17,000 but ten times less than the Costa Rican and five times less than the Nicaraguan and Jamaican ratios. With many fewer births (20 percent) being attended by a trained physician in Haiti as compared to those in Honduras (81 percent), Nicaragua (73 percent), and the Dominican Republic (92 percent), it is no wonder that the maternal mortality rate is 6 per 1,000 births.[7]

Malnutrition and morbidity persist in contemporary Haiti. The World Bank estimated in 1994 that fully half of Haiti's population had a caloric intake below 75 percent of minimum daily requirements; 25 percent of children exhibited signs of malnutrition—kwashiorkor, marasmus, and other conditions. From 1988 to 1990 the average Haitian caloric intake was slightly more than 2,000, considerably less than that in Cuba, Costa Rica, the Dominican Republic, and even Honduras.[8] The average U.S. caloric intake is 3,642 a day.

Not surprisingly, measles, meningitis, rabies, and anthrax are common in Haiti. Fewer than half of all children are inoculated against tuberculosis, and fewer than a third are protected against diphtheria. AIDS has become the primary cause of hospitalization in Haiti.

Haitians lack access to potable water and reliable energy. In 1992, only 1.5 percent of the population had piped water; 29 percent are said to have access to potable water from natural sources.[9]

Port-au-Prince, the nation's capital, received electricity only about six hours each day during 1995. Nationally, Haiti has one of the lowest per capita consumption rates of energy in the world—the equivalent of 47 kg of oil.[10] Average citizens of the Dominican Republic consume seven times as much energy (340 kg). In Honduras, energy consumption is the equivalent of 1,096 kg. Even during the rainy season, Haiti's hydroelectric plants generate only 199 megawatts of power, a sixth of the total generated in the Dominican Republic.

Only 8 Haitians per 1,000 have a telephone. Businesses use radio or satellite communication facilities, and many businesses have their own power-generating equipment. Only 5 households per 1,000 own a television set, compared to 62 in Nicaragua, 72 in Honduras, and 149 in Costa Rica.[11]

Electricity is in short supply, and so are paved roads and other infrastructural necessities. In 1989 Haiti had 3,200 km of roads but only 600 km were paved. In 1995 it was estimated that there were 4,000 km of roads in Haiti with 950 km paved, but only a fifth of the roads were adequately maintained.

During the 1970s and 1980s the growth of Haiti's manufacturing economy was able to absorb a large proportion of population increases and unemployment caused by declining agricultural productivity. After the death of President François Duvalier in 1971, small-scale assembly operations were introduced into Port-au-Prince by Americans and Canadians. They stitched baseballs and other sporting goods and produced inexpensive textiles, footwear, and electronic parts. Wages were low, and the dictatorship of Jean-Claude Duvalier prohibited trade unions. At the end of the 1970s, industrial output grew at 10 percent per year and GDP by 5 percent a year.[12]

After the second Duvalier was forced into exile in 1986, political leadership disintegrated into a succession of unstable military juntas, and many of the assembly plants transferred their operations to the Dominican Republic and other island states of the Caribbean. About 150,000 jobs were lost. In 1996, formal unemployment rates were at least 50 percent, and skilled labor was in short supply.

From 1986 to 1996, with a severe dip during the embargo period from 1991 to 1994, GDP fell drastically. During the first four years of the 1990s it fell by an accumulated 31 percent.[13] In 1995, heavy external assistance produced a GDP increase of 4.5 percent, but Haiti's GDP was still below the peak levels of 1980–1985. Legal exports fell from $202 million in 1991 to $57 million in 1994. Illicit drug smuggling may have made up some of the difference, but no figures are available.

If Haiti under Préval remains politically stable and democratic—two conditions that have never prevailed together in its history—the country's reconstruction can begin to make progress. But widespread poverty, the lack of urban jobs and rural sources of income, severe infrastructural and health deficits, rising urban crime rates, and continued population increases will act as severe brakes on even the most dedicated and innovative efforts of national reconstruction.

Furthermore, Haiti continues to suffer from a critical shortage of human capital. Illiteracy is still severe. In the early 1970s the country was believed to be 90 percent illiterate. In the 1990s, estimates range from 47 to 85 percent illiterate. No other country in the Western Hemisphere, and only a few in the world (for example, Ethiopia, Afghanistan, and Mozambique) have such high rates of illiteracy among adults. For Honduras the figure is 27 percent and in the Dominican Republic, 17 percent.

Haiti and Nicaragua have the lowest primary school enrollment rates in the hemisphere at 56 and 52 percent, respectively, of potential students. But Honduras has 82 percent of its prospective students enrolled, and the rates in most other countries are higher. Secondary and tertiary rates are also much lower in Haiti than elsewhere in the Hemisphere.[14]

The Préval government thus has much to do, which is what this book is about. If the government succeeds in making the economy of the country grow and providing greater employment opportunities in manufacturing, if it manages rapidly to open up and privatize the economy, if it can ensure increased security from crime, and if it begins to accumulate more than 6 percent of GDP (1995) in government revenues, then it can begin to spend more on basic services and lift up the least well off of its impoverished citizens. Foreign aid currently accounts for about two-thirds of government expenditures and may not continue at that level.

The chapters that follow in this book, including the introduction by Jennifer McCoy that reviews and frames the results of the original conference, provide an agenda for Préval and his successors. It is hardly a complete agenda, but it is a full one that considers both Haiti's political culture—its historical legacy and what that means for future reconstruction—and many of its most critical current political, economic, and social challenges.

In this book's first two chapters, Patrick Bellegarde-Smith and Michel-Rolph Trouillot present sophisticated arguments about the relevance of Haiti's past to its democratic future. Mats Lundahl reviews Haiti's economic history and explains how it has remained mired in poverty for so long. Donald Schultz examines the Haitian experience with state terror, coercion, and dictatorship. Robert Pastor's chapter is about Jean-Bertrand Aristide's interrupted presidency, his restoration to power, and the elections of 1995 and 1996. Robert Fatton focuses on the meaning of Aristide's presidency in terms of Haitian history. Robert Maguire discusses the new leaders of Haiti and the challenges that they have endured and will need to manage.

Michel Laguerre's chapter is about the contribution of Haitians in the diaspora and their role in contemporary Haitian politics. Clive Gray and Anthony Catanese offer alternative models for Haiti's economic growth and reconstruction. William O'Neill's chapter is about the judicial system and judicial reform. Marc Prou writes about the Haitian educational deficit and how it can be ameliorated.

This book derives (although all of the chapters are substantially revised and some are brand new) from a conference in Mayagüez, Puerto Rico, in 1995. It was a collaborative effort of the Haitian Studies Association of the United States, the University of Puerto Rico, and the World Peace Foundation. It was also supported in part by the U.S. Army War College and the Ford Foundation, for whose assistance the sponsors express great gratitude. Several members of the staff of the Haitian Studies Association, especially Alix Cantave, and of the University of Puerto Rico, especially Ann Howard de Tristani, contributed significantly to the conference and thus to this book. The staff of the World Peace Foundation, especially Ann Hannum, who managed the mammoth task of editing the volume, also contributed in major ways to its final production. Any of this book's positive outcomes are a tribute to all of those who participated in the conference as well as those who took part in the lengthy production of the book.

Notes

1. World Bank, *Trends in Developing Economies, 1995* (Washington, D.C., 1995), 148, 232, 236, 257, 322, 372, 575. For an earlier era in Haiti, see Robert I. Rotberg, *Haiti: The Politics of Squalor* (Boston, 1971), 9. Staci Warden provided substantial research support for this preface. Her assiduous efforts are gratefully acknowledged.
2. See Rotberg, *Haiti*, 12.
3. International Development Association (IDA) memorandum, June 1996.
4. United Nations, *Statistical Yearbook for Latin America and the Caribbean* (New York, 1994).
5. World Resources Institute, et al., *World Resources: A Guide to the Global Environment* (New York, 1996), 197.
6. United Nations, *Yearbook*; *Caribbean Insight*, XIX (April 1996), 8. For the 1970 figure, see Rotberg, *Haiti*, 11.
7. IDA memorandum. Some of the IDA and World Bank figures do not agree with the estimates employed at the World Peace Foundation's 1995 conference or with the numbers used in Jennifer McCoy's introduction (originally the report of the conference).

8. *Statistical Abstract of Latin America* (Los Angeles, 1995), XXXI, table 824; Economist Intelligence Unit (EIU), *Haiti* (London, 1995), 37.

9. EIU, *Haiti*, 37. See also World Bank, *Trends in Developing Economies, 1995*, 233.

10. World Bank, *Trends in Developing Economies*, 233; EIU, *Haiti*, 43.

11. *Statistical Abstract*, table 824.

12. IDA memorandum.

13. EIU, *Haiti*, 39.

14. United Nations, *Statistical Yearbook*; World Bank, *Trends in Developing Economies, 1995*, 233.

HAITI
RENEWED

Introduction: Dismantling the Predatory State—The Conference Report

Jennifer L. McCoy

FOR NEARLY 200 years Haiti was a classic predatory state. The state preyed on its people without providing political or economic goods. Lacking accountability, governments used their power to destroy rather than to create. The task in the late 1990s is to dismantle the remnants of the predatory regime, replacing it with a humane, democratic government that can respond to the needs of the nation, alleviating poverty and hunger, creating the basis for sustained economic growth and development, and providing justice and security for all.

To meet this challenge, the Haitian government and society must tackle daunting tasks:

—Create a unified national identity and forge a new social contract between the state and the nation.

—Revive the economy and reduce inequality, poverty, and violence, which impede growth.

—Reconceptualize the state and the division of responsibilities between the public and private spheres.

—Create a secure environment and justice for all.

—Nurture a democratic political culture and develop universal respect for the rule of law.

Achieving these goals will not be easy. At its independence in 1804 Haiti was a proud country, the first in Latin America and the Caribbean to achieve its independence, the first black republic in the world, and the

1

jewel of the colonial Caribbean economy. Today, Haiti is the poorest nation in the hemisphere, with an average annual income of less than $250; it is denuded of forests and soil; and it has a dense population that has been oppressed for decades by a small group of elites and the military.

Flying over the border between Haiti and the Dominican Republic, its neighbor on the island of Hispaniola, one sees a visible line where the lush green mountaintops of the Dominican Republic end and the bald mountains of Haiti begin. Stripped of trees by a population dependent on wood for charcoal fuel and cleared land for farming, the soil has gradually eroded to leave the mountaintops bare. Each year, the equivalent of 6,000 hectares (almost 15,000 acres) of land is lost to erosion, its soil carried pell-mell to the sea. Forest cover has been severely depleted in over 97 percent of Haiti. In a country where nearly 70 percent of the population lives in the rural sectors, the combination of rapid population growth and soil destruction has increased the already high rural population density on arable land and threatened the very existence of peasant agriculture.

Human security in Haiti is dangerously weak. The United Nations Development Program (UNDP) reports that life expectancy at birth is only fifty-six years, compared with seventy-six in Costa Rica and the United States. Fifteen percent of children die before the age of five. In 1993, the last year statistics were available, three-quarters of the Haitian population lived in absolute poverty, half lacked access to health services, 60 percent lived without safe drinking water, and 75 percent lacked sanitation facilities. More than half the population cannot read or write.

The physical infrastructure of the cities has also decayed in the face of financial constraints, which intensified from 1991 to 1994, swollen urban populations, and environmental degradation. The Inter-American Development Bank reports that less than 40 percent of the water needs of the capital are being met and that erratic gathering and disposal of solid waste in Port-au-Prince and Cap Haitien contribute to deplorable sanitation conditions. Roads and infrastructure in urban and rural Haiti are damaged by soil erosion and poor watershed management.

Finally, Haiti is a country of extreme political polarization, class divisions, and fractured national identity. Each inhibits the attainment of collective goals. The judicial system is nonexistent; the prison system is overcrowded and inhumane. Order and security depend on an international force that is scheduled to depart in mid-1997, leaving a potentially dangerous vacuum in its wake.

Despite this depressing picture, Haiti boasts some impressive accomplishments since the restoration of the Aristide government in 1994:

— resumed constitutional government;

— sharply reduced human rights abuses;

— dramatically improved overall security through the elimination of the army and the training of a new police force;

— a new, positive relationship with the Caribbean and the entire international community;

— development and implementation of the 1994 Emergency Economic Recovery Program ($668 million) within a viable macroeconomic framework, and pledges of more than $1 billion in foreign aid to fund it in 1995–1996;

— a tentative new sense among the Haitian people that the government exists to serve the people rather than to exploit and plunder them.

Even more promising are longer-term trends that may contribute to achieving the Herculean tasks of reconstruction and help overcome some of the obstacles described above. An emerging majoritarian culture may provide the basis for a shared identity in the whole society. A dynamic informal sector is emerging from the oppressive controls of the predatory state. With the elimination of disincentives for rural smallholders, peasant agricultural production is changing for the better. Grassroots organizations and a nascent civil society are budding, and these groups are demonstrating a willingness to cooperate to achieve collective goals at the local level, even if not yet at the national level. Finally, and most basically, the survival capacity of the Haitian people, demonstrated during the 1991–1994 repression, belies the deterministic forecasts of pessimists and doomsayers.

Nevertheless, at the conference Michel-Rolph Trouillot cautioned against seeing the restoration of Aristide's government as yet another opportunity for Haiti to start from scratch and build a new society, as some argued should have occurred in 1804, 1935, and 1986. We cannot ignore historical legacies, but we can recognize the breaks from the past and ask what other breaks are needed, and to build what? This volume starts from Trouillot's premise. The following sections discuss the challenges of reconstruction identified above:

— creating a national identity;

— achieving economic growth and alleviating poverty;

— reconceptualizing public and private roles;

— providing justice and security for all;

— creating a democratic political culture and institutions.

These efforts underlie a fundamental need: to dismantle the predatory state and replace it with a legitimate government that can successfully address the needs of the nation. This remedy implies both short-term and long-term objectives. Acknowledging that the required tasks cannot be completed overnight, this introduction indicates urgent, immediate steps that can and should be taken, and longer-term aims that will require significant planning and investment.

Creating a National Identity–"We're All in the Same Boat, and This Boat Isn't Going to Florida"

Trouillot reported that the most serious obstacle to rebuilding Haiti was the flawed relationship between state and nation; likewise, the most serious undertaking on the path to reconstruction is a social contract that repairs that relationship to the benefit of the nation. The fundamental issue is how to create a sense among Haitians that they are all in the same boat, and that if one group or class goes overboard, the whole boat will capsize. The problem is that Haitian elites honestly believe, and have believed for a century and a half, that they can survive without the poor, rural majority of Haiti.

The solution, contended Trouillot, involves a social contract between the state and society, or the nation, that lays out the obligations of each to the other. For Haiti, as for most countries, the state preceded the nation at independence. But, unlike other emerging democracies, the Haitian state did not achieve a social contract that could produce a sense of national unity. Instead, in nineteenth-century Haiti, elites reacted to the rise of the peasantry not with a package of social benefits that would have led the majority to believe that they were indeed in the same boat as the elites, but with a form of social apartheid. Elites believed that they could survive even if the majority did not. Thus, a sense of sameness across class lines—a sense of nationhood—was never achieved in Haiti.

Can a shared national identity be created in present-day Haiti, given its history of colonial enslavement, its color and class divisions, its absence of political culture, and its juxtaposition of Western and African cultures? To understand Haiti in the 1990s requires an understanding of its French colonial past and the struggle for freedom against slavery. Created during colonialism, and continued after independence, dichotomies between European and African, slaveowner and slave, slave and free people (*affranchis*), black and brown, French and Kreyòl (Creole), Catholicism and Vodun, were all fostered to maintain power and subjugation, primarily for the purpose of safeguarding wealth among the elites.

Yet, Patrick Bellegarde-Smith has argued that these dichotomies should be seen not as opposites but as part of a continuum along which all Haitians find themselves. Under colonialism, slaves united against slavery by minimizing their different national origins and by developing survival coping mechanisms: the Kreyòl language and the Vodun religion. Kreyòl was a compromise language derived from West African and French roots and served as both a contact language between French and African and a counterlanguage to that of the masters. It is a basis for a shared identity today, since all Haitians speak Kreyòl, while only 10 percent speak French. Likewise, Vodun, more a spiritual discipline than a religion, is today followed by upper and middle classes for its magical powers, and by the poor majority for its world view.

Considered as arranged on a continuum rather than as opposites, the cultural elements of language, religion, race, and ethnicity might finally prove to be the source of the national identity that has been so damagingly elusive in Haiti for two centuries. Yet, this forging of a national identity may only happen if the economic motivations for dominance and subjugation that underlie these forced dichotomies are replaced by an expanding pie. As many conference participants noted, the deepest roots of Haiti's problems lie in social inequality and economic maldistribution. In other words, creating a vision among Haitians that they share the same boat will require that Haitians all adopt new attitudes toward economic growth and distribution, that collectively they will all be better off, and indeed will survive, only if they work together to provide a sound basis for economic growth. Achieving these goals will necessitate dismantling the predatory state and replacing it with a democratic state that can serve the needs of the whole nation.

If creating a shared national identity is intertwined with addressing the fundamental economic problems of a grossly unequal distribution of a limited economic pie, what are the prospects for improving those conditions?

Economic Growth And Poverty Reduction

Although economists disagree over whether trickle-down economic growth or income redistribution is the best means to alleviate poverty, economic growth will clearly help to provide employment and resources that can improve the lives of the poor in Haiti. In turn, helping the poor by investing in human capital formation and expanding the domestic consumer market will contribute to economic growth and development. Thus, stimulating growth, reducing inequality, and alleviating poverty were themes interwoven throughout the conference.

Yet how, or whether, it is even possible to create a sustainable, growing economy in a country as ecologically and infrastructurally devastated as Haiti is one of the most challenging and debated issues among scholars and practitioners. In an economy with only a 0.9 percent per capita annual growth rate between 1965 and 1980, a -2.4 percent rate between 1980 and 1992, and an estimated 30 percent drop in GDP during the 1991–1994 military period, the need for massive economic reconstruction is starkly clear. The statistics on education, land-person ratios, and erosion do not engender much optimism. How should the Haitian society and the international community go about trying to stimulate economic growth while simultaneously trying to address the needs of an impoverished people?

Mats Lundahl described the Haitian economy as one locked into a low-level equilibrium characterized by high population growth and a very small stock of human capital.[1] To break out of the low-level equilibrium, a big push is required. What might be the source and focus of such a push?

Anthony Catanese posited that in a predominantly rural, agrarian society, the first priority should be to look at the prospects of revitalizing agricultural productivity. Yet, the analyses of Lundahl and Uli Locher offered a sobering conclusion: Traditional agriculture will not survive the cumulative effects of Haiti's steady population growth interacting with its rapid soil destruction. Haiti's predominant agricultural method of slash and burn, its use of charcoal from wood as a basic fuel, and its high population growth contribute to unchecked soil erosion, stemming from a basic need for more space, resources, and alternative methods of agricultural production for an expanding population. Even if population growth were reduced rapidly to zero, the dynamics of soil erosion would continue for decades. Furthermore, as the land-person ratio decreases, the very basis of peasant existence is threatened: In 1950 the arable land area per capita was 0.38 hectares; by 2000 it is expected to fall to 0.16 hectares, with food production at an all-time low and food imports at an all-time high. Agricultural exports also decline as the growing demand for food pushes farmers more and more into the production of subsistence crops.

Is there any way to halt the downward cycle? Lundahl proposed three possible ways of ending the destruction of the agrarian economy: slowing population growth, increasing job creation outside the agricultural sector, and encouraging emigration of the rural population.

The first option of slowing population growth is often advocated. The Becker-Murphy-Tamura model posits that, as income per capita over time is depressed, families choose how to adjust. They can reduce the family size to protect living standards or redistribute income within the family, usually to the detriment of the weakest and most vulnerable members, the children. If a mother enters the work force to maintain living standards, children lose either in consumption or in care.

In Haiti, the interaction of population growth and soil erosion tends to depress per capita income over time in a cumulative fashion. Unfortunately, redistributing resources within the family rather than reducing family size appears to be the more likely adjustment in the short term. To counteract this possibility, family planning and the education of young girls are urgently needed, since both are effective ways to slow population growth. To combat soil erosion, Paul Latortue advocated shifting food production to the flatlands and developing in the mountains tree crops such as oranges and avocados for export.

What of the prospects for the second option: Can sufficient manufacturing jobs be created to help offset job losses in the agricultural sector? Traditional import substitution in Haiti has not provided a viable base of employment in the past, while it has imposed high costs to consumers through inefficient and monopolistic industries protected by average nominal tariff rates as high as 200 percent in 1986. The assembly export sector generated high hopes for employment and foreign exchange as the share of manufactures in exports increased from 4 percent to 66 percent between 1966 and 1984. By 1990 employment grew to 46,000 in a labor force of 3.5 million. Nevertheless, political instability and international sanctions virtually eliminated these gains between 1991 and 1994. Although new manufacturing jobs can presumably be created, will this revival be sufficient?

The Haitian Presidential Commission on Economic Growth reported that 63 of the 145 export assembly plants that had operated in 1990 were reopened in 1995 and that 22 of 55 artisanal enterprises were also reopened. These data are positive indicators that business confidence is returning and that this sector may recover. Nevertheless, the labor-intensive manufacturing sector may give only a marginal boost to growth if low-value-added domestic enterprises and weak linkages with the rest of the economy continue to characterize manufacturing. Vulnerability to the whims of foreign investors also afflicts this sector, since plants can be moved out of the country at a moment's notice, as happened during the trade embargo.

The assembly sector appears to promise only low wages in a society with an unlimited labor supply. What, then, are the prospects for moving to the capital-intensive modern manufactures, as the Asian tigers have done, that tend to raise living standards? Lundahl's analysis again was sobering. Utilizing the Rodrik model, Lundahl explained that the profitability of a modern, relatively capital-intensive manufacturing sector depends on the range of intermediate goods available close by or available at low transportation costs, but the viability of intermediate production depends at the same time on demand from the modern sector.[2] In an economy specializing in traditional goods, neither the intermediate sector nor the modern will be established.

How can a country solve this chicken-and-egg dilemma? The answer is a coordinated, simultaneous movement of resources into both the modern and intermediate sectors. But in Lundahl's analysis, this option is also precluded, at least in the short-term. It presupposes both a sufficiently well educated labor force and a large enough capital stock, both of which are in short supply in Haiti. Latortue recommended developing tourism, in combination with Haiti's well-developed artistic and handicraft skills, as one alternative way to generate employment and foreign exchange.

The third option to slow the cycle of destruction of the agricultural sector is to encourage emigration of the rural population. Yet migration to the urban areas only puts further strain on overburdened cities, and emigration abroad is both difficult for individuals and insufficient to equalize Haiti's low wage rates, given its continued high population growth.

The dilemma remains: How can Haiti break the "traditional-goods deadlock" and move out of the low-level steady state? Although the new economic growth theory employed by Lundahl does not prescribe the solution to this dilemma, the implication is that an external shock is required to force the economy out of its low-level equilibrium: A massive investment in education and an infusion of capital appear to be prerequisites to break the deadlock.

Reconceptualizing the Role of the State

As North and Rotberg describe it, the predatory state extracts income from constituents in the interest of one group or class without regard to the impact on the wealth of the society as a whole.[3] Throughout the history of independent Haiti, the presidency served as a source of private income for the rulers. Characterized by either few productive expenditures or none, the state became, as Mats Lundahl comments in his chapter, at once too small and too big: "Too small in the sense that it has failed to create a policy environment conducive to productivity and growth; too large if one takes into account the number of public sector employees who have been taken into the service of kleptocrats to assist in the creation of private ruler income or have served solely as recipients of public funds without performing duties other than backing the ruler politically."

President Jean-Claude ("Baby Doc") Duvalier refined the predatory state by transforming public enterprises into the primary means of private access to government funds, especially through state monopolies in soybean oil, wheat flour, cement, and sugar. In other words, instead of simply skimming off the top of foreign aid funds or engaging in classic rent-seeking behavior through the distribution of government licenses and contracts, Baby Doc's government modernized the predatory state by exploiting government monopolies in basic goods. These enterprises provided a large source of income to the ruler, protected by nominal and effective tariff rates in 1986 that rose as high 200 percent and averaged 100 percent. This method thus created a direct transfer of income from the consumer to the state through exorbitant prices and lack of competition.

The old corrupt state must be dismantled before a new productive one can be built. The reasoning behind this argument is that graft and inefficiency are self-perpetuating, since the individual costs of corruption are low when the probability of being detected is low and when, even if a person is caught, the most punishment he or she will have to endure is to share the take with a detecting colleague. In other words, a corrupt administration tends to corrupt new employees. Therefore, the old state cannot be grafted onto or reformed, but instead must be dismantled before it can be recreated.

Consequently, criticisms of President Jean-Bertrand Aristide's administration for doing the bidding of the International Monetary Fund (IMF) in its attempts to privatize and dismantle old controls are ill founded. An open debate about what the new state will look like and what its responsibilities should be is important. But the first step must be to dismantle the old state controls and the public and private monopolies that formed the basis of the predatory state.

Unfortunately, it appeared that a deep distrust of international agencies and the United States, born of a long history of intervention and exploitation, clouded these issues in Haiti during the Aristide administration. Instead of taking the necessary steps to dismantle the old state and then focusing on how to reconceptualize the role of the new state and the division of responsibilities between the public and private sphere, at least one wing of the Aristide government appeared to continue to view the international community as adversaries rather than allies in the struggle to revitalize state and society. As a result, recommendations from the international community were treated with suspicion and disdain. Prime Minister Smarck Michel resigned on October 16, 1995, frustrated by political resistance to his program of privatization and economic reform and the reluctance of Aristide to commit himself to those reform efforts.

Once the old corrupt state and its disincentives to entrepreneurship and production are dismantled, a new one can be created. Conference participants engaged in a lively discussion about the respective responsibilities that could be borne by the state and the private sector, but viewed with some skepticism the potential for a private sector (that in many ways has also been parasitic) to replace the state in providing essential services. Out of this debate, however, emerged some basic principles and creative ideas that may contribute to a discussion in Haiti on reforming the state.

—Reconceptualize the role of the state and the relationships among the central government, local governments, communities, and NGOs. The new, direct election of municipal and section-level governments and the prevalence of NGOs in Haiti provide an opportunity to engage local communities in planning and decision-making about basic services, and to form innovative partnerships between public and private sector (both for-profit and nonprofit) organizations. Some specific ideas for health and education are discussed below.

—Consider new alternatives, such as contracting out some services. As the discussion over public and private sector responsibilities unfolds in Haiti, new types of relationships between the two spheres could be explored. For example, rather than simply privatizing some basic services, the government could contract out services in health or education to the private sector or to NGOs, while still maintaining an oversight, regulatory, and planning function.

— Improve the state's long-term regulatory, planning, and infrastructural development capacity. The Emergency Economic Recovery Program (EERP), created by the Haitian government in consultation with the major international donors in 1994, lays out the areas for immediate, short-term (twelve to eighteen months) investment for economic and social recovery in Haiti, and indicates areas for longer-term investment. Given the dire needs of the Haitian population, it is not surprising that the government has focused thus far on short-term programs that can begin to meet such needs. Yet public investment in urban and rural infrastructure, as well as basic services, requires a long-term perspective if the productive capacity of the country is to be stimulated.

Two sectors in particular were discussed at the conference and in this volume: education, and population and health.

Education

Education is critical for both democratization and development. In Haiti the state has clearly failed in its obligation to provide free and compulsory education as mandated by the 1987 constitution. Yet the demand for education is so overwhelming that private institutions have sprung up in the last two decades to fill the gap, and many poor families are willing to pay $25 a month to educate their children—this in a country with an average annual per capita income of only $250. Indeed, the high demand for education belies the Becker-Murphy-Tamura model, which predicts that a low supply of education generates low demand.

Charles Tardieu, director of the Haitian National Education Plan, reported that approximately 14 percent of GDP is devoted to education in Haiti, with only 1.9 percent of GDP coming from the state. Public expenditure on education in Haiti is lower than that in all but four developing countries included in the UNDP's human development index, and lower than the 3.2 percent average spent in Latin American and Caribbean countries. An astounding 85 to 95 percent of schools at the primary and secondary levels are privately owned.

Should Haiti invent a new model whereby the private sector and NGOs provide a service as vital as education with the efficiency and effectiveness of the public sector? UNDP statistics show that Haiti has relatively high rates of primary school enrollment for a low-income developing country, albeit still the lowest rates in the Western Hemisphere. Girls are enrolled in primary and secondary schools at rates equal or nearly equal to those of boys, again surpassing the average for developing countries.

Yet these figures hide severe problems. The issue is not a lack of demand for education nor the absence of sufficient supply. Instead, the problem is low participation (low attendance and graduation rates). There is also poor access to schools in rural areas. Instructional quality is poor throughout the country. Although the private sector has responded to the collapse of public schools, the historic lack of government attention to this sector has created a situation of unequal access and ineffective instruction. These problems call for a much greater state role in providing the infrastructure for education—teacher and administrator training, buildings, transportation to school—and in monitoring and regulating both private and public schools to improve graduation rates and the caliber of education.

The Ministry of Education is currently working on Plan 2004. It will provide an opportunity for Haiti to develop innovative new means of public and private sector cooperation, with local community involvement, to address specific problems, including:

— Low attendance rates and a gender gap. School enrollment figures do not measure actual school attendance among Haitian school children, which is estimated to be much lower. In particular, there is a marked gender gap. Although UNDP statistics show that the ratio of girls enrolled in primary schools is equal to that of boys, Locher reported that actual attendance of girls is only about one-third of the attendance of boys.[4] At the university level, women enroll at only one-third the rate of men, well below the average for developing countries.

— High dropout and repetition rates. The Inter-American Development Bank reports that only about one-third of the children entering primary school complete the cycle. Locher estimated that two-thirds of seats in primary schools are occupied by overage children who are repeating grades.[5]

— High student-teacher ratios. Marc Prou estimated a student-teacher ratio of 80:1 at some levels, indicating the pressing need for more trained teachers.

— Rural access problems. Although enrollments have grown over the past two decades, they are concentrated in Port-au-Prince and smaller cities. Access to schools in rural Haiti continues to be a severe problem. Better roads and public transportation are necessary in addition to the construction of schools in the countryside. Free school lunches would also avert the need for children to spend valuable time traveling to and from home for lunch.

—Lack of basic supplies. Haitian schoolchildren need textbooks, paper, and pencils. The international community is already helping, but these needs remain great.

—Imbalanced curricula and inadequate technical education. An overemphasis on the humanities at the secondary and university levels has deprived Haiti of trained workers in other areas. Technical education should be enhanced. An example of international assistance in this area is the Fodement program sponsored by UNESCO, wherein math and science teachers from Haiti are trained in Puerto Rico.

—Inadequate teacher and administrator training. The quality of the preparation of teachers and school administrators is woefully inadequate. Locher pointed out that of 3,000 new teachers employed each year, only 200 to 300 are fully qualified.[6] The state should improve training and techniques in these two areas.

—Adult illiteracy. Adult programs are needed to address the highest illiteracy rates in the Western Hemisphere.[7]

—Lack of basic data. Better data are needed so that national education planning can be effective. For example, traditional measures based on number of years in school do not measure actual language attainment—whether a person can read or remember what was learned. In addition, it is not clear whether literacy rates measure literacy in Kreyòl. Data on the number of children passing exams for graduation are also needed. Data on actual attendance of girls and boys, and rural and urban children, will help planning as well.

Population and Health

The demographics of population growth and migration affect all aspects of Haiti's development: health, environment, infrastructure, education, housing, and employment. The statistics are alarming. Locher reported that Haiti now has 7.5 million people; with an annual population growth rate of 2.4 percent (2.2 percent of whom remain in Haiti), the population doubles every 30 years.[8] Haiti's population density of 850 persons per arable square kilometer is near the record for the developing world. Likewise, urbanization is advancing rapidly, with the country's urban population now approaching 40 percent. Port-au-Prince grows 7 percent annually, a rate in the top third among developing countries.

The consequences of this population increase are obvious: Domestic food scarcity is now a major problem, with 40 percent of staple food needs imported. The stress on housing, urban infrastructure, and employment is severe.

Statistics on health are equally alarming, but do show some areas of improvement, as demonstrated by Marie-Andrée Diouf.[9] Infant mortality declined from 101 deaths per 1,000 infants in 1985–1989 to 74 in 1990–1994 in response to a focus on neonatal tetanus vaccination and oral rehydration therapy. Youth mortality (1–5 years), however, rose during 1990–1994 as a result of a measles epidemic and worsened nutrition accompanied by declining family incomes. A current campaign for measles vaccination aims to achieve coverage of 93 percent, as compared with only 20 percent before 1994. Increased use of contraceptives has reduced fertility from 6.3 children per woman in 1987 to 4.8 in 1994, with 13 percent of women and 17 percent of men using contraception.

The primary public health problems in Haiti stem from poor sanitation, inadequate nutrition, and unequal access to health care. Among the problems are the following.

—Infectious and parasitic pathologies. These include cholera (growing after the isolation of the embargo ended), dengue fever and malaria, diarrhea (first cause of infant mortality), acute respiratory problems (second cause of infant mortality), tuberculosis (growing, with the highest incidence in the world), and HIV (stable in urban areas at 7–10 percent; growing in rural areas at 3–5 percent).

—Maternal and infant malnutrition. One-third of infants suffer from chronic malnutrition, threatening their growth and capabilities.

—High rate of maternal mortality. With 80 percent of births occurring at home, and fewer than half of them assisted births, maternal mortality is high, at 4.5 per 1,000 live births.

—Lack of access to modern medicine. Forty percent of the population has no access to modern medicine, although everyone has access to traditional medicine. Public sector health care was destroyed completely during the last military regime.

Like education, most health services are fee based. With the collapse of the public health sector, Haitians are paying for health care in the private sector but are receiving low-quality care. Even immunizations are fee based, making Haiti an exceptional case globally. The question is what should be the responsibility of the government in a system that is virtually privatized?

Another dilemma presented by public health services in Haiti is how to incorporate traditional, or Kreyòl medicine, into the health system. As Johannes Sommerfeld argued, planners must recognize the medical pluralism that exists in Haiti and perhaps allow for traditional medicine as an alternative system of care, especially for problems not treatable with modern medicine.[10] In addition, traditional medical practitioners might be integrated into the modern biomedical system where appropriate, such as the training of birth attendants. The real challenge is to make modern medicine relevant in Haiti's plural medical culture.

One viable strategy for public health focuses heavily on a nonmedical strategy, community participation. The idea is to develop low-cost programs based on simple interventions, such as training citizens to be educators and local health monitors. Since health services will be effective only if proper sanitation is practiced at home, education and participation at the local level is absolutely vital.

A second strategy is partnerships in which some health services would be contracted out to NGOs or communities and the government would serve a regulatory and planning role, focusing on public health needs by providing a safe water supply, preventive medicine and immunizations, disease surveillance, and coordination across the different sectors.

For the first time, Haiti's health policy is based on equity and on providing access to health care for everyone. Although the government must take an active role in delivering health care and family planning, overall success is likely to depend on public-private partnerships, community participation, and long-term investment in improved medical practices.

Justice and Security

To dismantle the predatory state and create a successful democratic one requires, first, a universal respect for the rule of law. The underlying problem in Haiti is that the judicial system is completely dysfunctional and distrusted by the populace, and that the security created by the multinational force (MNF), the UN peacekeepers, is artificial. To move toward a political culture in which all Haitians respect the rule of law will require a justice system that works and is applied to all equally, a security force that is widely trusted and that respects human rights, and resolution of the dilemma of justice versus reconciliation.

Haiti faces formidable obstacles in accomplishing these tasks, as outlined at the conference by William O'Neill and Marguerite Laurent.

—Unequal access to justice. Most of the population has no access to the courts or legal representation. The Civil Code is elaborate, requiring the preparation of many written documents, and has not been translated into Kreyòl. Judges, who lack even basic writing implements, frequently charge plaintiffs for supplies as well as charging commissions to augment their meager salaries, making justice an expensive proposition for most Haitians.

—Uninhabitable courthouses and prisons. The physical condition of courthouses, prisons, and administrative buildings is deplorable. Prisons date from the eighteenth century and lack running water, toilets, and electricity. Most courts lack electricity and telephones, and many judges do not even possess copies of the Civil Code. Some progress, however, was made in the prisons in 1995. Among Haiti's fourteen detention centers, seven were rehabilitated; prison registries were being better maintained; and women and children were segregated from male prisoners.

—Illiterate, corrupt, and untrained judges. An international advisory team assessing the lower courts, where most of the population has its first contact with the judicial system, found that many justices of the peace were illiterate and simply made up the law. Compounding the problem has been the absence of local elected officials who could nominate new judges.

—Lack of due process. As O'Neill said, the Haitian justice system tends to follow the practice of "arrest first, investigate later." Haitian law still follows French law, allowing for public denunciation, although this practice was abolished in France long ago. Consequently, 88 percent of the prison population in 1995 was convicted of a crime and was awaiting either charges or trial. This figure is very high, even relative to earlier conditions in Central America, where 50 to 70 percent of prisoners await either charges or trial.

Use of illegal warrants in politically tinged cases is evident, although not widespread. Trials in absentia are also occurring. In contrast, the Rwandan and Bosnian international tribunals outlaw in absentia trials so as to protect the rights of defendants to face their accusers.

Finally, vigilante justice—instant executions—have occurred, although not on the scale that some had predicted. The UN/OAS human rights mission documented forty such cases in March and eighteen in July 1995, primarily involving mob killings of thieves.

—Fear of retribution as an impediment to justice. Many judges and prosecutors, especially in the countryside, feared retribution from the former paramilitary group, the Front for the Advancement and Progress of Haiti (FRAPH), after the UN peacekeepers departed. This fear precluded justice from being carried out and undermined the judiciary in the eyes of the population.

—Lack of leadership in the security forces. One of the biggest fears of Haitians and international observers alike was that the multinational army would leave a security vacuum when it departed. Although the newly trained police force is composed of better-educated recruits than the previous police force and is being warmly received by Haitians, training of the 5,000-person force will not be complete nor will it have experienced senior officers by the scheduled departure of the MNF in February 1997. Some 1,100 trained police were in the field as of September 1995, with 1,200 in training; the original goal was to train a total of 5,000 police by January 1996. Consequently, under the original plan, the most experience any police officer would have by February 1996 would be a year's worth.

In response to the lack of commanding experience, the MNF recruited former officers from the Haitian Armed Forces (FADH) into the interim security force in September 1995. The government was reportedly rethinking its prohibition on former FADH officers for the permanent police force, raising concerns about the integrity of the revamped police force and its likely respect for human rights.

—Unequal and unsustainable salaries. To recruit good candidates into the new police force, newly hired policemen were being offered salaries in 1995 that were at least twelve times higher than the average Haitian monthly income. The risk is that if the government is unable to sustain this salary structure, disgruntled policemen may resort to the old ways of extortion and theft to supplement their incomes. In addition, the discrepancy between generous new police salaries and low judicial salaries threatens to create resentment and temptations for corruption among the judiciary.

—Potential for nondemocratic forces to coopt the police. Even though the old security forces have been dismantled and are incapable of staging a comeback, there is still the risk that the new police force, with its monopoly on the use of armed power, could be coopted by monied or political elements to subvert the rule of law. As Robert Pastor argued, a civil democracy in Haiti is possible only where there is a nonpoliticized security force that is subordinate to the legitimately elected civilian leaders and obedient to the rule of law. Achieving these outcomes will in the medium term require a continued presence of international trainers and security forces, and in the longer term a functioning judicial system, a sense of national identity, a loyal police force, adequate financial resources, and local civilian oversight.

—Disjointed progress in legal and police reform. Although the new police force enjoys substantial legitimacy, the judicial system does not. This disjuncture threatens to undermine the entire criminal justice system. If criminals arrested are not convicted and the public lacks confidence in the judicial system, citizens will be tempted to take justice into their own hands, and the police will become demoralized.

—Justice versus reconciliation. Haitians must deal with a dilemma that faces every society emerging from a period of repression or civil conflict: how to balance the demands for the punishment of past abuses with national reconciliation. A Truth Commission has been established, similar to those in El Salvador and Chile, but it is underfunded and disorganized. The quality of its report, due in December 1995 but never released to the public, was expected to determine the ability of Haiti to balance the needs of both justice and reconciliation.

—Rural insecurity. Although the feared rural section chiefs (members of the army charged with policing rural areas) were eliminated by the Aristide government, police protection has still been concentrated in the urban areas, leaving rural areas unprotected.

In the face of these disheartening problems, how should the Haitian government and international community go about reforming the justice system? The first priority is an international security presence of some kind for at least five years, the bare minimum time estimated to put into place an adequate judicial system. The extension of the MNF presence until June 1996 and subsequently until mid-1997 was welcome, but still too short.

A second priority is to construct secure prisons that are not merely holding pens and to provide adequate offices and supplies for legal personnel. If international donors continue to be reluctant to contribute to this vital infrastructural need, the government may want to consider seeking a multilateral loan to finance the construction and renovation of buildings.

A third priority is the training of ministry personnel, judges, prosecutors, public defenders, judicial security officers, and investigative police. The international community is already involved in these training efforts and should do more.

Fourth, it may be desirable to reform the legal system to make it more accessible to the Haitian population. For example, the elaborate Napoleonic Civil Code is difficult to administer in a society with a high illiteracy rate and limited resources. At the minimum, it is absolutely essential to translate the legal code into Kreyòl for the use of judges and laypersons alike.

In the larger picture, the need for simultaneous reforms is evident, not only to link judicial reform to police reform, but also to address more fundamental causes of violence in society. As Donald Schulz argued, destroying the military structure is not sufficient to create security and justice. As long as the current inequitable economic substructure remains intact, the roots of violence will not be destroyed. President François (Papa Doc) Duvalier knew that he could buy desperate people cheaply. The FADH, itself, was an extractive institution: troops used their weapons to extort their fellow citizens. Creating a democratic political culture based on a more equitable socioeconomic structure is the key to providing justice and security in Haiti.

Creating a Democratic Political Culture

Robert Fatton argued that the predatory state becomes a source of private income for rulers through its total lack of accountability, which suppresses even the murmurs of democracy and forces civil society and political society underground. Creating accountability is the foundation of democracy.

A democratic polity is based on the presumption that all of the major forces in the society accept and abide by the rules. More specifically, winners of electoral contests must assure losers that they will have further chances to compete for power and that their views will not be ignored. Losers of electoral contests must assure victors that they will respect the authority of the winners and work as a constructive opposition. This mutual reassurance, known as contingent consent, requires strong political parties working within a framework of free and fair elections trusted by all; freedom of speech and press; and respect for political minorities.

The challenge is to create stakes in the system for all of the major players so that they come to view the benefits of participating as greater than the costs. In Haiti, this is doubly difficult because the society lacks a cohesive national identity and sense of collective purpose. Furthermore, it took international intervention to precipitate a change in the balance of forces in Haiti.

Building trust is the key to the success of this democratization process, and also the major challenge, given the history of Haiti. Changing a political culture is a long-term process, but it can be initiated by formulating rules acceptable to all and strengthening institutions to enforce those rules. Over time, through repeated trials and errors, confidence and mutual trust can be achieved. Two elements in particular contribute to building trust: transparent and respected elections, and the informal networks and social capital created in a civil society.

Electoral Process

Elections are an initial step whereby each political group tests the system to see if the rules will hold and be applied fairly. If the electoral process can be institutionalized and the rules agreed upon by all, the first step toward creating the mutual reassurances of contingent consent can be taken.

The June 1995 municipal and parliamentary elections provided a massive victory for Lavalas, the political movement that brought Aristide to victory in 1990 and was endorsed by him in the June elections. But the election procedures were questionable, risking the delegitimation of the newly elected institutions because of problems with the process. As Pastor documents, administrative and technical problems resulted in serious problems with the vote count, and the inattention of the Provisional Electoral Council (CEP) to party complaints and concerns before and after the elections reduced confidence to dangerously low levels. The result was that twenty-three out of twenty-seven parties condemned the results and asked for an annulment, and only 10 to 15 percent of the population voted in subsequent runoff polls.

The presidential elections scheduled for December 17, 1995, were the next test. President Aristide's tremendous personal popularity gave him a unique opportunity to legitimize both the next president and the nation's nascent democratic institutions. Yet he did nothing to address the opposition's legitimate requests for electoral reform, and he waited until two days before the election to endorse the Lavalas candidate, René Préval, and squelch rumors that he might accede to popular demand to stay in office for three more years. Préval was overwhelmingly elected with 88 percent of the vote, but with an opposition boycott and the uncertainty about the elections and the candidates, the turnout was only 28 percent.

The transfer of power from one elected government to another on February 7, 1996, ten years after the flight of Jean-Claude Duvalier, was a historic moment for Haiti. But the chaotic elections of 1995 did little to legitimize and strengthen Haiti's nascent representative institutions.

Civil Society and Social Capital

Putnam has written about the importance of social capital for democracy, the mutual trust built up through informal citizen interactions, from bowling leagues to neighborhood associations.[11] One of the most hopeful stories about Haiti today is of the maturation of grassroots organizations. Mobilization from below has grown in Haiti; as Robert Maguire said, the "muzzle has fallen" with the explosion of the voices of the grassroots and the silent civil society since 1986.

Grassroots organizers fall into two categories: those who work to improve the socioeconomic status of the poor, such as through collectively building silos, and those who work to improve politics, such as through civic education. Maguire pointed out a major change in the second type of grassroots organizers since the 1990 elections. In 1990 the electoral prize was the presidency, with local and parliamentary races virtually ignored. Political parties were mostly urban based, sending out nonresident representatives to local areas. Consequently, those races generated very little voter enthusiasm.

In contrast, by 1995 grassroots leaders had learned that each elected office was important, and they shifted from an attitude eschewing involvement in politics to one recognizing the need for such involvement in order to prevent the return of dictatorship. As a result, many grassroots leaders became candidates for local office in the June 1995 elections, and more would have run as independents if the electoral rules had not made it ten times more expensive to register as an independent candidate than as a member of a party.

Minister of Culture Jean-Claude Bajeux highlighted the fundamental positive changes in Haiti represented by the 1995 elections in spite of the electoral flaws.[12] First, the results indicated the strength of the popular sectors and the defeat of Duvalierism. All of the political formulas related to Duvalierism disappeared as a consequence of the elections. Second, the results represented the disappearance of the military and of a history of change brought about only by arms.

Bajeux argued optimistically that Haiti would not return to past practices because of the newfound strength of the popular sectors. He contended that illiteracy did not doom democracy, since in Haiti the proponents of democracy have always been illiterate, while its opponents have been among the best-educated people in the country.

But Haitian civil society has not yet forged the necessary links to political society that enable its citizens to gain control over public authority. Political society requires institutionalizing parties and movements. It requires institutionalizing uncertainty of outcomes, so that the results of political contests are not predetermined. In Haiti the party system is immature and weak. The strength of the Lavalas movement is gathered around a single individual, and it is not clear how the movement will survive after Aristide. Already the movement has fractured, with splits within the "family" leading to sometimes divisive struggles in the 1995 elections.

Another uncertainty for Haitian democracy is the role of the international community. If the democratic moment came only when international conditions were right, Fatton and Pastor argue (albeit with different emphases), what does this say for the future, when the international community no longer attends to Haiti? Are Haitians condemned to waiting for the next expression of international interest, or can they develop their own "technology of governance and power" that can sustain the moment of democracy and promise of development?

Role of the International Community

Although viewed by some Haitians as adversaries of change, the international community can prove to be allies in three key areas: security (the MNF), finance from international donors, and support and skills from the Haitian diaspora.

The MNF has been critical to the restoration of constitutional government and the creation of a climate of security. As discussed above, the development of an adequate judicial system will take several years. Conference participants spoke repeatedly of the need for the MNF to maintain a long-term presence to avoid turning a short-term tactical success into a strategic failure.

The international community has pledged $1.2 billion to help reconstruct Haiti, specifically to fund the EERP and to pay debt arrears for 1995 and 1996. Although this infusion of foreign aid is absolutely crucial to Haiti's recovery, several issues need to be taken into account. First, there is a problem of absorption capacity in Haiti, with limits on human resource and management capacity for projects. Second, many donors have sought to channel aid through NGOs, indicating the need to establish oversight of the 250 legally recognized NGOs already operating in Haiti. Third, there is some concern about the risk of a growing dependence on aid on the one hand, and the lack of a long-term commitment on the part of donors on the other hand.

The Haitian diaspora is potentially an important source of skills and financing for Haiti. Yet the lack of data on the composition and skill levels of the diaspora, return migration, and the value of remittances lead to varying interpretations about the likelihood that such potential will be achieved.

Aristide spoke of a "Tenth Department" composed of Haitian expatriates. This implies that Haitian emigrants retain a Haitian identity and loyalty to their country even after they migrate. The concept of the diaspora, however, allows for the possibility that Haitian émigrés assimilate into their countries of residence, and are unlikely to return to Haiti. Nor is the diaspora necessarily unified in its support of the Aristide government, with class differences in Haiti apparently replicated among emigrants abroad. These differences may also adversely affect the inclination of Haitian emigrants to invest in Haiti.

But despite the mixed evidence about the degree to which Haitian expatriates retain a Haitian identity and loyalty longer than other immigrant groups, it seems clear that many expatriates retain strong emotional ties to Haiti and a nostalgia, perhaps born of the country's history of external isolation. Even if Haitian emigrants are unlikely to repatriate, they can play important roles in Haiti's reconstruction by sending remittances, lobbying host governments on refugee issues and foreign aid, and providing expert training in Haiti.

Conclusions

The following were identified at the conference as urgent concerns for the long-term development of Haiti.

Long-term security can be provided only by a permanent Haitian police force accountable to the rule of law. To accomplish this objective, the MNF needs to maintain a presence and a training capability in Haiti for five years, the minimum time estimated to put into place an adequate justice system.

Judicial reform must accompany police reform. Uninhabitable courthouses must be refurbished, and prisons must be constructed. Judges, prosecutors, public defenders, and ministry personnel must be trained. The legal system should be made more accessible to the population, beginning with translating the legal code into Kreyòl.

Investment in physical infrastructure and human capital is essential to promote economic growth and reduce poverty. To accomplish this goal, the state must improve its long-term planning, regulatory, and infrastructural development capacity.

Massive investment in education and an infusion of capital are required to break out of the traditional goods deadlock. Economic controls that are legacies of the old predatory state must be eliminated to attract foreign and domestic investment and unleash an entrepreneurial spirit long inhibited by oppressive state regulations.

Control of soil erosion requires both slowing down population growth and developing alternatives to the traditional slash-and-burn agricultural practices. Developing tree crops for export and shifting food production to the flatlands will help to control soil erosion on the mountainsides.

In reconceptualizing the role of the state, Haitian public and private officials should explore innovative new partnerships between the public and private sectors, and among local communities, local governments, and the central government. The government should consider contracting out services in health or education to private sector businesses or NGOs, while retaining an oversight, regulatory, and planning function.

The state must play a larger role in providing the infrastructure for education—teacher and administrator training, buildings, and transportation to school—and in monitoring and regulating privately supplied education in order to improve the quality of education and graduation rates. Educational policy should strive to increase attendance at school, especially among girls, improve access to education in rural areas, provide textbooks and pencils, and expand technical training.

Improving public health and access to family planning is crucial for Haiti's recovery. Community participation and education of women will contribute to family health. Low-cost interventions such as training village women to teach nutrition and family planning are effective and should be implemented. The state should focus on providing a safe water supply, immunizations, disease surveillance, and coordination among private health providers, communities, and local and central governments.

The legitimacy of future elections is at stake so long as the parties' legitimate concerns about the electoral process are not addressed. All political parties should meet in a national conference or a private mediated session to reach agreement on electoral reforms that would permit all parties to participate fully in future elections.

Notes

1. In the Becker-Murphy-Tamura model, two steady states are possible. In a society with no human capital, the return on accumulating such capital is low, and parents will put a low value on each child's future utility. As long as the rate at which future consumption is being discounted is higher than the rate of return on human capital, little human capital will be formed, and the society will be stuck in the low-level equilibrium with high birthrates and no education. In a high-level steady state, on the other hand, increasing returns to human capital formation and increasing costs of rearing children produce an economy with a large stock of human capital, low birthrates and small families. Gary Becker, Kevin Murphy, and Robert Tamura, "Human Capital, Fertility, and Economic Growth," *Journal of Political Economy*, XCVIII (1990), S12–S37.

2. Dani Rodrik, "Getting Interventions Right: How South Korea and Taiwan Grew Rich," *Economic Policy*, XX (1995), 53–108.

3. Douglass North, *Structure and Change in Economic History* (New York, 1981), 22–28; Robert I. Rotberg, *Haiti: The Politics of Squalor* (Boston, 1971), 342–378.

4. Presentation at the conference on "Prospects for Political and Economic Reconstruction in Haiti," Mayagüez, Puerto Rico, September 1995.

5. Ibid.

6. Ibid.

7. Estimates of illiteracy vary widely, indicating the difficulty of obtaining reliable data on Haiti. In its *Economic and Social Progress Report: 1994*, the Inter-American Development Bank reported a 47 percent illiteracy rate for adults in 1990. In its 1995 *Human Development Report,* the UNDP estimated adult illiteracy in 1992 to be 57 percent. Haitian Director of External Cooperation Robert Jean estimated adult illiteracy at 65 percent in his paper for the conference. The U.S. State Department estimated total illiteracy to be 75 percent in *Background Notes* (November 1994).

8. Uli Locher, presentation at the conference Prospects for Political and Economic Reconstruction in Haiti, Mayagüez, Puerto Rico, September 1995.

9. Marie-Andrée Diouf, presentation at the conference Prospects for Political and Economic Reconstruction in Haiti, Mayagüez, Puerto Rico, September 1995.

10. Presentation at the conference Prospects for Political and Economic Reconstruction in Haiti. September 1995.

11. Robert Putnam, *Making Democracy Work* (Princeton, 1993).

12. Presentation at the conference Prospects for Political and Economic Reconstruction in Haiti.

CHAPTER ONE

Resisting Freedom: Cultural Factors in Democracy—The Case for Haiti

Patrick Bellegarde-Smith

The trees fall from time to time, but the voice of the forest never loses its power. Life begins.

—Jacques Alexis, *Les Arbres Musiciens* (Paris, 1957)

HAITIAN SOCIETAL development seems to be filled with paradoxes, contradictions, and enigmas. The process begun with the "encounter" of 1492 was profoundly corrupting in terms of cultural deflections to both the Old World and the New World and to established patterns of interaction everywhere between the powerful and the weak that are still evident today. Haitian history has been marked by struggle and by continuous acts of rebellion that, in more quiescent times, become passive resistance known by the Haitian label, *marronage*.

The Haitian Revolution of 1791, the most complete social revolution in the hemisphere until Mexico in 1910 and Cuba in 1959, was formed by two major distinct movements that coalesced in an unsteady alliance but never fully merged. The first movement, that of the enslaved, was the heir to all earlier slave rebellions, and was consistent with slaves' opposition to slavery and all forms of oppression. The second movement was that of the plantocracy of color. Using a combination of tactics and approaches such as warfare, guerrilla activities, and poisonings, this group terrorized the plantocracy. The leaders were often Vodun priests.

27

Boukman Dutty and a female priest are said to have officiated at a Vodun ceremony at Bois Caïman—doubtless one of many such ceremonies—inaugurating the insurrection of 1791. Makandal, an African-born Muslim with a reputation of being a *bòkò*, led the 1757 revolt.[1] Pierre Dominique Toussaint L'Ouverture, who later ruled, was also thought to be a *bòkò*. Makandal's sacred mission, like that of Zumbi of Palmares, was to rid the colony of its white inhabitants and to create an African kingdom in Saint-Domingue.

The social philosopher Dantès Bellegarde (1877–1966), who was most unsympathetic to Vodun, wrote the following about Makandal: "The certainty [that he had survived execution by the French] played an important role in organizing later uprisings. It maintained the trust of slaves who had found in the Vodun religion a particularly strong ferment to exalt their energies, since Vodun . . . had become less a religion than a political movement, a kind of 'black *Carbonarisme*' whose objective was white extermination and black liberation."[2]

Writing later about Toussaint L'Ouverture, Bellegarde stated: "Some have doubted the sincerity of the Catholic faith of Toussaint without offering a single fact to justify such a doubt." He continued in an apparent contradiction, "he knew from personal experience that the vodun ceremonies were only a pretext for political reunions where, in the secretive 'houmforts' [temples] and in the exaltation of ritual dancing, plots were being hatched against the authorities or, again, attacks against property; [Toussaint] had become the 'authority' [as governor] and had made himself defender of property, which article 13 of the Constitution had declared 'sacred and unassailable'."[3] Under capitalism, property is sacred and freedom of cultural expression can be curtailed in its defense. The slaves qua peasants had been forced to remain on plantations against their will. They revolted, as they would again and again *after* Haitian independence, for which they had fought. Most of the 100,000 deaths during the war for independence were from their ranks.

Toussaint L'Ouverture, as well as all of his successors at the helm of the Haitian state, realized Vodun's potential for challenging the power and authority of the state and the "mainstream" vision of society. Toussaint L'Ouverture was thought by his followers to be a believer in Vodun, reflecting the phrase that "Haiti is 80 percent Catholic, but 100 percent Vodun." This emphasizes the view that it need not be "practiced" to have a valid hold on most minds as a state of mind, a spiritual system, and a world view.[4]

By the time Toussaint L'Ouverture came to power, an awesome change in the nature of the struggle had already begun. The leaders of the first uprisings had died in battle, been assassinated, or been coopted by newcomers who were themselves Westernizers. Plymouth, Jean Biassou, Lamour Dérance, Jean-François Papillon, Romaine la Prophétesse, and, of course, Boukman Dutty, and countless other men and women were "dismissed" in a later phase of the struggle for independence. Westernizers in power have dismissed competing historical explanations of various events.

The majoritarian vision in Haiti, as elsewhere, was established largely on the collective experience of enslavement that, at its onset, had solely an economic purpose: to exploit the natural resources and human capital cheaply for the benefit of the metropolitan elites. Indeed, the colonial state—with intentional as well as unintentional results—set social policies to sustain economic exploitation in the plantation system by converting the enslaved population to Christianity and by assimilating a few to French cultural norms in order to enslave better. Some slaves saw the benefits of such a course of action. The majoritarian vision also developed from the peasants' shared language (Kreyòl) and religion (Vodun) which helped provide them with an ideological superstructure in form *and* content.[5]

Significantly, language and religion were inventions of the Haitian peasants that permitted them to face the power deficit between master and slave, oppressor and oppressed, and a dominant Europe and a subaltern Africa. In both Haitian language and Haitian religion, one finds the necessary compromises and subterfuges that the weak use to survive. They also reflect a "hybridity" built largely on deception, later referred to by some scholars as "Creole culture." But synthesis does not mean syncretism. Neither implies synergy, but sometimes its opposite.[6]

Kreyòl and Vodun are, in the final analysis, organized responses to oppression, created *from* African foundations. Kreyòl appears to have grammatical and syntactical roots in West Africa, notably in the Kwa language group, into which foreign words (such as French) were easily incorporated out of the necessity to communicate with those in power.[7] Kreyòl is conceptually rich, having borrowed from many sources to reflect new artifacts. At no time was Kreyòl "animal talk," "baby talk," "*petit nègre*," "*un français remis en enfance*," or "bad French," as long believed by many scholars. At no time was Vodun "*un Catholicisme mal digéré*," although it may have been *indigeste*. Both emanated from West

African societies remarkable for their overall cultural similarities, although there was certain preeminence achieved over time by a core of Fon, Ewe, Yoruba, and related peoples.[8]

The inclusion of non-African forms into the Haitian language and religion became a form of adaptation rendered necessary by circumstances. Kreyòl became, at once, a "contact" language and a "counterlanguage," the latter with its studied ambiguity, irony, satire, and wit, and its ability to *voye pwent*.[9] In one sense, it defeated the purpose of separating Africans from members of their ethnic group. As a contact language, it became the lingua franca in Saint-Domingue between French and Africans and between African and African. Today, all Haitians speak Kreyòl; less than 10 percent of the population is fluent in French, the other official language. As the national language understood by all, Kreyòl served as the language of widest communication throughout Haiti, particularly in the absence of widespread literacy.[10]

Born in the Americas, Vodun responded to the spiritual and temporal needs such as in health care and psychology of the majority population by amalgamating rituals from west, west central, and south central Africa. Here again, Dahomean and Yoruba elements predominated, with significant contributions from Kongo cultures and civilization.[11] A strong family resemblance exists within the religious systems, moral ideals, and social organizational structures of most African cultures, particularly as concerns ancestral veneration and the cosmic, esoteric, or occult interaction between worlds and universes. The significance of Vodun in the Haitian struggle for independence, in the slave uprisings that preceded it, and in subsequent peasant rebellions, cannot be overstated, nor its importance in most art forms such as music, dance, the plastic arts, and oral literature, as befits a system that is also the culture's repository for social thought, organization, and ideology.

The central role of religion in human affairs is fairly well understood for its explicatory value in all societies. Less a religion than a spiritual system and discipline, Vodun extends "naturally" and easily, permeating all systems, structures, and institutions in the large and subtle ways in which most Haitians view their world and all worlds, even as they migrate.[12] Indeed, Haitians need not be observant, initiated, nor believers to partake of that shared national world view fostered through Vodun.[13] As with Judaism in Israel and Shinto in Japan, Vodun helped define the Haitian nationality and ethos. Roman Catholicism, in its French variant, remained the official religion until 1987 and defined the state, the powers that structured it, and the elites who controlled it. Individuals who have decried Vodun or who have been embarrassed by it have hoped to attain a "higher standard," an interesting point of colonial psychology.[14] The ostensible rejection of Vodun, or any other African cultural marker, has been absurdly common among black populations throughout the Western Hemisphere, where physical oppression has been accompanied by the requisite imposition of European cultural norms, resulting in the marginalization of these groups. They have, in turn, internalized their apparent inferiority and have been given the status of a minority (not necessarily defined in demographic terms). Colonialism engaged all human faculties and has been a factor in all social science.[15] Eurocentric anthropologists, psychologists, and economists, typically anchored in their own civilization, have found it necessary thus far to divide the world between "primitive mentalities" and modern man, and in perfectly rational arguments support directly policies that subjugate most areas of the world.[16]

Power That Defines: Class, "Modeling," and Dominant Paradigms

The leaders who hijacked the twenty-one American republics in the nineteenth century, leading them to formal independence, had come from similar (if not identical) social backgrounds as *criollos* (in Spanish America) and colonists (in the United States). Both groups were descended from Europeans who settled these colonies after they had been "discovered" by their forebears, who had come as conquerors.

The Haitian struggle for independence, formally lasting thirteen years, led to the creation of the first independent Latin American state in 1804. It was, besides, the first "modern" state of African origin on the Western model, followed by Liberia, whose elites were established along identical premises.

The Haitian war of independence came about as a result of an amalgam of diverse movements and conflicts. The first movement arose on the part of the enslaved majority—about 90 percent—as a search for freedom and liberation, defined by them as cultural autonomy and the power of political initiative. The second movement erupted from among the middle groups whose existence came from the social order fostered by the encounter between the West and Africa in colonial Saint-Domingue, as elsewhere. Indeed, between the white apex and the black base of the societal triangle, there existed a level intermediate in status and color, which aspired to be closer to God.[17] Class interests dictated that the affranchis, as the free people were called, would lend their support to whichever group could buttress its insecure social position. Middle classes in all cultures have often felt inherently insecure. In perhaps 99 percent of the cases, they have exercised the option of lending their support in favor of the powerful upper classes. The French Revolution of 1789, *not* the endemic slave uprisings, had unleashed the affranchis' natural reserve, as they wished to remove the petty racial vexations of colonial social apartheid and to become *citoyens actifs* as the revolution had promised.

The affranchis had achieved a significant economic position despite French racism: One-fourth to one-third of the plantations and one-fourth of the slaves belonged to them. The white plantocracy had misgivings about the racial implications of the French Revolution with respect to colonial society. Consequently, many in the white plantocracy were royalists who had sided with France's arch rival, the United Kingdom. Spanish settlers in the Americas had had the same qualms about a liberalizing Spain (under Napoleonic rule), a concern that had led to Mexican independence under Augustín Iturbide, whose group came to power partly to forestall a social revolution from among the (Indian and mestizo) lower class in the early nineteenth century.[18] U.S. intervention in the Spanish-American-Cuban War had a similar genesis. The Haitian affranchis had achieved a status similar to that of the Spanish-American criollos and the North American colonists, with similar conflicts arising in Saint-Domingue as had arisen between criollos and *peninsulares*, the American colonists and the British. In Haiti that dispute carried an additional burden, that of biological "race." The white plantocracy opposed the granting of social and political equality to brown and black planters. What had been a family dispute among putative members of a potential same bourgeoisie would lead to a "racial" war because of the intransigence of white Saint-Dominguois and French racism.

Colonial societies such as Haiti, in which a segment of the population is often formed from the union between ruler and ruled and master and slave from disparate cultures, frequently have as a salient element of their psychology the self-hatred and sense of violation resulting from the cultural and emotional rape that took place. This sense of violation and distrust accounts for tensions in the existing relations between the governed and the social institutions of the country. By forcibly depriving people of their cultural heritage, colonialism sought willfully to structure and organize all social alliances, thereby instituting its domination over the norms and values of the colonized.[19] More often than not this domination resulted in feelings of inferiority among those who had been colonized, in part the very definition of a racial minority. The vanquished often exhibit a form of idolatry vis-à-vis the conqueror. This sort of psychological violence inherent in all colonization—and in religious conversion—together with most colonial administrative practices, goes a long way toward explaining the spirit and the reality of authoritarianism found in neocolonial societies. Often unable to transcend the conditions of their birth, Haitian elites are also victims of the clash between the Western old and a new non-Western world order. Furthermore, in contradistinction with the rigid racialist position of Anglo-Saxon cultures—de jure policies as well as de facto—cultural assimilation was promoted by the Latin powers. Anglo-Saxon societies openly excluded blacks; Latin societies, in theory, included them, but only according to a racialist argument that blacks could be salvaged, despite their having nothing to contribute culturally. Christianity everywhere adopted the Latin version of racism by actively seeking converts from among black populations. Under such odds, what was to be the rational response of Haitian elites?

The grand alliance between slaves and affranchis that culminated in Haitian independence fourteen years later, in fact, was a cynical and calculated effort to coopt the slaves' fighting power for the affranchis' own purposes.[20] That alliance was, nonetheless, the necessary condition for independence, although not for freedom.

The assessment of the philosopher Louis-Joseph Janvier (1855–1911) is particularly useful in this context. Commenting on Haiti's continued authoritarian tradition, he wrote at the turn of the century that "political freedom is an inferior good [compared to] national independence."[21] Ribeiro, the Brazilian scholar, synthesized the conditions left by colonialism, stating, "Each people, even each human being, was affected by and caught up in the European economic system or the ideals of wealth, power, justice, or health inspired by it."[22] This legacy also explained Emperor Jean-Jacques Dessalines' cry of anguish when former affranchis tried to appropriate all property that belonged to their white fathers (not to their black mothers): "What of the poor blacks whose fathers are in Africa, won't they inherit anything?" In the larger context, however, it meant slavish acceptance of liberal ideology as it sustained capitalism, which was seen as quintessentially "modern." In early nineteenth-century Haiti, French political influences, British social thought, and the example of the North American rebellion of 1776 aided in the formulation of Westernized ideologies that were viewed as rationalistic and the sine qua non of modern existence.[23]

The ascendancy of the former affranchis occurred shortly after independence. The consolidation of elite hegemony, starting in the 1820s under the long reign of President Jean- Pierre Boyer, led to the first major postindependence peasant uprising, in 1843. The Piquets, the "suffering army" as the insurgents called themselves, demanded land distribution, the dispossession of the rich, and "black" (peasant) political control. Beaubrun Ardouin, a historian (1796–1865), had claimed the Caribbean as a whole for the mulâtres (a new name for the former affranchis) who had nowhere else to go. Simón Bolivar had made a similar argument for Spanish America.

Despite the "revolutionary" message, there was the continuation of structures, the form and the spirit of colonial constructs adopted from the slave master. The historian Lespinasse (1811–1863) added to the analysis that the spirit of freedom was a mulâtre gift to the blacks— that the slaves had acquired a taste of independence from mulattos. But all must now unite for raison d'état.[24] These historians had rendered in a fairly sophisticated way—the first time this had been done by Westernized blacks anywhere in the world—even earlier analyses published by Haitian intellectuals. In 1817, for instance, Valentin Pompée de Vastey had defended the European colonization of Africa almost a century before it was fully under way.

Whether based on pre-Enlightenment ideologies, or liberalism, conservatism, positivism, or, much later, Marxism and modernization theories, all were ideas expressed by the small coterie of Haitian intellectuals that hoped to help define Haiti to the rest of the world, institute its policies, and define its raison d'être. All of these ideas came from a Western civilization that claimed universality, but in fact remained alien to most Haitians. Once translated into state policy, these ideas were never so broad as to incorporate broad segments of the polity into res publica—neither the very large peasantry, the small urban working class, or at its outset, the emerging middle classes.

The desire of one group to maintain power over others occurred through a brutal econo-political system instituted from the ideological base of a political culture dominated by an upper class, and not necessarily from a national political culture. Elites were fearful of relinquishing pieces of what was a limited pie, which, starting in the 1880s, was also additionally shared by expatriate European, North American, and Levantine elites.[25] Individuals and groups vied for preeminence within a restricted and restrictive social environment, in which perhaps 5 percent of the population counted.[26]

Among the elites, men (and a few women) argued in favor of the French language and of Roman Catholicism as the pillars upon which to erect Haitian culture; some mistook the dream for the reality. The obstacles to achieving this on a widespread basis eventually proved insurmountable. Most Haitians knew that Kreyòl and Vodun were the *poto mitan* (the center posts) of Haitian culture, the language they spoke and the gods they worshipped. The dichotomies in Haiti near the turn of the century between European and African, elites and peasantry, French and Kreyòl, and Catholicism and Vodun were vital echoes of earlier dichotomies between affranchi and slave, brown and black, creole and *bossale*, and civilized and primitive. The dichotomies informed a vision, a world view, and a mentality in which reality, to a large extent, was composed of opposites, and was viewed as such. Haitian society was in fact ordered according to a non-Western view in which knowledge of French and Kreyòl was part of a continuum, in which the majority worshipped the *Loa* (deities) while still going to church, and where shades of brown and black occurred within each extended family. In the final analysis, the national period reflected a continuation of social policies set by France during colonization that were, in a paradox more apparent than real, easier to pursue once the whites had been forcibly removed from the national scene.

The first American occupation of Haiti, (1915–1934), brutal at all levels, was a cultural shock as well.[27] In view of the proud and bellicose racism of the United States as it applied to the whole of Latin America, Haiti—*la France noire* of Jules Michelet—was believed by the United States to be inoperative. Early on, Simón Bolivar had stated that the United States, "so enamored of its own liberties, is already less fond of the liberties of others. Quite the contrary: it has made of this liberty an instrument for causing other people misery."[28] U.S. economic interests in its private sector, far more than strategic interests, had been a primary cause of the occupation.

In the shock of the occupation, emerging middle class intellectuals throughout Haiti rose against the cultural status quo, defending African norms and values adhered to by the majority of Haitians, despite knowing little about them. These efforts did not preclude widespread persecution of Vodun, however, nor did it signify an acceptance of Kreyòl. Hurt to the very core of their souls by an American army that had penetrated Haitian psychic defenses, intellectuals rebelled against the vision expressed by Bellegarde that Haiti was "an intellectual province of France." Later, in the heat of the culture wars he would add, "What would happen to a Dahomean islet in the heart of the Americas?"[29] The *Indigénisme* movement spread nonetheless, inching closer—but not too close—to a peasantry lauded in the abstract.[30] That peasantry had taken the brunt of the U.S. invasion and had responded to that invasion with an armed resistance movement. It appeared to the peasantry that the whites were reinstituting slavery.

Bellegarde's nemesis was his personal friend, Jean Price-Mars (1875–1969), whose works were well placed to "start" the worldwide movement of négritude, yet another literary movement of blacks who had been assimilated into French culture, and who had realized faintly what had been lost. The more radical members of these groups moved toward Marxism. But both Marxism and négritude were still solidly anchored in a Western ethos—an anti-Western Westernism, if you will— similar to Sartre's description of négritude as racist antiracism.[31] These Haitians retained an etic viewpoint; in the context of Haitian upper and middle classes and education, an emic quality remains elusive.

Not so paradoxically, the U.S. occupation shored up the Haitian upper classes, the best guarantors of U.S. hegemonic economic interests in the country, against the rising popular tide. It had been increasingly difficult to quell popular discontent against a status quo established in 1806. A series of ephemeral governments at key points in Haitian history had revealed the disarray of a ruling group faced by pressures from below. At times, only foreign intervention seemed able to maintain political stability.

By 1847, the system had already undergone tremendous stress, largely from the Piquets' uprising. The country had four presidents between 1843 and 1847. As the malaise continued to grow, and rural uprisings maintained pressure on Port-au-Prince—the Caco rebellions might be said to have lasted between 1860 and 1929—six ephemeral governments succeeded one another between 1911 and 1915. Later, additional pressures from the newly conscious middle classes, as distinct from the peasantry, led to five governments between 1956 and 1957. The crises became increasingly severe. After the fall of President Jean-Claude Duvalier in February 1986, five provisional governments took power between 1986 and 1991, and a prolonged military dictatorship under General Raoul Cédras took over, with three distinct administrations between 1991 and 1994.[32]

In each case, the crisis was resolved temporarily—by President and later Emperor Faustin Soulouque in 1847, the American occupation in 1915, the "selection" of President François Duvalier in 1957 with U.S. support, and the election of President Jean-Bertrand Aristide in 1991 and his restoration in 1994, with U.S. support. The United States proved to be a crucial player in the transition between upper class and middle class rule in 1957 and between middle class and "popular" rule in 1991, while its hegemonic interests remained intact or actually increased. A symmetry was being established: Desperate living circumstances would lead to revolutionary conditions, which, in turn, would lead to repression. Each response ultimately led to increased repression.

As If *le Peuple* Mattered: Democracy in Popular Culture

Demographics and class structure, as well as popular culture dictate that the impact of social movements upon the body politic and political culture be considered seriously. The objective had been to stymie popular participation in politics. Frequent declarations about the inherent lack of a democratic tradition in Haiti are ahistorical and are anchored in a Western social science tradition that rejects the reality of class, while itself remaining culture specific.[33] More significant in furthering an understanding of Haiti's political culture might be the study of the ideological superstructure ensconced in a metaphysical world view elaborated by Haitians. Palmares and other similar experiments in indigenous autonomy were destined to fail when at odds with the economic interests of the powerful. Indeed, the cry *"que deviendrait un îlot dahoméen . . . ,"* however ill intentioned and racist, acknowledged that Haiti could be recolonized *because* it was barbaric, as was Africa in the 1940s. The statement did not, however, question the basis for that assertion. The elites' best intentions notwithstanding, they did not preclude neocolonization starting in the 1880s or self-righteous efforts by the international Western community to civilize Haiti.[34] But belles lettres and belles manières did not suffice in saving the country from interference and intervention.

Middle class political control (as distinct from economic power) had incited great hopes in the 1940s. The middle classes did not bring with them the psychological baggage or the reservations of the previous ruling group regarding language and religion. And it claimed to represent *le peuple*. Cultural nationalism transmogrified into political nationalism, and were both a part of an anticolonial arsenal in which the master, nonetheless, remains the model, the *patron* (blueprint or boss) for one's action. These developments indicated that after two centuries of independence, Haiti and the still-colonized Caribbean countries were not far apart politically or culturally. The middle class faced social apartheid and petty humiliations of the kind suffered earlier by the affranchis, whose descendants and intellectual heirs they were now fighting. That middle class had been formed by the economic space created by beneficial worldwide conditions, the political stability provided by the U.S. occupation (that also discriminated against it on the basis of color), and the educational opportunities established by the governments of Philippe-Sudre Dartiguenave and Louis Borno. In fact, the middle class represented a new element in the equation in the *rapport de forces* that failed to live up to the expectations of many.

Although opposed to the first middle class government of President Dumarsais Estimé (1946–1950), the United States supported the second, that of François Duvalier. The United States seemed fairly comfortable with a racial rather than a class analysis, since it could and did blunt class differences while augmenting the "political class" and giving the appearance of expanding democracy. The United States had followed a similar course in Cuba and the Dominican Republic with success. As was later proven within the confines of the United States proper during the Civil Rights movement, an obsession with the social construct "race" (as a form of nationalism), is more easily a part of a conservative and traditionalist agenda than not.[35] The old guard, nonetheless, had viewed the replacement of cherished cultural positions (Haiti as Christian, French, and a part of the Western world), as challenging a national identity, disguising class interests.

The issue of a national identity (hence, personal identity) had a profound impact and implications in all other areas.[36] But for two centuries, the debate took place in a rarefied atmosphere in which the majority of Haitians had no voice. Despite real cultural dislocation, as the intelligentsia peregrinated from Pan-Americanism, to Pan-Caribbeanism, to Pan-Africanism, indigénisme, negritude, and now to Antillanité—all a search for a middle ground and a sustainable identity—the people seemed remarkably unconcerned. The uprisings of yesteryear seem to have been replaced by a form of passive resistance, a *marronage*, reflected in religion, language, and fairly uncontrollable institutions and activities that set the province apart from the "République de Port-au-Prince," the countryside from the urban center when the center's centripetal force was increased purposefully during the occupation.[37] The "*gouvenman lannuit*" was harder to sustain, as the reach of the central government became more realizable.[38] And the widespread and generalized movements that led to the overthrow of the dictatorship in 1986 had come from all segments of the population, including the Catholic Church, the *hounfò* (Vodun temples), Duvalierists (who attempted Duvalierism sans Duvalier), and the army. But because of irreconcilable differences, the grand alliances broke as soon as they coalesced. The popular movement remained unimpressed by political parties (a sine qua non of Western definitions of democracy) until Lavalas came upon the national scene.

But where there is intrusion there is resistance. Only in the area of culture can an oppressed population find a playing field. That resistance was exemplified and illustrated in a culture that was often countercultural and would become the dominant culture if there were a change in the socioeconomic system of the sort that might have been sustained if the Haitian Revolution had survived the assassination of Jean-Jacques Dessalines in October 1806. President Jean-Bertrand Aristide was conscious of both symbol and reality when he took the oath of office in Kreyòl, and received the presidential sash from a *manbo* (female Vodun priest) in February 1991, with symbolic forms of greeting that resonated deeply within the population. His deliberate use of Kreyòl indicated a break and discontinuity in cultural patterns that was strangely symbolic of the synthesis in Vodun and dealt blows to both the elite language (true language, French) and the elite religion (true faith, Catholicism).[39] Subsequently, in 1995 Aristide further evened the playing field between Vodun and Christianity. When he flung open the gates of the presidential mansion to serve food to beggars personally, he simultaneously transformed a white house built on the model of the Petit Trianon into a national palace.

In all fairness to France, the spread of the French language, which was essential in establishing the commonweal, was incomplete by the time of Haitian independence. France was not fluent in French. The French Revolution and the Napoleonic Wars were the context in which that language spread inside France, creating the modern nation state and nationalism as we now understand it. Haiti was linguistically unified before France. The adoption of French (rather than English, which Henri Christophe might have wished) rendered that language a language of differentiation and, in the process, made Kreyòl the language of countercultural resistance. The manichean dichotomy, which is not found in the Vodun religion, need not have occurred: A linguistic continuum has always existed, illustrated by the expressions *parler pointu* and *parler plat*.[40] Language has "color" and becomes a marker for limiting access to power.

Carew, the Guyanese novelist, said that "we have misperceived ourselves since Columbus."[41] But it is also true that criollos and affranchis in Latin America developed a nativism and a nationalism ahead of much of Europe. Why? The answer lies partly in the hybridization of cultures and the deracialization of race in which race remains a factor, and in which the concept of miscegenation acquired a positive cast that it did not acquire in North America. (In the United States, nationalism takes the form of white ethnic chauvinism.) Haitian racial definitions were borrowed from those of northern Europe (France, England, and the United States), and *mulâtres* became "blacks" except when at home, where they became *blan peyi* (local whites)—elsewhere, *blanco de la tierra* (in Spanish), and *branco da terra* (in Portuguese)—raising the specter of caste-like social arrangements and quasi-ethnic differences.[42] *Limpieza de sangre* (purity of blood, clean blood), is but an approximation of desire. New peoples arose in the colonial contexts, different from the lower classes—the raw material for new sociocultural formations. The latter retained a "different" outlook, and their original culture evolved as counterculture.

In religion, the other primary cultural element defining nationality, Haiti's early break with Africa not so paradoxically reinforced Africanisms in which content remains strangely familiar today to Ewe and Fon populations. As in Quebec with French Catholicism, that Vodun remained vital to most forms of political resistance cannot be disputed. The armed resistance to the U.S. occupation, which came exclusively from the countryside, was anchored in the national religion, as seen in this exchange in December 1921 between Monseigneur Jean-Marie Jan, the French Roman Catholic Bishop of Cap Haitien, and Senator Medill McCormick, a member of the U.S. Senate commission that investigated the reports of atrocities leveled against the occupation:

Senator: Your comments on the U.S. occupation of Haiti?
Bishop: The occupation was an act of kindness. . . .
Senator: The war against the Americans, how do you explain it?
Bishop: The people were pushed to desperation by [American] arbitrariness, injustice and mistreatments. It proclaimed its right to self-defense. Does the United States want to impose Protestantism by force?
Senator: The Washington government will never attack Haiti's [Catholic] faith. Can you provide information on Vodun, its practices and status? Has it diminished since the occupation?
Bishop: It has increased. . . . The greatest cause for this is that the bocors *(bokò)* were the soul of the insurrection.[43]

In the battle between French and U.S. imperialism, the French bishop had expressed the well-founded fear that U.S. missionaries would weaken the French traditional advantage in Haiti. At the same time, Edwin Denby, the U.S. Under Secretary of the Navy, was writing E. O. Watson, the director of the U.S. Council of Churches, that "Haiti is within the sphere of the United States . . . and the Churches and the missionary societies can be of very real help. . . . The Navy Department will be happy to facilitate your work in any way possible."[44] The very serious efforts to convert the Haitian population to American Protestantism should be an indication that others have understood the importance of Vodun. The persecutions orchestrated by many Haitian presidents (although themselves believers in Vodun), following Toussaint L'Ouverture's recognition that resistance and conspiracies could well come from these quarters, should provide similar indications. It seems certain that Haitians have found the millenary religion to be a source of empowerment over the past five centuries. Less a religion than a spiritual discipline sustained by awesome rituals, Vodun, as with Kreyòl, provides a fluidity, a cultural continuum and a bridge between those in the upper and middle classes who follow it for its *magie* (magical powers) and those at the bottom who recognize it as a world view sui generis.

The dichotomies between European and African, slaveowner and slave, brown and black, French and Kreyòl, elite and peasant, and Christian and servant of the Loa were created largely out of the necessity for a small minority to subjugate the majority and maintain control for the primary purpose of acquiring wealth. The gulf created through these juxtapositions would seem to be insurmountable, sapping the very notion of "nation." Having their genesis in colonialism, these bifurcations should be seen not as opposites, but as part of a spectrum and a cultural continuum in which Haitians find themselves. Neither Indian Hinduism, Japanese Shinto, nor Native American spirituality has suffered the indignities born by Vodun. The Japanese context in which Buddhism and Shinto have their spheres is instructive. One acknowledges generally the singular importance that Vodun has on all Haitian arts, although not in other domains such as science and psychology.

Questions regarding the issue of identity have been the concern mainly of elites in Haiti, as have questions regarding the power to define, for as new hybrid cultures were developing from the clash of civilizations in the Americas, no such worries occupied the collective minds of le peuple. The issue becomes important, however, when tied to power and class. It needs to be resolved, furthermore, when liberation—subsuming freedom and democracy—is at stake. One must not in the process jettison the outstanding achievements, norms, and values created in the West that could help in the evolution and development of Haiti. A redefinition of both *form* and *context* must take place, however, based on the ethos of a people neglected far too long. A society in which the haves crush the have-nots can never be democratic nor can it be a community, no matter how numerous the elections. And within the purview of a well-organized state, structure and institutions must be willing to address the well-being of the majority in order to ensure some sense of belonging, a modicum of stability, and social peace. Repression inevitably occurs when oppression remains strong; it also occurs when institutions created by the majority are not respected but are instead targeted for destruction. Democracy in Haiti will be an Africanizing process, as the structures of the state come to reflect the institutions of the nation.[45] One might well assume that ancestral values and norms will not be prized as they resurface in the body politic after a lapse of two centuries. New intellectual paradigms in Haitian scholarship are in the offing.

If Haitian history teaches us anything at all, it is the inordinate love for democracy in a people that has never stopped fighting against those who would deny them that freedom. That history is little understood by scholars outside Haiti; the concept of political culture has hence been misapplied; and democracy, seen as the preserve of Western societies, has been defined improperly.

Notes

1. Boukman Eksperyans, a "roots" (racine) band with a high octane "world (African) beat," is named after him. A bòkò is a Vodun priest in the north of Haiti, or a root doctor or magician, elsewhere.

2. Dantès Bellegarde, *Histoire du Peuple Haïtien* (Port-au-Prince, 1953), 59. Carbonarisme refers to a secret Italian society that met in the woods to plot that country's unification in the nineteenth century under the leadership of Guiseppe Garibaldi (1807–1882).

3. Bellegarde, *Histoire,* 77. It was understandable that enslaved Africans—considered to be property—declared war on property.

4. See Patrick Bellegarde-Smith, *Haiti: The Breached Citadel* (Boulder, CO, 1990).

5. As an aside, when unable to find the solution to an algebraic problem in English, I turned to French. This artifice allowed me to gain a fresh perspective on a given question. Language— and a rich vocabulary—can frame an argument.

6. That Vodun and Kreyòl comprise non-Africanized forms reflects in part an admission of fear and lack of control on the part of a large group subjugated to a powerful smaller group. It also demonstrates the necessity of using "new" words for new things. Additionally, in Vodun, the absolute necessity of hiding what was already a mystical religion demanding initiation came as the result of colonial interdiction and as the recognition of the validity of all spiritual systems. (The relationship between Buddhism and Shinto in Japan or perhaps that between Hinduism and Buddhism serve me well here.) I do, however, accept the validity and reality of a "Creole culture" as defined by anthropologists.

7. There are numerous explanations for the development of Creole languages in general and of Kreyòl specifically. I accept the logic of the arguments made by linguistics scholar Marie-Marcelle Buteau Racine and the research of independent scholar, Thérèse Roumer, on these matters. Why would enslaved Africans born in Africa "forget" the structure of their languages? Kreyòl is not a romance language, as stated in Webster's Dictionary, as Yiddish is Germanic.

8. My experience in West Africa would seem to support this argument, where I stunned Africans by demonstrating "pure" Ewe behavior while I was dancing. Many others have spoken of Kreyòl in similar terms.

9. Voye pwent is a feature of Kreyòl that allows a speaker verbally to attack someone indirectly by innuendo. Kreyòl shares these linguistic features with other fairly autonomous African-derived languages and dialects in the Western Hemisphere, notably, black English (or Ebonics) in the United States. "Playin' the dozens," "signifyin'," and "testifyin'" are common examples of kinds of discourse in black English. See the works of Geneva Smitherman.

10. The Kreyòl lexicon is overwhelmingly French although it comprises far-reaching contributions from various African languages, English, American, Spanish, Dutch, and Portuguese. Similarly, although its base is Germanic, English owes much of its vocabulary to Norman French, Latin, and Greek. All Haitians speak Kreyòl; 10 percent know French, and as many or perhaps more, know English. Approximately 5 percent are fluent in Spanish.

11. In the religion these rituals are kept separate, and in various parts of Haiti different rituals dominate. See Robert Farris Thompson, *Flash of the Spirit: African and African-American Art and Philosophy* (New York, 1983).

12. It is common to find Vodun practitioners in most families that purport to despise Vodun. Commonly, one member of an extended family will continue the Vodun rituals for all family members, even among elite families. My personal and academic interests in this subject led me to discover similar behavior among most Haitian presidents and their family members.

13. When a religion is a part of the ethnic patrimony, which is typical in the African setting, it needs no name, since all individuals participate in its rituals at various levels. In Haiti, Vodun (Voodoo, Vaudou, Vodou) is an "invention" necessitated by the presence of other religions in the landscape.

14. See Frantz Fanon, *The Wretched of the Earth* (New York, 1968); Aimé Césaire, *Discours sur le colonialisme* (Paris, 1955); and Albert Memmi, *Portrait du colonisé, précédé du portrait du colonisateur* (Paris, 1957).

15. This view is factored into the academic discipline of africology, but not necessarily in other, more Eurocentric disciplines. Africology complements other disciplines that are Eurocentric in thrust. The africological subfield in psycho-social inquiry is particularly à propos here.

16. See James M. Blaut, *The Colonizer's Model of the World* (New York, 1993), 97–100.

17. An illustration is found in Euzhan Palcy's film "La Rue des cases nègres" (Sugar Cane Alley), about Martinique in the 1930s, in which the son of a white planter and a mulatto woman with aspirations for her son, turns against the colonial structure altogether, embittered by the "irrationality" of his father's racism. God is the white man, and the God of Christians is represented—as he should be—as a white man.

18. The revolution had been planned by two Roman Catholic priests, Miguel Hidalgo and José-Maria Morelos. They paved the way for priests Camilo Torres (Colombia) and Jean-Bertrand Aristide (Haiti), who later led populist social movements.

19. While U.S. President Ronald Reagan bemoaned the missed opportunity to have resolved the Native American "problem" once and for all, they were not "forcibly" assimilated. They were, in large measure, however, assimilated culturally, racially, and linguistically. They were also the victims of widespread genocide.

20. Official Haitian historiography relates the creation of the blue and red flag in 1803 as symbolizing the union of the blacks (mostly slave, represented by the blue) and affranchis (mostly mulatto, represented by the red), and the motto "L'Union fait la force" ("In unity there is strength"). There are alternative popular explanations of the same event.

21. Louis-Joseph Janvier, *Les Constitutions d'Haiti* (Paris, 1886), 32.

22. Darcy Ribeiro, *The Americas and Civilization* (New York, 1971), 49.

23. See my lengthy treatment of that subject in *In the Shadow of Powers: Dantès Bellegarde in Haitian Social Thought* (Atlantic Highlands, NJ, 1985).

24. Beauvais Lespinasse, *Histoire des affranchis de Saint-Domingue* (Paris, 1882), 15–16.

25. See Brenda Gayle Plummer, *Haiti and the Great Powers* (Baton Rouge, 1988), 41–66.

26. See the analysis in Bellegarde-Smith, *In the Shadow of Powers*, 30–53.

27. Roger Gaillard, *Les Blancs débarquent: la guérilla de Batraville* (Port-au-Prince, 1983), 238. An English text is Hans Schmidt, *The United States Occupation of Haiti* (New Brunswick, NJ, 1971), 135–153.

28. Cited by Germán Arciniegas, *Latin America: A Cultural History* (New York, 1967), 379.

29. Dantès Bellegarde, *Haiti et ses problèmes* (Montreal, 1941), 17.

30. My experience with the major poets Léon Laleau and Jean F. Brierre and the Guyanais Léon-Gontran Damas over the years has shown me how tenuous the African connection was. At the end of their lives, all three recanted their negritude to me, personally.

31. Jean-Paul Sartre had written this in a preface, "Orphée noire," to Léopold Sédar Senghor, *Anthologie de la nouvelle poésie nègre et malgache* (Paris, 1948), xx.

32. The ephemeral presidencies were the following: 1843–1847: Rivière Hérard, Philippe Guérrier, Louis Pierrot, Jean-Baptiste Riché. 1908–1911: Antoine Simon, Cincinatus Leconte, Tancrède Auguste, Michel Oreste, Oreste Zamor, Davilmar Théodore, Vilbrun-Guillaume Sam. 1956–1957: Joseph-Nemours Pierre-Louis, Franck Sylvain, the "collégial," Daniel Fignolé, General Antonio Kébreau. After 1986: General Henri Namphy, Leslie Manigat, "Namphy II," General Prosper Avril, Ertha Pascal-Trouillot—after seven months of Jean-Bertrand Aristide(René Préval)—General Raoul Cédras between 1991 and 1994, with three "distinct" presidents or prime ministers: Emile Jonassaint (and Jean-Jacques Honorat), Marc Bazin, and then Aristide II, with Robert Malval, Smarck Michel, and Claudette Werleigh.

33. See Bellegarde-Smith, *Breached*, 175.

34. Major efforts were undertaken by the French Roman Catholic Church after 1862 and by U.S. Protestant missions from 1922 to the present.

35. The leadership of President François Duvalier in Haiti, President Léopold Sédar Senghor in Senegal, and African-American nationalists buttress my position.

36. At a conference of the Association of Caribbean Studies in Martinique in 1984, Roger Toumson, a Martinican thinker speaking on Caribbean identity, stopped in mid-sentence to exclaim: "Only in the Caribbean could we argue about identity after 500 years of colonization. The issue of identity is alien to the French and to most Europeans."

37. The creation of the Haitian army by the United States in 1916 is a part of that movement. See Sidney W. Mintz, "Preface," in James G. Leyburn, *The Haitian People* (New Haven, 1966), v–xxxvi.

38. This is translated as "government-at-night," referring to secret neo-African societies that "govern" the country when the Westernized urban authorities are asleep. Brazilians have a saying, "the country grows when the government is asleep."

39. My impression is that, when given a chance, Haitians become fluent more easily in Spanish and English than in French, since these languages do not carry the psychological baggage of the last.

40. To speak in sharp, crisp Parisian tones versus speaking flatly, in grammatically correct but Haitian-French intonations.

41. Conversations with Jan Carew, Manaus, Brazil (July 1995).

42. See the analysis in Bellegarde-Smith, "Rum as Cognac: Fluidity of an Ethnocultural Crisis—Haiti," *Kaleidoscope II* (Milwaukee, 1994), 13–18.

43. Jean-Marie Jan, *Collecta III* (Port-au-Prince, 1995), 340–344.

44. Ibid., 350–351.

45. Bellegarde-Smith, *In the Shadow of Powers,* 107.

CHAPTER TWO

A Social Contract for Whom?
Haitian History and Haiti's Future

Michel-Rolph Trouillot

"It is evident that I must consider myself . . . as a member of a larger body, on the survival of which my own survival depends absolutely."

—Jean-Jacques Rousseau

THE ILLUSION that Haiti can start from scratch is an old one. Fifty-five years ago, in a pathbreaking book, Leyburn, an American sociologist, wrote: "If ever a country had an opportunity to start absolutely fresh in choosing its own social institutions, Haiti had that opportunity in 1804. . . . The Haitians might (theoretically, at least) have invented an entire new little world of economic, political, religious, and social life. All paths were open to them."[1] Leyburn concludes that, unfortunately, President Jean-Jacques Dessalines's mental limitations set the Haitians upon the road to disaster.

Dessalines himself, the first Haitian chief of state, and his closest advisors (Boisrond Tonnerre, for instance) also believed, though perhaps less than Leyburn, that Haiti could shed most of the burdens of its colonial past. Less than two years later, President Alexandre Pétion and

This paper was completed while the author was a Fellow at the Center for Advanced Study in the Behavioral Sciences. I thank the National Science Foundation, which supported my fellowship at the Center (NSF #SES-9022192) and the Hopkins-Georgetown Haiti Project, which provided logistical support.

others thought that they could erase the legacy of the Dessalines years. President Louis Lysius Félicité Salomon thought he could erase President Boissond Canal. President Dumarsais Estimé thought he had erased President Elie Lescot. President François Duvalier tried to erase everyone else. Similarly, in 1915 the first U.S. occupation was supposed to give Haiti a new start. So was the 1934 departure of the Marines, which was saluted as the "second independence."

In short, alleged new departures are not new to anyone aware of Haitian history. And that should be the first lesson from the past. It is an important lesson in the current context. In 1986, after the fall of the Duvalier dictatorship, euphoric talk of a "second independence," echoing the slogan of 1934, revamped the assumption that Haiti was in for a new start. We learned better between 1986 and 1990. Hopes of new beginnings returned, quite understandably and quite legitimately, with the electoral landslide of President Jean-Bertrand Aristide. They resurfaced with Aristide's own return from exile, declined somewhat at the end of 1995, and continued well into the presidency of René Préval. Similarly, the illusion of an economic tabula rasa that could serve as a new starting point lingers behind most proposals of economic restructuring.

Haiti is not a prisoner of its history. No country is. Nor has Haiti been without a significant political break since 1986. The end of the Duvalier years (1986), the first genuine presidential landslide in Haitian history (1990), the dismissal of the army (1995), and the first transmission of power between two elected presidents (1996) are all important markers of change. Rather, assuming these breaks, I am asking: What else must we break from and to build what? And what must we do to achieve such breaks? In slightly different terms: What are the most serious obstacles impeding Haiti's reconstruction? What are the assets available? What are the most fundamental undertakings?

This is, of course, a huge agenda that no single analyst can exhaust. Yet there are two critical issues within that agenda. I argue that the most serious obstacle to rebuilding Haiti is the flawed relationship between the state and the nation. I also argue that the most serious undertaking on the path to reconstruction is the forging of a social contract that repairs this relationship to the benefit of the nation.

The context is critical. The Haitian nation is fundamentally rural in its demographic distribution. Haiti's so-called *arrière-pays* is most of Haiti. Even more important, both in structural and quantitative terms, is the fact that thus far the majority of Haitians have survived primarily because of what can be called the rural economy. The social, economic, cultural, and political effects of this rural grounding are fundamental and cannot be wished away. Any social contract needs to take that fact into account.

The notion of a social contract evokes political philosophers from Thomas Hobbes and John Locke to David Hume and, especially, Jean-Jacques Rousseau, who popularized the term with his famous title.[2] Although my arguments are flavored by Rousseau's particular view of the social contract, they do not require an exegesis of Rousseau's writings or a central commitment to his political theories.[3] Two ideas that are essential—though not unique—to Rousseau's thinking are nevertheless of crucial relevance to my reading of Haiti. The first is the now banal ideal that only the general will can guide the state toward the common interest. The second is that the emergence of this general will is tied to the citizens' recognition of their absolute interdependence.[4]

These ideas are directly relevant to the Haitian situation for two reasons. First, it is certain that the Haitian state has never represented the general will of the citizenry, however defined. Indeed, the schism between state and nation has led the state to crush systematically the common interest of the Haitian people. Second, the notion of a necessary interdependence within and, especially, across classes is largely foreign to Haitian social and political practice. To put it most simply, few Haitians feel—and act as if—all Haitians are in the same boat. Rousseau saw a strong sense of interdependence and the personal renouncements that it entails as necessary to his ideal social contract. I suggest that Haiti will not move decisively toward democracy without a minimal recognition of interdependence on the part of its elites. I suggest further that only a national debate on the future of the country may convince elites that this recognition is necessary to their own survival.

Social Contracts and Nationhood

When Haiti became independent in 1804, there was no Haitian nation. There was a political project, freedom, and independence, embodied in the alliance between Pétion and Dessalines. There was also a state apparatus embodied in the army. Both of these were legacies of the Toussaint Louverture years, modified to fit the alliance and the changing circumstances. Louverture first built an army between 1793 and 1797. Between 1797 and 1801, he consolidated the political and administrative apparatus built with and around that army. This militarized state apparatus was the key institutional asset with which Dessalines began independence in 1804.[5]

Historically speaking, Haiti did not start as a nation. It began, instead, as a rebellion that begot an army. The army begot a national apparatus. That militarized apparatus, in turn, begot the state. The nation trailed behind. Or, to pursue the metaphor to its bloody end, the state miscarried the nation.

Yet contrary to what most people may think, the Haitian story is not that exceptional so far. Many modern states grew out of either a military—often feudal—apparatus or out of a colonial—often militarized—apparatus. Most such states evolved before the modern nations we associate with them. That is the case certainly of India, of most African and Latin American states, and even of China. That is also the case of nations of the Middle East, with the notable exception of Israel, where a transnational nation can be said to have claimed statehood. It is even the case of most of Europe—Britain, Spain, Portugal, and, certainly, France. Francis I used the violence of the absolutist state to convince his subjects that they were Frenchmen. It took three centuries, a revolution, and, in particular, Napoleon—that most foreign of French leaders—to build the French nation as it now stands. The outstanding European exception may be Italy, where the nation can be said to have consolidated before the state. On the western side of the Atlantic, only in the case of the United States is there serious debate about whether the nation came before the state.[6]

Thus, the chronology sketched above does not at all imply that the Haitian nation was doomed from the start. It does suggest, however, that nation building would first occur within the limitations imposed by that militarized state apparatus, at least in the immediate aftermath of independence. A concrete and obvious example is the militarized agricultural system, the so-called *caporalisme agraire* deployed by Toussaint Louverture. Emperor Dessalines, King Henri Christophe, and President Jean-Pierre Boyer tried to revamp it with decreasing degrees of success. Less obvious, but no less concrete, is the military handling of most matters related to the social and cultural life of the nation, from language to marriage to religion.[7]

The demise of the plantation system and of the related military organization of agricultural production could have provided an opportunity to reshuffle Haiti's social landscape. After 1804 there was a chance for the nation to enter into a dialogue with the state on terms more beneficial to the majority. There was, especially, a chance for those who controlled the state to make a deal with the nation.

Such a deal typifies the countries that are today, in different ways and to different degrees, models of democratic states. At some point, most often in reaction to a new economic order, political reshuffling, or a combination of both, dominant classes backed up by the state offer the nation a package that is palatable to the majority. That package is never final, but it entails a broad sense of economic, political, and social direction. Although it is rarely, if ever, devised for the total benefit of the majority, the package usually contains enough social, economic, cultural, and political concessions to a working class majority for that majority to adhere to it.

What seals such adherence is, indeed, the capacity of the state and the dominant classes, usually the upper bourgeoisie, to convince the majority that they are all in the same boat. To some extent, the upper classes themselves must believe in that package. Indeed, they know, however awkwardly, that they cannot survive if the majority is completely destroyed. Thus beyond the recognition of sameness, however genuine, is the recognition of a necessity of interdependence. Well-known adages confirm this recognition: "politics is the art of compromise"; "half a loaf is better than none." These sayings pertain to the political sphere and describe correctly what happens in that sphere, because political life reflects the deeper interaction of social and civil life.

Rousseau's reflections aside, I am not arguing that citizens go about their daily routine thinking about interdependence. Rather, they engage in civil life as if a number of social bargains were taken for granted; their daily practice, in turn, confirms some of these assumptions. Thus although the degree of interdependence varies greatly in practice, it is the recognition of its necessity that drives to the negotiating table those who could yield absolute power.

This give-and-take among various segments of the society, sealed as it is by state power, the conviction of national sameness, and, not least, the necessity of survival, is what I mean by a social contract. The allusion to Rousseau is obvious, though my objective is more modest than Rousseau's ideal projection.[8] If nations are, indeed, imagined communities sealed by the practice of daily life,[9] social contracts are among the most solid building blocks of that imagination. A social contract is the confirmation of nationhood, the confirmation of civil society by the state, and the confirmation of sameness and interdependence across class boundaries.

Apartheid and Dictatorships

What happened in nineteenth-century Haiti was the opposite of a social contract. The reaction of the urban elites to the rise of the peasantry was to turn away from anything that would resemble a package of entitlements for the majority. Rather, the choice was to turn to a system of social apartheid.

By "choice," I do not mean necessarily to investigate the individual motives of historical actors long dead. I do mean, however, that the institutional arrangements put together by the Haitian elites aimed at particular results. I mean that social and economic apartheid was premised on these results and that at least some within these elites knew it and did not care. Slowly but surely, from the first tax proposal of Général Bonnet, the leader of the self-appointed Senate of 1807, during the presidency of Pétion, to the timid reforms of Salomon, the minister of finance under Emperor Soulouque, most measures taken by the Haitian state only confirmed apartheid. Half a century after independence, the Haitian urban elites, political and economic, had given up the very idea of a social contract that would seal the nation across classes. By the time that the U.S. Marines landed in Bizoton in 1915, the elites and the state had learned to live only at the expense of the nation.[10]

To the extent that the absence of a social contract continues to plague Haiti today and undermines the legitimacy of the state, this is not a lesson from the past. Unlike the elites and upper classes in most of the countries that could be labeled democratic, those in Haiti intend to succeed whether or not the majority of the nation survives. If some within the majority happen to eke out a living, so be it; if most of the majority does not make it, tough luck.[11]

In the context of Haiti's increasing poverty, that attitude now horrifies many foreign observers. They see with contempt people who insist on having the whole loaf, even if that means the destruction of their own country. Thus, in the early 1990s the Haitian elites earned the label "morally repugnant elites" (MRE). It was used in the U.S. press to describe them. Moral judgments aside, however, the analytical point is that those who rule Haiti economically and politically never offered a social contract to the rest of the nation. They never developed a historical sense of interdependence, even minimally. The MRE label is recent; the indifference it describes is long-standing. What characterizes Haiti is an economic elite and a political class that *sincerely and honestly believe they can survive and reproduce regardless of what happens to the nation.* That peculiar phenomenon has less to do with morals unique to Haiti than with the socioeconomic organization of the country and the positioning of the Haitian state. It predates the Duvaliers' dictatorship. It has survived the *déchoukaj*. It has survived and may continue well beyond the transmission of power from Aristide to Préval.

The Past and the Future

The absence of a social contract in Haiti fundamentally undermines the legitimacy of the Haitian state, regardless of the popularity of the government of the day. It dooms all attempts to introduce democracy via a mere institutional reform or through a populist consensus.[12] Indeed, Haitian politics from 1986 to the present demonstrates the chronic weakness of the state. Lavalas and Aristide signified the entry of forgotten segments of the population onto the political stage.[13] Yet neither the president nor his movement was able to rechannel the tremendous political will that had made them possible.

During Aristide's tenure, Haiti enjoyed the double luxury of a popular and legitimate president. Yet the legitimacy of Aristide's presidency never extended to his government or, to be more precise, to measures taken by his government. The second Aristide government drafted, designed, and started to implement a social and economic program that was received with suspicion by large segments of the citizenry. The government never dealt with this suspicion in a democratic manner, however. The program was not submitted to the Haitian people, either through Parliament or through any other kind of public forum where it could have been debated properly. Regardless of what we think of the relative merits of the Paris Plan, it is generally accepted that the first hurried attempt at implementation was not an illustration of democracy at work.[14]

No government can be more legitimate than the state it embodies. Because of the lack of legitimacy of the Haitian state, every single political leader, from the president to a minor legislator, always has to renegotiate from scratch his or her right to govern. President Préval, for instance, has discovered that he has to negotiate anew both the representativeness of Lavalas and his own right to lead the movement. Will he manage to keep intact the fragile parliamentary alliance assembled by

Aristide? President Aristide was not able to guarantee the legitimacy of his office or to pass on a mantle of legitimacy to his successor. Only his extraordinary popularity masked the weaknesses of his office.

Little time is left before issues of legitimacy limit further the field of maneuver of the Préval regime. That time can be used to set an agenda that goes beyond Préval's tenure. It can be used by President Préval, former President Aristide, as well as grassroots leaders to set an agenda and open a debate that transcends the politics of the new regime and aims directly at a repositioning of the Haitian state. President Aristide lost the historic chance of implementing such an agenda, at least during his first term.[15]

Aristide came to power with as much chance as anyone since Dessalines to unify the Haitian nation. To say this is not to minimize the deep divisions that coalesced around his presence in the National Palace. On the contrary, precisely because these divisions were voiced, precisely because the Haitian elites felt threatened as never before and had to reveal all their cards—including the extent of their indifference to the suffering of the common people— the president could have paved the way for a civil debate about these divisions. He had the popular support necessary to steer such a debate to a peaceful conclusion.

President Aristide missed that opportunity, mainly for three reasons. First, and most importantly, the coup robbed him of his due chance. There is no way to know how an Aristide presidency would have evolved without the coup. In that sense, the Haitian military and its elite backers wounded the nation much more than they hurt Aristide himself.

Aristide's two other wounds, however, were self-inflicted. Coming, as it were, from different sides of his political persona, they also reveal the limits of the Lavalas movement both before and after the coup. Before the coup, the first Aristide regime needlessly adopted a leftist rhetoric and a populist style of governance that genuinely scared many Haitians who could have been convinced that a national debate was necessary. After the coup, the second Aristide regime proceeded as if the debate had taken place. Aristide's populist credentials and extraordinary charisma masked the social direction of his second regime.

Aristide, Préval, and the entire Lavalas movement missed another golden opportunity during the 1995 presidential elections. Few observers had doubts that the Lavalas candidate, whoever he or she was, would easily win at the polls. In the absence of serious opposition, Lavalas had the luxury to develop its own platform without political risk. It had a chance to use the platform as a working document for a conversation about Haiti's future and the construction of a full-fledged political party. Alas, the campaign was uninspiring. Yet many of the questions swept under the table both before and after that campaign resurfaced as Préval started to put his own stamp on matters of governance.

The Préval government moved much faster than the second Aristide regime toward the implementation of the new economic program. Yet by the president's own admission, his government had avoided public debate about the contents and objectives of its otherwise publicized negotiations with the IMF and the World Bank. By April 1996 the substantial part of the middle class that depends on government salaries had voiced its increasing dissatisfaction with the government. By May, protests and demonstrations had increased in the capital and in the other towns. More importantly, by mid-1996 there were obvious cracks within the Lavalas movement. Some grassroots leaders were calling for a new *déchoukaj*. Others shunned Préval's closest advisers or key members of the Lavalas platform. In the future, antidemocratic factions from the right may use any growing cracks within Lavalas to attempt another coup. Whatever the scenarios, the new president will not benefit from the popularity that shielded Aristide.

Aristide enjoyed a teflon effect similar to that of Ronald Reagan. Criticism, fair or unjust, and even obvious political mistakes did not much curtail his popularity. Further, influential voices within the political class preferred to blame Aristide's advisers or ministers than to criticize the president himself.[16] Very few Lavalas leaders, including Préval and even Aristide, perhaps, if he runs again, will benefit from such a teflon effect.

In short, the lack of legitimacy of the Haitian state, partly masked by Aristide's popularity in the 1990s, will continue to haunt any government until the political class publicly understands the need for an enduring social contract.

The Peasantry and the Nation

Any social contract requires a clear and explicit acknowledgment that Haiti is foremost a rural country, that this rural grounding is more than merely demographic, and that it is the reality whether or not we like it.

Lest I am accused of romanticizing the peasantry, let me say loudly and clearly that I am not sure that Haiti has a peasant future. At the very least, I fully agree that rural Haiti as we know it is doomed. But that is not the issue. The issue is that the future is in the present just as the present is in the past. And, at present, Haiti's social and economic reality is fundamentally rooted in its rural world. That is where we start, especially if we want to change that reality. For Haitians cannot be in the same boat if the Haitian peasants who represent a majority of that population are not in the boat as well.

There is an illusion among some observers, especially foreign observers, that the reality of the peasantry can be bypassed politically. That illusion rests on two arguments, sometimes intertwined, and always complementary. The first stresses the economic frailty of the peasantry. It assumes that the Haitian peasantry cannot play a political role in the construction of democracy because of its structural economic weaknesses. The urban poor and an urban working class yet to be built would be the prime driving forces behind democratic change, making the peasantry irrelevant.

This contempt for the rural world makes strange bedfellows. It is shared equally by orthodox marxists echoing Karl Marx's disregard for the "sack of potatoes," and by orthodox capitalist planners who dream of a Western-style Haitian working class. The difficulty, of course, is the agonizing interval between the rise of that working class and the slow death of an entire country. Even if the formulas most acclaimed by armchair economists actually guaranteed growth—a promise that remains to be fulfilled—we would need to flesh out what this actually meant for a country like Haiti, lest we believe it possible for a country to grow while its majority dies.[17]

While the first argument complies with economic determinism, liberal or marxist, the second is rooted in cultural determinism. It assumes that, for a number of reasons from illiteracy to traditional values to belief in the supernatural, the Haitian rural world is not ready for an accountable system of governance. The illusion duplicates that of Haitian reformers of the nineteenth century (notably, the Parti Libéral leaders) who thought that good politics could be only urban based in a country like Haiti. The fate of the Parti Libéral itself is a good antidote against that illusion. Frustrated by years of fruitless struggles and damaged by political bruises, many of which were self-inflicted, these enlightened gentlemen concluded that only military force could further their democratic goals. They launched an ill-fated invasion against the Salomon government. Liberal elitism died with them, until it was resurrected under U.S. influence at the end of the 1915–1934 occupation.

The Haitian rural world may never be at the forefront of electoral or activist politics as segments of it tried to be in the early nineteenth century. But the political support of the rural population is vital in Haiti, and is a sine qua non of any fundamental change. National politics requires locating what politicians call "the heart of the nation." Democracy will not last long in Haiti without national support. That support will not come if a majority of the Haitian rural population does not believe that the state, for the first time, is on its side and that all Haitians are finally in the same boat.

Reforms are costly, regardless of their orientation. Sweeping reforms are even costlier, both in social and cultural terms. Why should any majority support such efforts if that majority does not believe, rightly or wrongly, that it will collect some of the dividends of such reforms, at least at some future point?

The post-Aristide period can be used to evoke that future publicly. Haiti needs a national debate that goes beyond the individual disputes that typified its tormented history, beyond even the cyclical discussions that mark electoral campaigns in formal democracies. That debate was possible in 1986–1987. Haitians missed the opportunity. That opportunity emerged again immediately after Aristide took office: The president could have used the momentum of his landslide victory to call all Haitians to participate in a conversation on the future of Haiti. He did not do so. This chance was missed again during the 1995 presidential elections. It should not be missed again.

Lavalas's political leaders have revealed their capacity to move wide segments of the population. They can use that same capacity to assure that the next Haitian government engages the entire nation in a debate about its future. President Aristide achieved the much needed reconciliation between his government and the Haitian elites. Let his successor at least begin the even more needed reconciliation between the state and the rest of the nation.

Conclusion

The deepest roots of Haiti's political problems are not in the country's politics. Institutional reforms will not erase them. Nor are these roots to be found in cultural factors, fictitious or real. As an anthropologist, I find scientifically dubious and often racist all cultural explanations of the

Haitian quagmire.[18] To be sure, Haiti faces a number of cultural problems on the road to accountable government. The moral turpitude of the elites is real, but its roots are in the socioeconomic organization of the country. Illiteracy, also, is a very serious concern and a contributing factor, but not *the* stumbling block to a balanced political system. Nor, for that matter, is an all-too-real tradition of extreme partisanship to be blamed for Haiti's political distress.

The deepest roots of Haiti's political problems lie in social inequality and economic maldistribution. The political sphere will follow if these most important issues are addressed. There is no guarantee that democracy will emerge from a new social arrangement. Even if that new arrangement ensures growth in productivity, as it should, Haiti's infrastructural problems are so enormous that future governments will have a hard time in maintaining the balance across classes that is implicit in any social contract. Thus a new social arrangement will be difficult to initiate and even harder to maintain. But therein lies the only chance that the Haitian state may gain the legitimacy that it never achieved. Therein, too, lies the only chance that most Haitians will start feeling that they are in the same boat, and that the boat is not going to Florida.

Notes

1. James G. Leyburn, *The Haitian People* (New Haven, 1941).

2. Thomas Redpath, "Réflections sur la nature du concept de Contrat social chez Hobbes, Locke, Rousseau et Hume," in idem, *Etudes sur le Contrat Social de Jean-Jacques Rousseau* (Paris, 1964), 55–65.

3. For rich interpretations of Rousseau's *Social Contract*, see *Etudes sur le Contrat Social.*

4. The need for that recognition comes out repeatedly in the *Social Contract,* but Rousseau expresses it most clearly in the *Lettres à Sophie:* "Now that my life, my security, my freedom and my happiness depend on the collaboration of my peers, it is evident that I must not consider myself anymore as an isolated individual being, but as part of a larger whole, as a member of a larger body, on whose survival my own depends absolutely, and that cannot be deranged lest I myself experience this disorder." *Rousseau, Oeuvres Complètes* (Paris, 1839), IX, 367 (trans. by Trouillot).

5. Tadeusz Lepkowski, *Haiti*, 2 vols. (Havana, 1968–1969).

6. On state formation and the relationship between state and nation, see Benedict Anderson, *Imagined Communities: Reflections on the Origins and Spread of Nationalism* (London, 1983); Michel-Rolph Trouillot, *Haiti: State Against Nation. The Origins and Legacy of Duvalierism* (New York, 1990).

7. An interesting exception is the regime of Dessalines, which was liberal and, at

times, progressive on social and cultural issues, notwithstanding his reputed brutality. S. Linstant De Pradine, *Receuil général des lois et actes du governement d'Haïti 1804–1808* (Paris, 1886).

8. My social contract comes closer to what Rousseau, always suspicious of illusory freedoms, labeled a false social contract. It has the advantage of realism.

9. Anderson, *Imagined Communities*.

10. For a full development of the institutional arrangements behind this schism, see Trouillot, *State Against Nation*.

11. That feeling is encapsulated by the saying, *Ayiti mèt kraze*, which was easily revamped by the coup leaders. *Ayiti mèt kraze, Aristide pap tounen*: Haiti may disappear, Aristide should not return. But the coup leaders only expressed feelings that had been expressed repeatedly in different contexts throughout a century and a half. An illustrative analogy is the way most whites in the United States approach their black compatriots, not necessarily as individuals, but rather as a corporate group. From that corporate viewpoint there is no doubt about the belief that the United States can succeed without its black minority. And, for all I know, this may be correct—if not morally, at least in sheer cost accounting terms. The difference in Haiti, as in South Africa for that matter, is that we are not talking about a demographic minority, but about the bulk of the nation.

12. Michel-Rolph Trouillot, "Etat et duvaliérisme," in Gérard Barthélémy and Christian Girault (eds.), *La République haitienne: Etat des lieux et perspectives* (Paris, 1993), 189–192.

13. Michel-Rolph Trouillot, "Aristide's Challenge," *New York Review of Books* (November 3, 1994), 39–40; Robert Fatton, "Haiti's Road to Democracy: Contradictions and Paradoxes," Haiti Papers, Institute for Global Studies, Johns Hopkins University (Baltimore, 1995).

14. I have dealt elsewhere with the merits of this program; see, for example, Trouillot, "Aristide's Challenge."

15. Aristide is young enough for us not to rule out the possibility that he may seek national office in the future.

16. In 1994–1995, for instance, *Haiti en Marche*, which staunchly supported president Aristide, increasingly criticized the social and economic agenda of "Smark Michel's government." By late 1995, many pro-Lavalas sectors launched war against Michel without ever criticizing the president.

17. From a social viewpoint, growth is an empty category, void of historical actors. Let me hasten to say that it is a necessary one, but by no means the sole measure of national health. After all, on sheer quantitative grounds, Haiti itself in the eighteenth century was the richest colony of the Western world. Only when the numbers are broken down and the social reality is examined does it become clear that "rich" actually meant "profitable." In short, "growth," like "democracy," whatever else it may mean, is significant to the nation only if it trickles down to the well-being of the average citizen.

18. Trouillot, "Aristide's Challenge," 39–40; idem., "Rural Localities, National Realities," Haiti Papers, Institute for Global Studies, Johns Hopkins University (Baltimore, 1996).

CHAPTER THREE

The Haitian Dilemma Reexamined: Lessons from the Past in the Light of Some New Economic Theory

Mats Lundahl

A GOOD PART of our knowledge of how economies develop can be attributed to historical observation, and only the historical "laboratory" is large enough to offer the development economist the variety required for generalization and construction of theories of wide applicability.[1] Unfortunately, the economics profession has often failed to recognize this reality, and has proceeded instead in an armchair fashion.

Economists are not the only ones to blame, however. Economic historians often do a poor job interpreting their data for lack of an appropriate theory. Their historical analyses frequently take place in a theory-less vacuum or overemphasize the historically specific circumstances of a particular phenomenon while overlooking important general aspects that may be brought to bear on a wider range of situations.

The present chapter constitutes an attempt to make use of both economic theory and historical observation. It deals with economic and political lessons from Haiti's past as they emerge from the application mainly of some of the most recent strands of growth theory and political economy to the historical material. The intent is to offer insights with respect to the obstacles that must be overcome if Haiti is to break out of its present low-income equilibrium.

Thanks are due to Clive Gray, Paul Latortue, Robert Maguire, Ferauld Maignon, Robert Rotberg, and Charles Tardieu for constructive criticism of the original version.

The Rise of Saint-Domingue: A Staples Episode

A series of critical events was responsible for shaping the course of Haiti's economic history.[2] One was the creation of the French colony of Saint-Domingue during the seventeenth and eighteenth centuries. Let us begin by highlighting some of the salient characteristics of the colonial economy with the aid of the staples theory of economic growth.[3]

A staple is defined as a product with a large natural resource content, the production of which, in some sense, must take place on the spot, and which furthermore does not require any elaborate processing demanding special skills or large amounts of capital. It is valuable enough to bear transport costs and it is in international demand.[4] Typically, staples are either minerals or agricultural products, and they enter international trade either because a natural resource has been discovered, because the capital or knowledge or both necessary for the exploitation of a known but hitherto unexploited resource is made available, or because the demand for the resource in question increases enough to make its production worthwhile.

If we limit our attention to agricultural produce, staples episodes—notably the opening of the economy to international trade—tend to conform to a pattern. Historically, this has been the case with the *regions of recent settlement*, like Canada, United States, Australia, and Argentina; with *plantation economies*, like Malaya or Costa Rica; as well as with *peasant export economies*, like the Gold Coast or Burma.[5] Saint-Domingue is another case in point: a plantation economy par excellence. The common features are rising international prices and expanding markets, the existence of a land frontier—that is, uncultivated land that has to be cleared at a cost in terms of labor and capital—and the generation of a demand for labor and capital that has to be satisfied, at least in part, by foreign sources.

The most important staple of Saint-Domingue was sugar (with coffee following close behind at the end of the colonial period.[6] Sugar had already been introduced by the Spaniards at the beginning of the sixteenth century. It had been considered a luxury item in medieval Europe, but with the Spanish and Portuguese conquest of the Atlantic islands, larger quantities could be made available at a lower price, and its consumption spread to ever wider circles of European society. By the early eighteenth century a strong international demand had been established.

The colony of Saint-Domingue was in an excellent position to respond to this demand. The climate was ideal for sugar production. Moreover, Saint-Domingue had a land frontier. The Spaniards had first destroyed the indigenous population and thereafter, from the early seventeenth century, left the western third of Hispaniola virtually uninhabited. The French moved into this vacuum, and, in time, a sugar economy was established. During most of the eighteenth century, sugar plantations remained an attractive investment in the colony, with French sugar driving its English competitor out of the continental European market between 1720 and 1740. In 1883 the sugar production of Saint-Domingue was almost equal to that of all the British Caribbean colonies combined. The capital required for establishing the plantations and their crushing mills came from France, and the necessary labor was imported from Africa.

Other plantation crops were introduced as well, following the staples pattern: coffee, indigo, cocoa, and cotton, all requiring less capital and less labor. Saint-Domingue never became a monoculture economy, and toward the end of the colonial period, the value of coffee exports was almost as high as that of sugar exports.[7] In 1789 Saint-Domingue was producing as much as 60 percent of the world's coffee.[8] This coffee was produced with the aid of the best technology of its day. By the eve of the slave uprising that triggered the wars of liberation in 1791, the French planters of Saint-Domingue had already pioneered new techniques of coffee cultivation (pruning, drying, and cleaning) which had established a reputation for quality second to none in the world. French planter society possessed some unique skills that were used to excellent effect in coffee production.[9]

The sugar story is slightly different. The main characteristic of sugar technology was the indivisibility of the crushing mill that made for both the (relatively large) optimum size of the plantation and the corresponding optimum size of the slave labor force needed to cut the cane and bring it to mill.[10] Whether the technology employed by the French in Saint-Domingue was superior to that used by their competitors elsewhere is somewhat of a moot point. Rotberg and Clague offer the following summary:

> Whether the competitive edge of Saint-Domingue over the British islands was due to the superior fertility of its soil or to the skill and industry of the French is a matter on which the British and the French disagreed. Edwards estimated the sugar yields per acre to be two-thirds greater in Saint-Domingue than in Jamaica, but he

attributes this to the better irrigational possibilities and superior soils in Saint-Domingue. Vernault de Charmilly asserts that the French planters were more innovative and industrious, in part because absenteeism was less prevalent than in Jamaica.

Ragatz, who is very critical of the entrepreneurial failings of the British planters, indicates that the French might have been more enterprising. He attributes inertia in large measure to absenteeism. Perhaps one reason for the industry and enterprise of the Saint-Domingue planters was the migration there in the seventeenth century of French Protestants.

Saint-Domingue also had the benefit of a somewhat more enlightened colonial policy than that applied to the British islands. . . . Still, that Saint-Domingue was more prosperous was not solely a function of differences in colonial policy vis-à-vis the British-held islands. Saint-Domingue's soils were fertile and extensive, and her French owners had put their talents and their savings to work to create an impressive and efficient economic machine.[11]

At any rate, there seems to be no evidence to suggest that the techniques employed in Saint-Domingue were any less advanced than those used elsewhere, even though few people were involved in the high-level technical and managerial operations.[12]

When the wars of liberation broke out in 1791, Saint-Domingue was a plantation economy that in many ways was at the technological forefront of plantation agriculture. During the course of these wars, and during the decades that followed, the country underwent a technological retrogression.[13] It can even be argued that the agricultural technology that prevailed during the last decades of the colonial period was superior to the practices available to present-day peasants.

During the nineteenth century, the unit value of Haitian coffee sold abroad declined relative to that of the produce of other coffee-exporting countries. Apparently, this was the result of the adoption not only of less labor-intensive techniques but also of inferior technology. Elaborate French practices could no longer be maintained when the small peasant family farm replaced the large colonial plantation.

Since then, little progress has been made. Today's agricultural technology has much more in common with nineteenth- than with eighteenth-century practices. Attempts undertaken during the American occupation (1915–1934) to upgrade the technological level of agriculture by way of education failed completely, as did attempts to introduce new varieties of some of the most important crops. Later efforts fared no better. The Haitian peasant continues to work his land with the aid of techniques selected from a technological spectrum that is far from the efficiency frontier. In fact, it is difficult to find examples of successful innovations in the Haitian countryside.

The obvious question at this stage is: What caused this technological retrogression with consequences that continue to have an impact to this day? To answer this question, I will make use of an approach to knowledge and economic growth that incorporates endogenous population growth as one of its main features. The purpose is to demonstrate how Haiti may have turned from a high-knowledge, or high-technology, economy, where population growth was no problem, into a low-knowledge, low-technology economy with a rate of population growth that perpetuates such a low-level equilibrium.

Children versus Education

In a model that incorporates both endogenous fertility and accumulation of human capital, Becker, Murphy, and Tamura point to the conflict between having more children and educating the ones you already have and explore the implications for economic growth.[14] The model is one of overlapping generations with parents who, to varying degrees, are altruistic with respect to their children. These parents derive utility from their own consumption in the present but also from the utility their children obtain in the future, when they themselves are no longer around. The latter is discounted with an altruism factor that is lower the larger the family.

Child rearing requires both material (consumption) goods and time (care). If, in addition, the children are to accumulate human capital, they must be taught, and how much they accumulate depends, on the one hand, on how much time the parents' generation devotes to teaching them and, on the other, the parents' endowment of human capital. The parents may also choose to produce consumption goods, which requires both time and human capital.

Two problems face the parental generation. First it must decide how many children to have, given that children require both time and consumption goods and hence compete with the parents' own consumption. Second, it must decide how to divide its time between simple child rearing, education of the children, and production of consumption goods. These two decisions are interdependent. (The problem may be simplified by assuming that the time and material goods required per child for simple child-rearing are both constant.)

How many children will then be born, and how much human capital will be accumulated? The answer to these questions is that two steady states are possible.[15] To see how this works, assume that society has no human capital at all. This means that the return to accumulating such capital is likely to be very low. Human capital has a special feature in that it displays increasing returns to the already accumulated stock. The better educated a society, the easier it is to accumulate more human capital, at least up to some point where "it becomes increasingly difficult to absorb more knowledge."[16] Possibly, accumulation can go on indefinitely without reaching this point.

This means that in a society with no human capital, relatively more time is available for rearing children, that families will be large as a consequence, and that the value the parents attach to each child's future utility will be low. The rate at which the future is being discounted is then likely to be higher than the rate of return on human capital, and no accumulation of human capital will take place. The economy is stuck in an undeveloped or underdeveloped state with high birthrates and no education.

This low-level equilibrium is locally stable. Small additions to human capital will be of no avail: The economy simply returns to the original steady state. To break the deadlock, human capital formation is required that is large enough to raise the rate of return to the point where it is higher than the rate of discount on future consumption. Unless more human capital is being accumulated in each period than that which wears out, the economy will always fall back to the zero human capital position.

For a breakthrough to be possible, exogenous forces must come into play. Individual, marginal decisions do not suffice. A jump or big push is necessary. Once this jump has been achieved, however, increasing returns to human capital formation in combination with increasing costs of rearing children will guarantee that accumulation will proceed, either indefinitely, at an eventually constant level, or until a high-level human capital stock is reached in a steady state where the return to further accumulation equals the discount rate, which has fallen as the average family size has decreased. The high-level state corresponds to the developed economy, with a large stock of human capital, low birthrates, and small families.

Whether an economy ends up in the low-level or the high-level state very much depends on where it started. One of the most prominent features of the model is that it displays path dependence. Thus, major exogenous shocks are required to make the economy move from one type of steady state to another.

The Haitian economy has been exposed to at least one such shock: the wars of liberation of 1791–1803. The French had managed to build the most prosperous colony in the world in Saint-Domingue with the aid of an agricultural technology that was both elaborate and intricate. The wars of liberation destroyed both physical and human capital, and, what is more important in the present context, virtually eradicated the entire educated labor force of the colony. Those with technical and administrative expertise either emigrated or were killed off.[17] This result drastically altered the human capital situation in Haiti. In terms of the Becker-Murphy-Tamura (BMT) model, the economy received a shock, "as when a conqueror kills off the educated class," that propelled it toward stagnation.[18]

Subsequently, exactly as the model predicts, Haitians remained uneducated.[19] Emperor Henry Christophe and Presidents Alexandre Pétion and Jean-Pierre Boyer showed some interest, but little came of their efforts. As it seems, the demand for education remained weak throughout the entire nineteenth century. Even the private school system stagnated. When the American occupation began in 1915, literacy rates in the countryside were close to zero.[20] American efforts to change the schooling system failed, and the return to a domestic administration again brought little progress. Today, the situation is much the same. Haiti continues to have the lowest enrollment and literacy rates in the Western Hemisphere. Less than 50 percent of the children between five and eleven years attend school, and between 65 and 80 percent of the Haitian population is believed to be illiterate.[21]

Elsewhere I have analyzed at some length the reluctance of Haitian governments to address the education problem, and the next section will shed some more light on government action (and inaction).[22] The lack of education stands out not only as a supply problem, but as one of insufficient demand that is linked to insufficient supply through increasing returns to human capital formation. It is a version of Say's law in reverse: The lack of supply holds demand back as well. Or, to put it slightly differently, a cumulative process has already run its course. The lack of supply has made for low returns on investment in human capital, and, hence, for a weak demand for education. This, in turn, has held back supply, and so forth, in a cumulative fashion until a low-level steady state has been reached.[23]

The demand trend may recently have been broken, however. Household expenditure figures show that, on average, urban households in 1994–1995 spent between 1,300 and 6,700 gourdes on education, either directly or indirectly, and rural households somewhere between 1,300 and 3,200 gourdes. Insofar as these figures are representative of the overall situation in Haiti, they indicate that households spend approximately 15 percent of their income (12 percent of GDP) on education.[24]

Assuming that the figures are reasonably correct and therefore that a substantial demand for education actually exists in Haiti, it becomes important to investigate the causes of this demand and their economic implications. The "simplest" interpretation is that Haitians are envisaging a better future in the wake of the recent political changes and hence are willing to undertake long-term educational investments. There may be a grain of truth in this explanation, but it is not likely to provide us with more than part of the picture. Another, at least complementary, and presumably more plausible, hypothesis is that education is demanded with emigration in mind. The return to human capital formation may be too low inside Haiti to warrant substantial investment, but once the possibility of settling elsewhere is taken into account, the benefit-cost ratio may be much higher for the individual—but not for Haitian society as a whole.

The Predatory State: Too Small and Yet Too Large

As Mintz points out, the nineteenth century was crucial for Haiti.[25] Not least, it determined the political course followed to the present day. Between independence in 1804 and the beginning of the American occupation in 1915, a predatory state evolved, one that has continued to plague the country until very recently. The rise and logic of the predatory state is a topic examined at some length elsewhere.[26] A central feature is the modeling of ruler behavior in a situation where a balance has to be struck between concerns for income and security. Given that the ruler derives satisfaction from both these elements, he selects the size of polity or governing clique that maximizes his utility in a situation where increased income can only be obtained at the cost of an increased probability of being deposed by outside revolutions or inside palace coups. The consequences of this behavior have been distorted resource allocation, reduced national product, and highly unequal distribution of wealth and income. One aspect that has not been addressed, however, is the extent to which the predatory state has also displayed productive features, that is, whether government was an unqualified evil or its behavior contained any redeeming features. Was there anything about the logic of the predatory state that also allowed for productive behavior, and, if so, what conclusions can be drawn?

Findlay and Wilson have constructed a model of the state that incorporates both the predatory and the productive aspects of government behavior.[27] Their model contains two sectors: a private one that produces goods and services (national income) with the aid of labor and capital, and a government sector that, using only labor, contributes to the social and physical infrastructure in a way that increases private productivity. Government activities are subject to diminishing returns. Increasing the size of the public sector also has a negative effect on private production, one that has to be weighed against the positive contribution to productivity, since it takes labor away from work in the private sector. National income is maximized when the influences of these two forces balance each other at the margin.

The ruler in the Findlay-Wilson model taxes his citizens by retaining a fixed percentage of their incomes. This assumption means that gross tax revenue is maximized at the same size of public employment as the national income, declining thereafter as the value of private production decreases. Tax revenues may be used for financing public employment, that is, for wage payments in the government sector, and for consumption and wealth accumulation by the ruler. Government expenditure increases monotonically as the size of the public sector increases. The reason is that wages will increase, first, because when the public sector bids away labor from private activities it can do so only at an increasing wage, and, second, because increasing the public sector increases the overall productivity level of the private sector.

The optimal level of taxation in the Findlay-Wilson model is that which maximizes national income. The ruler already knows the optimal size of the public sector. He also knows the wage required to arrive at precisely that size. Equipped with this knowledge, he can calculate the optimal tax level. The optimal tax is that which suffices to finance optimum employment in the public sector, and nothing else. A benevolent ruler with the good of his people in mind will choose that level. But will a predatory ruler do so too?

If he does, the distributional implications will be different. A benevolent ruler would use taxes just for his wage bill. The predator instead aims at maximizing his own income. If he is free to set the tax level, he will choose the optimum size of the public sector, because this maximizes national income, that is, it gives him the largest possible cake upon which to feast. Findlay and Wilson suggest that the citizens will get only as much as they would if there were no public sector at all. Wages and capital income will both be taxed until they are no larger than their level in this "state of nature." So long as this is the case, the incentives to topple the ruler will be weak. It is only when the people become worse off as a result of state action that they are likely to rise up.

The ruler may, however, choose not to expand the public sector to its optimum size. Paradoxical as it may seem, this case is likely to arise when the ruler is subject to some degree of control by the population. For example, he may be allowed to set the tax at a level just sufficient to pay for optimal public employment, because this maximizes national income. If so, he will, however, *not* choose this public employment level because he will then be left without any net income for himself. With the assumptions made by Findlay and Wilson, given the optimum tax rate, the expenditure curve will cut the tax revenue curve from below at the size of the public sector that maximizes national income. At that level, all government revenue is spent on wage payments. The ruler will therefore stop short of this point, at the size of the public sector that makes his marginal tax revenue equal to his marginal wage expenditure, since that is where the difference between revenue and expenditure, the surplus accruing to the ruler himself, is maximized. The size of the public sector thus becomes smaller than optimal.

What Findlay and Wilson have shown is that with a predatory government, the state either becomes too small or it reaches its optimum size but leaves the citizens no better off than the Hobbesian state of nature— without any government at all. What are the implications for Haiti?

In principle, Haiti has been a predatory state ever since its birth as a sovereign nation. The first rulers had to satisfy both their own demands for income and those of the coalitions that backed them and extract sufficient government revenue in foreign currency to be able to purchase the arms required to prevent a French return. To this end, the Haitian population was taxed through a crop-share tax of one-fourth of agricultural output and through levies on exports and imports. (Pétion abolished the crop-share tax, but the duties on exports and imports had come to Haiti to stay.)[28]

It may very well be that the taxes imposed were those that maximized national income in the Findlay-Wilson fashion during the early years of independence. The early governments did make a contribution sui generis to private productivity by placing agricultural laborers under military supervision, and perhaps what the rulers did to defend the country belongs to the productivity-raising category of outlays as well, freeing the private citizens from the responsibility of handling this problem themselves.[29] However, it is also clear that the policy of Toussaint L'Ouverture, Jean-Jacques Dessalines, and Christophe was one of maximizing the surplus of public revenue over public expenditure in the sense of Findlay and Wilson (that is, expenditure that increased private productivity). The situation may not have been that different from the one in which the ruler maximizes national income but only leaves to the citizens what they would have received in the absence of any productivity-raising state intervention. Dessalines, in particular, was known to have been extraordinarily greedy, something that no doubt contributed to his eventual downfall, since his greed was instrumental in keeping down both the wages of workers and soldiers and the income of the estate owners.[30]

The early rulers represented only the beginning of the predatory state in Haiti. The nineteenth century was to witness a rapid succession of kleptocratic rulers, especially after the fall of Boyer in 1843, who viewed the presidency as no more than a source of private income. Their other main concern was how to remain in power so as to be able to continue their plunder of the Haitian population. This continued until the beginning of the American occupation in 1915. The pursuit of income resulted in a neglect of security, with the result that the period in office of the majority of those presidents was short-lived, and those who lasted for longer periods made special efforts to increase security.[31]

What insights does the Findlay-Wilson model offer with respect to the turbulent period of Haitian history from 1843 to 1915? Hardly any of these rulers did anything to stimulate private production, that is, agriculture. It is hence unlikely that national income ever increased above the level that it would have reached in the absence of a Haitian government, if that state of events can be imagined. Still, there was taxation, mainly of foreign trade.[32] There was government expenditure as well, but not on productivity-enhancing activities. The bulk of it consisted of repayment of a foreign debt that, among other things, had been created to stuff the pockets of the rulers and was accumulating rapidly during the last quarter of the nineteenth century, and of payment to the army and the police to increase ruler security.[33]

Nineteenth-century governments made national income decrease in Haiti because they absorbed and wasted resources that could have been used for the production of goods and services for the citizens instead, simply for redistributive purposes.[34] In terms of the Findlay-Wilson model, the latter half of the nineteenth century and the first fifteen years of the twentieth represent a "corner solution," with next to no resources devoted to boosting production, but with taxation and with expenditures of an unproductive kind, with national income below that of the "no-government state" and with a disastrously skewed income distribution.

A strict interpretation of Findlay and Wilson suggests that the state was too small because it had a public sector that was too small to allow maximum national income to be reached. In another sense, however, the state was far too large, because it served no purpose. The vast majority of the government employees were people who worked the extractive machinery or who were employed to share the spoils of office or both. The distinction between productive and unproductive bureaucrats is of supreme importance when one attempts to understand Haiti's plight.

The predation of the governments of Haiti on the population did not end with the American occupation. The occupational forces made some half-hearted attempts to create a functioning physical and social infrastructure, along the lines depicted in the Findlay-Wilson model, but taxed much of the productivity gains away via forced repayment of the country's foreign debt.[35] At any rate, the occupation was nothing but a parenthesis in Haiti's history. Once it was over, the predators were back in the nation's driver's seat.[36]

Predation escalated dramatically during the 1940s and the 1950s, reaching an all-time high during the era of the two Duvaliers.[37] It cannot be denied that presidents Sténio Vincent (1930–1941), Elie Lescot (1941–1946), Dumarsais Estimé (1946–1950), and Paul Magloire (1950–1956) made some efforts to develop the country's productivity-increasing infrastructure.[38] However, none put national income before plunder. What this means, simply, is that the size of the productive public sector remained too small from the end of the occupation to the coming of François ("Papa Doc") Duvalier in 1957. During this period, the Haitian governments were in the "intermediate" position of the Findlay-Wilson model. Tax rates were more or less determined by the precedent that had already been established, and the rulers concentrated on maximizing the surplus of government revenue over expenditure on the productive bureaucracy, preferring to keep the net revenue for themselves or distributing it to the unproductive parts of the public administration.

With the Duvaliers, the situation changed again, this time for the worse. Despite the promises delivered during the election campaign of 1957, Papa Doc did next to nothing to boost productivity in the economy. Instead, he concentrated on devising different ways of preying on the citizens. The new president was an innovator in the predatory state.[39] When his son succeeded him in 1971, it appeared for a while as if the worst features of Duvalierism were gone, with technocrats taking over the ministerial portfolios from the tonton macoute dinosaurs that had served under Duvalier père. This change, however, was purely cosmetic. If anything, predation escalated and became more refined than ever. Haiti entered what Maingot aptly termed "the fine tuning or modernization" phase of predation, where the main private access to government funds was via the public enterprises.[40] Basically, the economy was back to the Findlay-Wilson corner solution, with next to no productive state action but plenty of predatory activities, a situation that remained virtually unaltered during the politically turbulent years of military government that followed.

The sketch of Haiti drawn with the aid of the Findlay-Wilson framework should of course not be taken literally. Still, from the application of this model, it is possible to gain some fairly robust insights. In most instances the state in Haiti has been both too small and too large at the same time: too small in the sense that it has failed to create a policy environment conducive to productivity and growth, and too large if one takes into account the number of public sector employees who have been taken into the service of kleptocrats to assist in the creation of private ruler income or have served solely as recipients of public funds without performing any duties other than backing a ruler politically.

The policy conclusions are very clear. In some circles Presidents Aristide and Préval have been accused of being the errand boys of "neoliberals" and "big business" because of their cutbacks of public administration. This hardly provides an accurate picture of what is going on. Transition in an economy must always involve an element of what might be termed constructive destruction. This is evident from the experiences of the former communist countries of eastern Europe. The reform process has had great problems in taking off where the implementation is still dominated by the old *nomenklatura* or, for that matter, by bureaucrats who stood to gain from the now discarded system. Haiti constitutes an exact parallel. It would be utterly naive to believe that the old structures built with predation in mind could suddenly turn productive in the way described by the Findlay and Wilson model. These structures have to be put aside before new and better ones can be put in place. Attempting to impose the latter with the former still in place leads nowhere. Attempting to institute new structures while the old structures are still in place is, in fact, dangerous. Corruption tends to breed corruption.[41] A public employee is always faced with the choice of remaining honest or becoming corrupt. The factors involved in this decision are (1) his salary; (2) the incidence of corruption among other bureaucrats; (3) the probability of detection; (4) the size of payments received for rendering corrupt services; and (5) the rate at which future income is being discounted when compared with present income. The salary determines what he stands to lose in the future if he is caught and dismissed for being corrupt. The discount rate determines how much he values his future salary in comparison to an addition to income in the present by being corrupt. The size of the bribe determines how much he can add to his salary by being corrupt. The probability of being detected influences his possibility of getting away with illicit practice. Finally, if he is caught by a colleague who is also corrupt, he will presumably not lose his job, but simply have to share some of his illicit income with the latter.

The crucial element in the Haitian context is the overall incidence of corruption in the public administration. Other things being equal, if most of his colleagues are corrupt, the probability of any given bureaucrat following suit is high, since the chances of being caught and punished tend to be low. Through this mechanism, an administration that is basically corrupt also tends to corrupt new employees. Graft and inefficiency become self-perpetuating, and it becomes impossible to ever create a developmental state. Short of brainwashing, or milder forms of ideological retraining, which all face an incentive problem, the only way out of this high-corruption deadlock is to reduce the old public sector in principle to zero before starting to set up a bureaucracy that has something to contribute to productivity and welfare.[42]

Alone against Nature: The Haitian Peasant

Following the land reform policies initiated by Pétion in 1809, plantation agriculture gradually disappeared in Haiti. During the course of the nineteenth century, a peasant economy based on the family farm evolved. This economy has displayed remarkable resistance to attacks from outside forces, notably those attempting to reintroduce large-scale agriculture to the detriment of the peasants.[43] This conclusion does not mean, however, that the Haitian peasant is without problems. Equipped with little technology and little, if any, education, he is at a clear disadvantage when it comes to eking out a living. The *otorite* (authorities) have not cared too much about him, except in his capacity as a generator of revenue. His dilemma is further compounded by population growth, which tends to make it increasingly difficult to reduce poverty with every passing year. The relationship between population growth and rural per capita income constitutes one of the main themes of my book, *Peasants and Poverty*.[44]

The most serious problem facing the Haitian peasant is that population growth and soil destruction interact in a cumulative way to depress rural incomes over time. This insight can be reached with the aid of one of the standard theorems of international trade: the Rybczynski theorem.[45] It states that in a setting where two goods are produced with the aid of the same two factors, and neither of the two lines of production displays any increasing returns to scale, and one of the factors grows while the endowment of the other factor remains constant, at constant commodity prices, the output of the good employing the growing factor intensively increases while that of the other good contracts in absolute terms.

Translated into the Haitian setting, peasants produce land-intensive export goods on the one hand, and labor-intensive food crops on the other. As the population and the labor force grow, this practice, at constant prices (given, for example, by the level prevailing in the world market), makes the production of food crops increase while coffee production, for example, shrinks. Coffee is a perennial crop with a root system that binds and protects the soil, while the cultivation of food crops makes it necessary to lay the soil bare for planting when the rains come, which increases the risk of erosion, given Haiti's topography.

In other words, the available land shrinks, and this, in terms of the Rybczynski theorem, means that once more, the man-land ratio is altered. Again, population pressure on the land increases, more food crops are produced, and so on. Even without further population growth, the process will continue in a self-sustaining and cumulative fashion. Once set in motion, erosion will keep feeding on itself, and sooner or later per capita income will decline in the Haitian countryside, as it has for at least half a century, and presumably for much longer. It should also be noted that the Rybczynski theorem only requires constant relative commodity prices, but in Haiti, the cumulative process has received further impetus from a decline in the relative price of export crops, notably coffee.[46]

This process is extremely serious, since it threatens the very base of peasant existence, and more so every year. The question is: How much longer will it continue? Socioeconomic systems as a rule do not have truly explosive features, that is, cumulative processes do not go on forever. Sooner or later they lose their momentum. In the Haitian case, one may think of three different brakes: slowed population growth, employment outside the agricultural sector, or emigration of the agrarian population.

The BMT model provides some idea as to whether population growth can be expected to slow. In the low-level steady state prevailing in Haiti, very few efforts have been made to increase human capital stock. In practice, available time is devoted either to production or to child rearing. In this model, the simplest way to interpret the erosion process is as a reduction of the efficiency of the production of consumption goods. To do so leaves four adjustment options: Adult consumption of goods decreases, fewer children are born, the time devoted to child rearing decreases, or the amount of consumption goods devoted to each child decreases. The choice among these different adjustment mechanisms is an open one. The outcome is not necessarily slowed population growth, because the opportunity cost of a large family is not simply lower adult consumption. It could easily be that instead children suffer a reduction of their standard of living, either in terms of consumption or in terms of care.

Unfortunately, the latter possibility appears realistic, judging from past evidence. In a survey of nutrition research in Haiti up to the late 1960s, King concluded it was "clear that the present national food resources preclude the possibility of a really well nourished nation. On the other hand, the resources that are presently available are enough that no one need to starve to death. In spite of this, thousands of Haitian infants do not get their fair share of calories and protein from the family pot."[47] With falling per capita incomes, reduced altruism over time is a realistic possibility. This result also follows from traditional capital theory, as expounded by Fisher.[48] In this theory the rate of time preference (the opposite of altruism in the BMT model)—that is, the extent to which at the present time an addition to present income is preferred to an addition to future income—is determined mainly by three factors: the size of income, its distribution over time, and its probability or uncertainty (but not by family size alone as in the BMT case).

People with low incomes are likely to value the present very highly. This is most apparent at very low income levels. Staying alive today is an absolute prerequisite for being able to enjoy any income whatsoever in the future. Thus, in looking at income size alone, one should expect the Haitian peasant to be strongly in favor of present over future income, and even more so the closer he is to the subsistence level.[49] This argument could be even more valid when future income will be enjoyed not by the peasant himself but by his offspring.

The second factor, time distribution, presumably works in the opposite direction. The erosion process is cumulative, which means that incomes should decline faster and faster over time, making additions to future income relatively more attractive. Again, however, the matter is complicated by the fact that future income accrues to future generations. This effect may then easily be swamped by the size effect.

Finally, there is the question of uncertainty. Reduced probability of receiving a given income is synonymous with impoverishment in the eyes of the income earner. Also, most people would tend to regard their immediate incomes as more certain than their future incomes, since information about the present is better than information about more distant time periods. This speaks in favor of additions to future income, but again, these additions accrue to someone else.

Thus, population growth tends to depress per capita income over time in a cumulative fashion through its interaction with erosion. Possibly, in due course this growth will be reduced as households have to adjust their size to counteract the falling standard of living, but not necessarily. The adjustment mechanism may very well be one of redistribution within the family, to the detriment of the most vulnerable members: the children.

The Failure of Import Substitution

The second possible remedy to falling incomes is employment outside agriculture. Historically, the road to higher living standards has almost always involved some degree of industrialization.

The first and largest industrial sector to be created in Haiti was the import-substituting segment. This enjoyed substantial protection from 1949 to 1986.[50] According to traditional trade theory, which analyzes competitive situations, import substitution should have led to an inefficient allocation of resources and welfare losses in the economy. However, a new approach to international trade centers on the existence of markets dominated by imperfect competition.[51] In this context, the optimality of free trade from a welfare point of view has been called into question. That, of course, raises the question of whether this bears on the Haitian case as well, that is, of whether import substitution behind tariff walls constitutes an efficient way of boosting nonagricultural employment.

The call for intervention in international trade has basically centered on two cases.[52] The first focuses explicitly on the possibility of stimulating technological change. The argument is the following: Certain industries are intensive in research and development activities, that is, they generate new knowledge. Knowledge, in turn, is a public good. It is nonrivalrous because the fact that one firm uses it does not preclude another from doing so. It is also, to a large extent, nonexcludable in the sense that once the knowledge is spread, the firm that originated it cannot prevent other firms from making use of it. With imperfect patent legislation, knowledge spills over from those who developed it to their competitors.

Hence, especially in cases where the investment needed to produce the knowledge is high, firms may tend to underinvest in research and development activities. Then, one way of ensuring that innovating firms that contribute to growth by creating positive knowledge externalities are allowed to capture at least some of the profits that arise from being able to sell in a noncompetitive environment is to give them monopoly status in the domestic market, behind protective tariff walls.

The argument is dubious, however, and especially so in the case of Haiti. In the first place, the argument has mainly been advanced in the context of economies with a large domestic market, such as Japan or the United States, and not for small countries with a severely limited purchasing power. In Haiti this erroneous argument could easily lead to the creation of small firms that never reach large enough scale economies to make their efforts profitable. Second, domestic customers will suffer, exactly as in the competitive case, since tariff (or quota) protection will increase the prices that they have to pay. Third, and most importantly in the Haitian case, the kind of industries that give rise to important externalities have never existed. The industries that received protection were mainly of the simple consumer goods type: soap, detergents, shoes, cement, plastic and metal housewares, steel rods and corrugated sheets, textiles, paper products, cooking oil, flour, milk, matches, tomato paste, cigarettes, soft drinks, beer, and so forth, which do not rely heavily on continuous technological development.[53]

The second argument for strategic intervention in international trade refers to the case in which a foreign firm captures large rents in an imperfectly competitive industry that could be transferred to domestic producers, consumers, or the government. (These rents would show up either as high profits or as high factor rewards—for example, wages.) The typical case would be that of a foreign monopolist who exports to a domestic market where either there are no domestic producers at all or where domestic production takes place under competitive conditions but where the domestic producers are not efficient enough to outcompete the foreign monopolist completely.[54]

The problem is one of making the monopolist supply his product at cost, not at cost plus monopoly profit. The remedy is to impose a price ceiling on imports. With imports coming from a monopolistic supplier, the marginal import cost always exceeds the marginal cost for the monopolist of producing the good in question, provided that the latter cost is rising. As more units are imported, the import price increases, not only on additional imports, but also on inframarginal imports. The price of imported goods to the domestic consumer should thus be put equal to the marginal import cost, while the foreign seller should receive only his marginal cost of production times the imported quantity. The difference may be collected as a tariff.

The foreign monopoly case is hardly representative of the Haitian reality either. Tariffs on manufactures have never been imposed to maximize the sum of consumer surplus, domestic producer surplus, and government revenues. The Haitian story is an altogether different one. No monopolies have threatened domestic producers. On the contrary, the products that received tariff protection could all be obtained at a given, competitive, price in the world market. Thus, one simply has the traditional case of import substitution behind tariff walls. Instead of using tariffs in combination with import price ceilings, domestic monopoly or near-monopoly firms were created in a number of consumer goods industries. According to Fass, "Under industrial development policies established and modified from 1949 onwards, any substitution industry that could produce enough to supply a substantial share of the local market was protected from import competition by stiff tariffs or outright import bans and from competition from other local producers by their inability to obtain operating licenses after one or a few firms took over the market."[55]

So long as domestic demand was not saturated, the output of import-substituting industries grew rapidly, in some instances up to the 1970s.

Thereafter, however, the rate of expansion slowed down, being determined by rising incomes. The growth impulse provided by tariff protection had faded.

As Fass explains, the basis of import substitution was unsound from the very beginning:

> The cost of cornering the market, given that equipment and supplies could be had duty-free, was low. An individual with initiative, resources, and the necessary kinds of connections to assure that government would provide the operating license and then impose and maintain the protective clauses of policy could take control of supplying most or all of local demand. The first investor into a market therefore claimed the profits of other importers and of pre-existing local producers too small to benefit from policy, and monopoly rents from consumers. The only marketing skill required was that of selling the idea to the right people in the right places, not a difficult thing to do by definition if someone already had sufficient resources in hand.[56]

The situation became even more aggravated between the end of the 1970s and the mid- 1980s, when the Haitian government established direct ownership of five major firms in soybean oil, wheat flour, cement, and sugar (two factories). Inefficiency became endemic in the public import-competing sector. None of the companies created or taken over by the government was ever allowed to function according to conventional business management principles. They were all turned into vehicles for grinding out illegal incomes for the presidential family. None ever became economically viable. The sugar and flour operations were, in addition, undercut by illegal imports that formed part of a smuggling racket presumably organized by Ernest Bennett, the president's father-in-law.[57]

In 1986, when the Duvalier dictatorship fell, import-competing manufacturing in Haiti displayed high rates of both nominal and effective protection. The former rates could be as high as 200 percent and the latter 100 percent on average, being the result not only of tariffs but of quantitative import restrictions. Some 10 percent of the industrial output value enjoyed an effective protection of more than 300 percent.[58] This protection was harmful because it made consumers pay more than they would have under conditions of free trade and it misallocated resources in the domestic economy to the production of goods in which the country has a comparative *dis*advantage.

From the point of view of technological change as well, tariffs under the traditional assumption of competitive markets are likely to do more harm than good. As is well known from comparative studies of manufacturing in developing countries, excessive tariff protection tends to breed inefficiency and low capacity utilization.[59] The lack of exposure to international competition means that import-substituting industries are not forced to think of means of cutting their costs, for example by innovating processes, inputs, or products. They make profits and stay in business because tariffs make for high prices of their outputs and because tariffs on imported inputs are usually low.

The Haitian government that took over in February 1986 set out to reduce protection levels so as to lower the average effective rate of protection to less than 40 percent, closed one of the sugar factories and the soybean oil factory, and revoked the monopoly concessions of the cement and flour operations. Import-competing industries entered a difficult period of adjustment to marketlike conditions, a period that was to be further aggravated by the political turmoil of the 1990s and the subsequent international embargo, and that is not yet over.

Haiti has a long way to go before domestic producers in general are in a position to compete efficiently with imported goods without government support. Indeed, the effects of protection in the Haitian case closely mirror the situation described by traditional trade theory, compounded by predatory manipulations of those in political power. Clearly, this situation had very little to do with the potentially (but not necessarily) favorable sequence of events envisaged by more recent approaches of trade theory. The import-substituting segment of Haitian manufacturing never became economically sound. Protectionism is not the way to gainful employment. The costs it imposes on the economy are too high, a lesson that is as relevant for the future.

The Assembly Export Sector

The fact that import substitution behind high tariff walls was not a proper industrial strategy or employment strategy was also borne out by the experience of the export-oriented assembly industries. These industries constituted a dynamic and fast-growing segment of the Haitian economy during the 1970s and the 1980s. Between 1966 and 1984, the share of manufactures in exports increased from a mere 4 percent to 66 percent. By the latter date, employment in the sector amounted to about 30,000, a figure that was to increase to 46,000 in 1990.[60]

The growth of the assembly sector did not take place in splendid isolation. On the contrary, the government intervened in a number of ways. Some of those ways were dubious, such as preventing labor unionism under the two Duvaliers, which positively served to strengthen Haiti's comparative advantage in the form of low wages.[61] Others were more legitimate: exemption of import duties on inputs and export duties on outputs, and income and license taxes for determined periods, as well as the provision of infrastructure.[62] Against these gains, however, the anti-export bias created by the protection of the import-substituting industries was not removed until 1986.

Furthermore, a long list of obstacles connected with the general underdevelopment of Haiti had to be overcome. Fass has listed the various complaints that were voiced at one time or another between 1949 and the late 1980s:

inadequate numbers of qualified government workers, entrepreneurs, managers, supervisors, and skilled workers; inadequate or overpriced infrastructure services; insufficient investment, promotion, training, or credit; haphazard and arbitrary application of regulations concerning taxes, investment incentives, tariffs and labor; inappropriate legislation with respect to these issues; inadequate coordination among government agencies, among businesses, and between government and businesses; insufficient data or research; inappropriate or irrelevant advice from foreign technical assistants; insufficient coordination among foreign-assistance agencies; too many foreign economists without business knowledge; too many local investors without sufficient economics; poor quality control; absence of clear or rational planning in either the public or private sector; excessive tax evasion by the private sector and graft in the public sector; minimum wages too high for international competitiveness or too low to maintain worker productivity, purchasing power, and stability; and always, there was the inadequacy of the general investment "climate."[63]

In spite of all these obstacles, Haiti developed into an exporter of labor-intensive assembly products. "The accomplishment was in fact remarkable," concluded Fass.[64]

The assembly sector survived the increased organization of factory workers that came in the wake of the fall of Jean-Claude Duvalier in

1986. The upward pressure on the wage level that resulted could be accommodated.[65] Far less easy to handle were the political disturbances that resulted when the 1987 elections approached.[66] When the military regime was subjected to external pressure through increasingly tight sanctions after the coup against Aristide in 1991, the goose that had laid the golden egg was all but killed by the representatives of the predatory state. Value added in the assembly sector fell from $4 million in September 1991 to $0.06 million in January 1992.[67] The number of firms in the sector fell from 252 in 1990 and 145 in 1991 to less than 30 in early 1994, with employment being reduced from more than 40,000 to about 6,000 to 8,000 over approximately the same period. Toward the end of 1994, operations in this sector had virtually come to a standstill.[68]

Notwithstanding the difficulties faced by the assembly sector over the past four or five years, presumably it can be rebuilt substantially over the course of the next few years, provided the political temperature remains within tolerable limits. The comparative advantage remains the same—low wages—and so do, for that matter, many of the obstacles the sector has to overcome.

If Haiti enters a phase of political stability, assembly production, with all its problems, will provide an alternative to agriculture in terms of employment—in fact, one of the few outside the informal sector and the public administration. In the long run, however, other problems have to be tackled. The main complaints lodged against the assembly sector have to do with low wages and weak linkages with the rest of the economy.[69] To the extent that these complaints are true, the assembly sector only constitutes a marginal advance on traditional pursuits. The question then is whether better alternatives may be available in the future.

One of the facts of economic development is that developing countries specializing in the production of relatively capital-intensive modern manufactures tend to have higher national incomes per capita than countries specializing in traditional, labor-intensive products (manufactures or agricultural goods). The prime examples are the so-called Asian tigers of the Pacific Rim.

Using this observation as a starting point, Rodrik constructed a model that focused on when countries begin to develop a modern sector and become exporters of nontraditional goods.[70] The Rodrik model contains two tradable final goods: a labor-intensive, "traditional" one, produced with the aid of labor and capital, and a "modern" good produced with capital and a range of intermediate goods that are imperfect substitutes for each other, both produced under constant returns to scale. The inter-mediates may be thought of as producer services ("skilled and special-ized workmanship") or specialized inputs or technologies.[71] For example, extensive communication may be needed between the produc-ers of modern goods and the suppliers of intermediaries before arriving at specifications that fit the suppliers. "A salient aspect of these exchanges is the dependence of the outcome on extensive interaction between suppliers and users in iteratively changing both process and product characteristics."[72] Thus, both geographical proximity and variety matter. The wider the range of specialized intermediates available to the final-goods producers, the lower the unit costs of the firms in the modern sector.

The proximity requirement makes the intermediates nontradables. They are produced with the aid of skilled labor alone and under increas-ing returns to scale, because of the fixed costs that are required to develop the specialized skills—that is, under conditions of monopolistic competi-tion (each intermediate being produced by a single firm). The higher the skill level, the lower the unit cost of the intermediate in question.

This creates a catch-22 situation. The profitability of the modern sector depends on the range of intermediates available, but the viability of intermediate production simultaneously depends on the existence of a demand from the modern sector. Thus, in an economy that specializes in the production of traditional goods, neither the intermediate sector nor the modern one will be established, since it does not pay for individual producers of intermediates to establish themselves, for lack of demand.[73] It would take a coordinated movement of resources into modern and intermediate production to break away from specialization in traditional goods, but this in turn presupposes the existence of both a sufficiently well educated labor force and a large enough capital stock.

Should the Rodrik model constitute a good approximation of reality, countries such as Haiti are caught in a double trap. The lack of education not only produces a high rate of population growth, as in the BMT frame-work, but it also puts the economy in a traditional-goods deadlock that cannot be broken by gradual change, that is, by marginal efforts of indi-vidual producers. In the worst case, the political situation remains turbu-lent and the assembly sector fails to recover, with investors going else-where inside or outside the Caribbean. If so, Haiti is back to a traditional economy in which agriculture and informal urban pursuits constitute the only alternatives—a gloomy situation, indeed.[74]

Migration

The retrogression to a purely traditional economy leaves only the third alternative when it comes to slowing population growth: emigration. This is already the main adjustment mechanism. The erosion process triggers migration via the reduction of incomes.

One recent model that focuses on this feature in a growth context has been developed by Braun.[75] At the center of Braun's analysis is the existence of some natural resource that is in fixed supply and becomes congested as the population grows. This resource could be thought of as land in the Haitian context. It imposes diminishing returns to scale for labor and capital. It also makes the wage earned in the domestic economy a function of how much of this resource is available on a per capita basis: The more there is, the higher the wage. The production function of the economy also contains a standard efficiency or technology parameter, which may be interpreted, as in the Findlay-Wilson model, to depend on government policies. This parameter influences the wage rate in basically the same way: The higher the level of the technology, the higher the domestic wage.

The migration decision in the Braun model depends only on the wage differential between the rest of the world and the domestic economy, since capital is taken to be completely mobile across national boundaries and a single rate of return prevails everywhere in the world. In the case of Haiti, of course, there is a low availability of land per capita as well as a low level of technology. Hence, the prevailing wage rate can be expected to be low from an international perspective, which is also the case empirically. Haiti then becomes a country with net emigration, even in the absence of population growth.

The Braun model, however, may also be linked to the BMT model. This explains the low technological level as a result of conscious decision-making. It also makes for endogenous population growth that in turn influences the domestic wage level. In the Braun model, as people move out of the country, land gets less congested and the wage rate tends to rise. As long as the economy stays in the BMT low-level equilibrium with high population growth, however, one should not expect wages to rise. Wage rates will remain low, land will continue to be congested, and people will continue to leave Haiti. Wage rates will not be equalized between Haiti and the rest of the world, and the incentive to migrate will remain.

Conclusions

The French colony of Saint-Domingue was the richest of its kind in the world. Present-day Haiti is the poorest country in the Western Hemisphere. The shock received when the country lost its skilled labor force during the wars of liberation heralded an end to the staples-led economic expansion in the nineteenth century. Haiti became a low-technology economy that failed to create an educational system that could put an end to retrogression. Low returns to human capital formation coupled with government passivity concerning educational matters threw the country into mass illiteracy. Secular stagnation gradually set in with diminishing returns to labor, soil erosion in agriculture, and political degeneration. The peasantry was squeezed between a rock and a hard place, between the relentless forces of nature and a relentless state.

Import substitution in the industrial sector has failed, both for economic and political reasons. It never made any sense in the first place to foster high-cost ventures producing for a small domestic market, and once that sector became a playground for kleptocratic political interests, it virtually collapsed.

Today the Haitian economy may be in the worst place of its history. Per capita income has declined to a level of $250–$260 or less.[76] The only sector displaying any dynamism over the past two decades—assembly manufacturing for export—received a terrible blow as a result of political turmoil and international sanctions. At the same time, agricultural exports have become increasingly difficult, as the interplay between population growth and erosion pushes the rural economy more and more toward the production of domestic crops. The country's economic structure may be locked into a low-level equilibrium that offers no easy way out. This equilibrium is characterized by high population growth and a very small stock of human capital that tends not to expand.

As Locher pointed out, traditional agriculture hardly has any future: "There is a pervasively pessimistic undercurrent in virtually every recent assessment of Haiti's likely future. I think it is time to face up to the facts and realize that rural Haiti as we know it is doomed."[77] In 1950 the arable land area per capita was 0.38 hectares. With the trends that prevailed at the time Locher made his assessment in 1988, it would appear that the population in the year 2000 would amount to 7.5 million and that the arable area per capita would reduced to 0.16 hectares. Food production would be lower than ever and aid-financed food imports would reach an all-time high.[78]

Locher is right, and what is worse, as of 1997 there are no viable alternatives, with the possible exception of a revitalized assembly sector. Assembly production may not be able to do very much, either. It is a low-wage sector and has a virtually unlimited supply of labor (in the sense of Lewis) on which to draw.[79] Without a substantial stock of solid human capital, it is impossible to move into high-growth industries with more advanced technologies, but human capital formation may be locked into a low-level trap. Even with a larger stock of human capital, "trading up" may be difficult in the context of an internationalized economy. As Bardhan has observed, "trade may reduce the profitability of R&D in the poor country as it places local entrepreneurs in competition with a rapidly expanding set of imported, differentiated products and may drive the country to specialize in traditional, possibly stagnant, industries which use its relatively plentiful supply of unskilled workers."[80]

This is already the case in Haiti.

The future looks gloomy. Demographic pressure is exhausting the available soil at an increasing pace. The assembly sector is down to less than 10,000 jobs. Per capita income is falling and would fall even quicker were it not for emigration. Moreover, emigration takes place under exceedingly difficult circumstances.

The old, or traditional, aggregate neoclassical theory of economic growth reduced long- run growth of per capita income to a matter of population growth on the one hand and technological change on the other, both exogenously derived.[81] The new theory of economic growth escapes the determinism of the old growth models. Most importantly, it endogenizes technological change.[82] What it does *not* tell us is how to bring about this change. In the present chapter, the new growth theory explains important parts of Haiti's economic reality. But that is also where the story ends. As pointed out by Krugman, "New growth theory has been preoccupied with a different question than high development theory [of the 1950s and 1960s]: how to explain the persistence of growth rather than how to get it started. . . . So while the philosophy of new growth theory is in essence a rediscovery of high development theory, it has not returned to the same questions."[83]

Unfortunately, it is precisely in this area that development practitioners must concentrate their efforts, finding ways of breaking out of the interlocking traps that have been exposed in this chapter. It is clearly not an easy undertaking. In the worst case, it is an impossible one. Still, it must be attempted.

At least the unwilling government that was previously the constraint dominating all other constraints has been removed. This fact, however, creates not just new opportunities but also new problems. This chapter has dealt only with nonconvexities and externalities relating to the production of goods and services and not with the "massive costs of collective action in building new economic institutions and political coalitions and in breaking the deadlock of incumbent interests threatened by new technologies."[84] Even well-intentioned governments with a purged, honest, bureaucracy have a Herculean task in this respect. It would be unrealistic to expect any miracles.

Notes

1. Theodore W. Schultz, "On Economic History in Extending Economics," in Manning Nash (ed.), *Essays on Economic Development and Cultural Change in Honor of Bert F. Hoselitz*. Supplement to *Economic Development and Cultural Change*, XXV (1977), 245–253.

2. Mats Lundahl, "Five Decisive Events in the Economic History of Haiti," Department of Economics, Stockholm School of Economics, 1995.

3. See Mats Lundahl, "Staples Trade and Economic Development," *EFI Yearbook 1991* (Stockholm, 1991), 66–86; and Ronald Findlay and Mats Lundahl, "Natural Resources, 'Vent-for-Surplus,' and the Staples Theory," in Gerald M. Meier (ed.), *From Classical Economics to Development Economics* (New York, 1994), 68–93, and the references cited there, for an overview and formalization of the theory.

4. Processing, however, is not excluded. Gerald Helleiner, *International Trade and Economic Development* (Harmondsworth, 1972), 15–16.

5. See Findlay and Lundahl, "Natural Resources."

6. The following builds on Mats Lundahl, *Peasants and Poverty: A Study of Haiti* (London, 1979), 256–259.

7. Robert I. Rotberg, *Haiti: The Politics of Squalor* (Boston, 1971), 28.

8. Ibid., 29.

9. Lundahl, *Peasants and Poverty*, 563–566.

10. Ibid., 257–258.

11. Rotberg, *Haiti*, 30–31.

12. A summary description of the sugar production techniques employed in Saint-Domingue and their evolution is offered in *Paysans, systèmes et crise. Travaux sur l'agraire haïtien. Tome 1: Histoire agraire et développement* (Clamecy, 1993), 70–75. See also Robert E. Baldwin, "Patterns of Development in Newly Settled Regions," *Manchester School of Economic and Social Studies*, XXIV (1956), 161–179.

13. Mats Lundahl, "Les obstacles au changement technologique dans l'agriculture traditionelle haïtienne," *Conjonction*, CXXXV (1977), 69–85; idem., *Peasants*

and Poverty; idem., "Peasants, Government and Technological Change in Haitian Agriculture," in Hans F. Illy (ed.), *Politics, Public Administration and Rural Development in the Caribbean* (Munich, 1983), 61–93.

14. Gary S. Becker, Kevin M. Murphy, and Robert Tamura, "Human Capital Fertility, and Economic Growth," *Journal of Political Economy*, XCVIII (1990), 512–537. .

15. A steady state is defined as a situation in which the various quantities grow at constant rates.

16. Becker, Murphy, and Tamura, "Human Capital," 516.

17. Robert Lacerte, "The First Land Reform in Latin America: The Reforms of Alexander Pétion, 1809–1814," *Inter-American Economic Affairs*, XXVIII (1974–1975), 78–79; Rotberg, *Haiti*, 48.

18. Becker, Murphy, and Tamura, "Human Capital," 532.

19. Lundahl, *Peasants and Poverty*, 453–501; and Charles Tardieu, *L'éducation en Haïti de la période coloniale à nos jours (1980)* (Port-au-Prince, 1990), survey the educational history of Haiti.

20. Lundahl, *Peasants and Poverty*, 463.

21. Academy for Educational Development, *Diagnostic technique du secteur éducatif haïtien*. Version provisoire (Port-au-Prince, 1995), 3, annexe onze, 5.

22. Lundahl, *Peasants and Poverty*. The public school system remains undeveloped. Approximately 84 percent of all preschools are private, and the private schools account for 65 percent of all children in primary schools and 82 percent of all those in secondary schools (1991–1992). Academy for Educational Development, *Diagnostic*, 5, annexe six.

23. Quite likely, many households in Haiti are also facing a liquidity constraint, which makes it impossible to finance education to the extent desired (Academy for Educational Development, *Diagnostic*, 3–4). As demonstrated by Vicky Barham et al., "Education and the Poverty Trap," *European Economic Review*, XXXIX (1995), 1257–1275, this could produce a poverty trap: "Once a member of a family decides not to invest in education, all of that individual's descendants will be uneducated also" (1267).

24. Academy for Educational Development, *Diagnostic*, 4.

25. Sidney W. Mintz, "Introduction," in James G. Leyburn, *The Haitian People*, 2d ed. (New Haven, 1966), v.

26. See Lundahl, *Peasants and Poverty*; idem., *The Haitian Economy: Man, Land and Markets* (London, 1983); idem., *Politics or Markets? Essays on Haitian Underdevelopment* (London, 1992).

27. Ronald Findlay and John D. Wilson, "The Political Economy of Leviathan," in Assaf Razin and Efraim Sadka (eds.), *Economic Policy in Theory and Practice* (London, 1987), 289–304. See also Stanislaw Wellisz and Findlay, "The State and the Invisible Hand," *World Bank Research Observer*, III (1988), 59–80.

28. Lundahl, *Peasants and Poverty*, 392. The economic systems of Toussaint and Dessalines are analyzed in Lundahl, "Toussaint L'Ouverture and the War Economy of Saint- Domingue, 1796–1802," *Slavery and Abolition*, VI (1985). See also Lundahl, "Defense and Distribution: Agricultural Policy in Haiti during the Reign of Jean-Jacques Dessalines, 1804–1906," *Scandinavian Economic History Review*, XXXII (1984), 77–103.

29. Stefan Hedlund, Mats Lundahl, and Carl-Hampus Lyttkens, "The Attraction of Extraction: Three Cases of State versus Peasantry," *Scandia*, LV (1989), 45–71, analyzes the agricultural system of the early rulers as one of short-run extraction rather than one aiming for production in the long run. A similar view is presented in Gérard Barthélemy, *Le pays en dehors. Essai sur l'univers rural haïtien* (Port-au-Prince, 1989).

30. See Lundahl, "Dessalines," for details.

31. Mats Lundahl, "Government and Inefficiency in the Haitian Economy: The Nineteenth Century Legacy," in Michael B. Connolly and John McDermott (eds.), *The Economics of the Caribbean Basin* (New York, 1985), 175–218.

32. Lundahl, *Peasants and Poverty*, 393.

33. Lundahl, *Peasants and Poverty*, 366–370, 375–379.

34. The activities of the nineteenth-century governments were mainly directly unproductive profit-seeking activities undertaken simply to redistribute income from the population in favor of the various governing cliques without producing anything wanted by the citizens. See Jagdish Bhagwati, "Directly Unproductive, Profit-Seeking (DUP) Activities," *Journal of Political Economy*, XC (1982), 988–1002. These activities tend to be very costly to the economy in terms of production forgone; Mancur Olson, *The Rise and Decline of Nations: Economic Growth, Stagflation, and Social Rigidities* (New Haven, 1982), 42–44). Haiti constitutes no exception to this rule (Lundahl, "Nineteenth Century Legacy").

35. See Hans Schmidt, *The United States Occupation of Haiti, 1915–1934* (New Brunswick, NJ, 1971); and Suzy Castor, *La ocupación norteamericana de Haití y sus consecuencias (1915–1934)* (México, 1971), for the detailed picture.

36. Lundahl, "Nineteenth Century Legacy."

37. Lundahl, "Papa Doc: Innovator in the Predatory State," *Scandia*, L (1984), 39–78; Anders Danielson and Mats Lundahl, "Endogenous Policy Formation and the Principle of Optimal Obfuscation: Theory and Some Evidence from Haiti and Jamaica," *Comparative Economic Studies*, XXXVI (1994), 51–78.

38. See Lundahl, *Peasants and Poverty*, 302–308; idem., *Kleptokrati, socialism och demokrati* (Stockholm, 1993), 177–259.

39. Lundahl, "Papa Doc," gives the details.

40. Anthony P. Maingot, "Haiti: Problems of Transition to Democracy in an Authoritarian Soft State," *Journal of Interamerican Studies and World Affairs*, XXVIII (1986–87), 83. Cf. Elisabeth Abbott, *Haiti: The Duvaliers and Their Legacy* (New York, 1988), 250.

41. See Jens Christopher Andvig and Karl-Ove Moene, "How Corruption May Corrupt," *Journal of Economic Behavior and Organization*, XIII (1990), 63–76.

42. It should be stressed that I am not arguing for a minimal public sector. That should be a transitory state of affairs. The "new" bureaucracy should be of the size that is optimal in the Findlay-Wilson sense, that is, the size that maximizes national income.

43. See Gerald Francis Murray, "The Evolution of Haitian Peasant Land Tenure: A Case Study in Agrarian Adaptation to Population Growth" (Ph.D. dissertation, Columbia University, 1977); Lundahl, *Peasants and Poverty*, 255–295; and Barthélemy, *Le pays en dehors,* for an analysis of the causes of this strength and the mechanisms employed to defend peasant property.

90 MATS LUNDAHL

44. Lundahl, *Peasants and Poverty*, 187–254.

45. T. M. Rybczynski, "Factor Endowment and Relative Commodity Prices," *Economica*, XXII (1955), 336–341.

46. See Lundahl, *Peasants and Poverty* 187–254; Yves Bourdet and Lundahl, "Patterns and Prospects of Haitian Primary Exports," *Latin American Issues*, IX (Akron, 1991); International Monetary Fund, *Haiti—Recent Economic Developments*, SM/95/43 (Washington, D.C., 1995), 3.

47. Kendall W. King, "Nutrition Research in Haiti," in Richard P. Schaedel (ed.), *Research and Resources of Haiti. Papers of the Conference on Research and Resources of Haiti* (New York, 1969), 187.

48. Notably Irving Fisher, *The Theory of Interest* (New York, 1930). This theory is applied to Haiti in Lundahl, *Peasants and Poverty*, 503–555.

49. See Lundahl, *Peasants and Poverty*, 226–227, 514–515.

50. Mats Lundahl, "The Haitian Economy Facing the 1990s," *Canadian Journal of Latin American and Caribbean Studies*, XVII (1992), 5–32.

51. See, for example, Elhanan Helpman and Paul Krugman, *Market Structure and Foreign Trade: Increasing Returns, Imperfect Competition, and the International Economy* (Cambridge, MA, 1985); Elhanan Helpman and Paul Krugman, *Trade Policy and Market Structure* (Cambridge, MA, 1989); Paul Krugman (ed.), *Strategic Trade Policy and the New International Economics* (Cambridge, MA, 1986); Paul Krugman, *Rethinking International Trade* (Cambridge, MA, 1990); Gene M. Grossman and Elhanan Helpman, *Innovation and Growth in the Global Economy* (Cambridge MA, 1991). Elhanan Helpman, "The Noncompetitive Theory of International Trade and Trade Policy," *Proceedings of the World Bank Annual Conference on Development Economics 1989* (Washington, D.C., 1990), 193–216, gives an introduction to the field.

52. These are discussed extensively in the articles contained in Krugman, *Strategic Trade Policy*.

53. Simon M. Fass, *Political Economy in Haiti: The Drama of Survival* (New Brunswick, NJ, 1988), 33.

54. See Helpman and Krugman, *Trade Policy and Market Structure*, for a formal analysis of this case.

55. Fass, *Haiti*, 33.

56. Ibid.

57. Lundahl, "Haitian Economy," 5–32.

58. World Bank, *Haiti. Staff Appraisal Report. Industrial Restructuring and Development Project* (Washington, D.C., 1989), 5.

59. Notably Ian Little, Tibor Scitovsky, and Maurice Scott, *Industry and Trade in Some Developing Countries* (London, 1970); Jagdish N. Bhagwati, *Foreign Trade Regimes and Economic Development: Anatomy and Consequences of Exchange Control Regimes* (New York, 1978); Anne O. Krueger, *Foreign Trade Regimes and Economic Development: Liberalization Attempts and Consequences* (New York, 1978); Michael Michaely, Demetris Papageorgiou, and Armeane M. Choksi, *Liberalizing Foreign Trade: Lessons of Experience in the Developing World* (Cambridge, MA, 1991), .

60. Lundahl, "Haitian Economy Facing the 1990s," 16; Inter-American Development Bank, *Emergency Economic Recovery Program. Haiti*, Report of the Joint Mission (7–20 November 1994), (Washington, D.C., 1995), 4.

61. Mats Lundahl, "The Rise and Fall of the Haitian Labour Movement," in Malcolm Cross and Gad Heuman (eds.), *Labour in the Caribbean. From Emancipation to Independence* (Basingstoke, 1988), 88–119.

62. Lundahl, "Haitian Economy," 15–16.

63. Fass, *Haiti*, 39.

64. Ibid., 43.

65. Ibid., 44–45.

66. World Bank, *Economic Recovery in Haiti: Performance, Issues and Prospects*, Report 7469-HA (Washington, D.C., 1988), 14–15.

67. Gabriel Verret, *Haiti—Financial Update* (Port-au-Prince, 1992).

68. Inter-American Development Bank, *Emergency Economic Recovery Program, Haiti*, 36; International Monetary Fund, *Haiti—Recent Economic Developments*, 3.

69. Fass, *Haiti*, 41; Joseph Grunwald, Leslie Delatour, and Karl Voltaire, "Offshore Assembly in Haiti," in Charles R. Foster and Albert Valdman (eds.), *Haiti— Today and Tomorrow: An Interdisciplinary Study* (Lanham, MD, 1984), 231–252.

70. Dani Rodrik, "Getting Interventions Right: How South Korea and Taiwan Grew Rich," *Economic Policy* XX, (1995), 55–107.

71. Ibid., 80.

72. Howard Pack and Larry E. Westphal, "Industrial Strategy and Technological Change: Theory versus Reality," *Journal of Development Economics*, XXII (1986), 110; quoted in Rodrik, "Getting Interventions Right," 81.

73. This argument applies not only to specialized intermediates. It is easy to envisage a similar situation in the case of infrastructure. Building roads, railroads, or power stations is typically associated with a large fixed cost and may hence not take place unless there are many industrial units using these facilities; Kevin M. Murphy, Andrei Shleifer, and Robert Vishny, "Industrialization and the Big Push," *Journal of Political Economy*, XCVII (1989), 1003–1026. Without industrialization, there is no pressure to build the kind of infrastructure analyzed by Findlay and Wilson, and without infrastructure there may be no industrialization.

74. These are examined in detail in Fass, *Haiti*.

75. Juan Braun, "Essays on Economic Growth and Migration" (Ph.D. dissertation, Harvard University, 1993). Here, I discuss one of his models as presented by Robert J. Barro, and Xavier Sala-i-Martin, *Economic Growth* (New York, 1995), 300–308.

76. International Monetary Fund, *Haiti—Recent Economic Developments*, II; Inter-American Development Bank, *Emergency Economic Recovery Program, Haiti*, 28.

77. Uli Locher, "Land Distribution, Land Tenure and Land Erosion in Haiti," paper prepared for the Twelfth Annual Conference of the Society for Caribbean Studies, Hoddesdon, Hertfordshire, July 12–14, 1988, 16.

78. Ibid., 15–16.

79. W. Arthur Lewis, "Economic Development with Unlimited Supplies of Labour," *Manchester School of Economic and Social Studies*, XXII (1954), 139–191.

80. Pranab Bardhan, "The New Growth Theory, Trade and Development: Some Brief Reflections," in Göte Hansson (ed.), *Trade, Growth and Development: The Role of Politics and Institutions* (London, 1993), 24; Bardhan, "The Contributions of

Endogenous Growth Theory to the Analysis of Development Problems: An Assessment," in Jere Behrman and T. N. Srinivasan (eds.), *Handbook of Development Economics* (Amsterdam, 1995), IIIB, 2987.

81. Notably, Robert M. Solow, "A Contribution to the Theory of Economic Growth," *Quarterly Journal of Economics*, LXX (1956), 65–94, and the literature derived from this work.

82. See, for example, Paul M. Romer, "Increasing Returns and Long-Run Growth," *Journal of Political Economy*, XCIV (1986), 1002–1037; idem., "Endogenous Technological Change," *Journal of Political Economy*, XCVIII (1990), S71; and Robert E. Lucas, Jr., "On the Mechanics of Economic Development," *Journal of Monetary Economics*, XXII (1988), 3–42, as well as the works cited in the present chapter.

83. Paul R. Krugman, "Towards a Counter-Counterrevolution in Development Theory," *Proceedings of the World Bank Annual Conference on Development Economics 1992* (Washington, D.C., 1993), 31. See also Bardhan, "Contributions of Endogenous Growth," 2992.

84. Pranab Bardhan, "Contributions of Endogenous Growth," 2995.

CHAPTER FOUR

Political Culture, Political Change, and the Etiology of Violence

Donald E. Schulz

"The institutions of Haiti are Jacobin and Voodoo, watered in blood under the Tree of Liberty."

—Robert Heinl and Nancy Heinl, *Written in Blood*

WHAT ARE the prospects for political stability and democracy in Haiti? The Haitian state has traditionally functioned as a parasitic force, siphoning off economic resources from the peasantry through draconian taxes and other means, and enforcing its will through a multiplicity of controls, including the threat and the use of force. It is in this sense that one speaks of the state versus society, with the military operating as both a repressive arm of the government and as a semiautonomous actor with interests of its own.[1]

Have the restoration to power of President Jean-Bertrand Aristide and the subsequent election of René Préval as his successor fundamentally changed these realities? It has been suggested that the one major, con-

The views expressed in this report are those of the author and do not necessarily reflect the official policy or position of the Department of the Army, Department of Defense, or the U.S. government. I am indebted to Rachel Neild, Robert Maguire, Gabriel Marcella, John Fishel, and Robert Caslen for their incisive comments on an earlier draft of this chapter. Any sins of omission or commission are entirely my responsibility.

crete change that Aristide made during his second coming was the abolition of the armed forces (Forces Armees d'Haiti, or FADH). Haiti, it is
said, is being transformed. The old institutions of repression have been
dismantled. New democratic organizations, including an apolitical, professional police force, are being created. Will they transform the nature
of state-society relations fundamentally?

As important as the abolition of the military may be, I argue that the
optimistic view seriously underestimates the many obstacles to change.
The current situation in Haiti is an artificial one. Order is being maintained by UN and U.S. peace keepers, while Haitian police are being
trained to assume that duty when the foreigners leave. But once the UN
exits, Haiti may fall apart. This might occur fairly quickly or it might be
gradual. A structure of violence undercuts the Haitian socioeconomic and
political order; it has been only partially uprooted. Until much more
progress has been made, democracy and political stability will be very
iffy propositions.

A Dysfunctional Political Culture

Political beliefs, values, attitudes, and behavior—political culture—
matters. Among political scientists, this is virtually taken as a given.[2]
Among Haitians and those who study Haiti, however, it is a hotly con-
tested issue. There is a tendency to regard cultural explanations for
Haiti's political and economic underdevelopment as insulting (some
would say racist), and sometimes they can be. Still, unless one is willing
to argue that political beliefs, values, attitudes, and behavior are unim-
portant, one is forced to take them seriously.

To say so is not to imply either that cultures are monolithic or
immutable, much less the product of some congenital disease that defies
rational explanation. On the contrary, culture is the product of socializa-
tion and experience, which, to one extent or another, differs from person
to person and group to group. The political culture of elites may be
expected to be significantly different from the political culture of the
masses. (Precisely how is a question for empirical research.) If the political relationships between classes change, the dominant political culture
may also change. Or, at least, a window of opportunity will open.
Whether Haitians will be able to take advantage of that opportunity when
and if it occurs is one of the most crucial questions facing today's Haiti.

The road will not be smooth. In Haiti a deeply embedded culture of predation has fostered autocracy and corruption, extreme social injustice, and economic stagnation. In this sense the Duvaliers and Duvalierism were not aberrations, but rather the culmination of a particular set of historical experiences, including those provided by traditional African culture, slavery, a bloody war of liberation, the reimposition of relations of elite dominance and mass submission, chronic cycles of tyranny and chaos, and the effects of a prolonged U.S. occupation. The result has been the development of an elaborate syndrome of destructive and self-destructive political behavior marked by authoritarianism, paternalism, personalism, patronage, nepotism, demagogy, corruption, cynicism, opportunism, racism, incompetence, parasitism, rigidity, intolerance, rivalry, distrust, insecurity, vengeance, intrigue, superstition, volatility, violence, paranoia, xenophobia, exploitation, class hatred, institutional illegitimacy, and mass apathy, aversion, and submission.

These and associated traits have been identified and commented on elsewhere; they are all too familiar to students of Haitian history and politics.[3] What is more relevant for our purposes is a clear understanding of the constraints that these traits place on political and economic development.

Notwithstanding Aristide's return, Préval's subsequent inauguration, and the dissolution of the FADH, to a very considerable extent, Haiti's future is likely to be dependent on the same elites who have dominated its past. They have the education, wealth, and other resources that are critical to pulling the country out of the quagmire of underdevelopment in which it has long been trapped. Yet, their past behavior provides scant basis for optimism. Predators do not change their habits overnight. Even today, the mulatto elite retains many of the values of the eighteenth-century plantation owners. It is an aristocracy with no sense of noblesse oblige.[4] Traditionally, its members have tended to view themselves as superior by dint of the color of their skin. They disdain manual labor and those who engage in it.[5]

Haiti's black elites have not been any better. President François ("Papa Doc") Duvalier's efforts to promote *négritude* merely opened the door to upwardly aspiring predators with a different shade of skin who, once in positions of power, proved to be just as violent and corrupt as their predecessors. Indeed, under Papa Doc terror became a way of life. Nor was there any effort to improve the economic lot of the masses or to educate them so that they might better themselves in the future. The culture of predation did not allow for such sentiment. The only "development" that was held to be desirable was that which benefited the country's political and economic elites.

Furthermore, is Haiti really a nation? The evidence suggests that it is not—or at least that its nationhood is severely underdeveloped. Haiti lacks a true sense of community, a feeling of shared values and common interests sufficient to overcome the differences that divide people from one another. Thus, urban elites have always considered peasants the *moun andeyò*, the people on the outside. Nor has this sense of estrangement been limited to class relationships. As Rotberg observed, mistrust has been the traditional "response of Haitians of all classes to all other Haitians." Peasants distrusted other peasants and pursued a dog-eat-dog (*chin manje chin*) existence. Until fairly recently, moreover, "to call a peasant a Haitian was to insult him grossly; a man had very specific ties to a locale, and no supralocal or national links to which he gave real credence."[6]

Historically, this has meant that politics has been a zero-sum game: The winner took all. Power—when it has not been used simply to accumulate more power and spoils—has largely been a negative phenomenon: It has been used to obstruct or destroy rather than to create. At the national level, at least, Haitians have had extraordinary difficulty in cooperating for programmatic ends. In the words of Maingot, they "can never fight the large wars [against poverty or gross injustice]; instead, they are geared only toward fighting the next political battles."[7]

To overcome this legacy and remain on the path of peaceful democratic evolution will require nothing less than a cultural revolution, and it was precisely that which was attempted under Aristide's leadership. Aristide expended much time and energy promoting national reconciliation and democracy. He wooed the bourgeoisie in an attempt to enlist its cooperation in his efforts to promote economic development. At the same time, he pleaded with his followers to forgo vengeance in favor of the justice that he hoped would be attained with the establishment of a renovated judicial system. In effect, he tried to create a social contract between state and society where one had never really existed. To this end he sought to educate the populace about the importance of democracy and encouraged the construction of new democratic institutions that would bring the *moun andeyò* into the political process and replace the traditionally one-sided and exploitative state-society relationship by one based on government responsiveness and accountability to the masses.

To what extent did he succeed, and what are the prospects for the future? To raise once again the question posed by Rotberg at the September 1995 conference, Haiti: Prospects for Political and Economic Reconstruction, is Maingot's observation still true? Or have Haitians finally learned to work together to fight the larger wars against poverty and injustice?

While it is much too early to render any definitive judgments, there are some signs that Haiti's political culture is indeed changing. The relative lack of large-scale, revenge-motivated violence is encouraging. Furthermore, the extraordinary renaissance that is occurring in grassroots organizing and the spillover of these activities into the political arena at all levels suggest that new patterns of political participation and recruitment have emerged. These grassroots efforts are the continuation of a process that began well before Aristide came to the presidency but that was interrupted during the Raoul Cédras years (1991–1994), when all such activities were suppressed. This resurrection has been accompanied by an important shift in political attitudes and behavior: Previously, whereas local leaders shunned conventional politics and institutions and tried to bring about change outside the system, today they are increasingly moving into the political system, joining parties, running for office, and serving in the executive branch as well as Congress and municipal government. One anticipates that their presence may inject a much greater degree of responsiveness and accountability into Haitian political institutions.[8]

This being said, other signs are less favorable. The June 1995 legislative and municipal elections were a near-disaster. Marred by an unresponsive and incompetent Provisional Elections Council (CEP), by organizational chaos, some evidence of fraud, and a few isolated cases of violence, the balloting undercut the legitimacy of the Haitian government and the nascent democratic experiment. The government's slowness in dealing with the opposition's legitimate complaints only made matters worse. Most of the opposition parties repudiated that vote and refused to participate in the subsequent makeup and runoff elections (although many candidates ran anyway). The result was an overwhelming Lavalas victory.

In short, Haitians apparently still could not put aside their power struggles for the sake of national interest.

In perspective, the legislative elections represented a return to the zero-sum politics of the past. In the months that followed, moreover, there were other indications that all was not right. There was an upsurge in political violence, and death squad activities increased. Most of it was aimed at people associated with the Cédras regime or the FADH, but this was not always the case: In early November 1995, Jean-Hubert Feuillé, a newly elected legislator, and cousin and former bodyguard of the president, was gunned down in what was widely presumed to be a political assassination. At his funeral, an emotionally distraught Aristide ordered the police to disarm the macoutes and their sponsors, and he called on his supporters to help them. ("Go to the neighborhoods where there are big houses and heavy weapons.")[9] There followed an outbreak of rioting that left at least ten people dead and over a score wounded. Dozens of Aristide's foes had their homes torched or looted. A radio station critical of the president was attacked. Vigilantes erected roadblocks, burned tires, and searched vehicles. In Gonaïves, UN soldiers were attacked by an angry mob.

Meanwhile, in spite of a long-standing pledge to step down from office at the end of his term, Aristide did little to dissuade his supporters from launching a campaign to extend his stay. Indeed, at times he seemed openly to encourage them. In late November, before a "national dialogue" conference that had passed resolutions calling for a term extension, he proclaimed that "if you want three [more] years, I will not ignore you." He promised to present the resolutions at a cabinet meeting the following week.[10]

These were disturbing developments. Aristide's political foes interpreted them as a prelude to the cancellation of the election, or at least as an attempt to create a climate of intimidation that would render the balloting meaningless. (Some were threatened or attacked by Lavalas partisans.) Subsequently, Aristide, under heavy pressure from the United States and the international community, reiterated his pledge to follow through with the elections as scheduled, but by then much damage had been done.

Whether one interprets Aristide's behavior as a calculated attempt to test the United States and the international community to see how far he could go, or as an effort to contain internal schisms within Lavalas and prevent violence, the net result was disastrous: U.S.-Haitian relations were damaged. Anti-American feeling increased, as the president's followers blamed Washington for forcing Haiti's "savior" from office. U.S. observers—both critics and supporters of the Clinton administration's policy—had their worst fears reinforced. CIA claims about Aristide's lack of stability, which had been largely discredited, regained plausibility. Within Haiti, moreover, frightened members of the bourgeoisie began to leave the country or at least shelved any plans they might have had to invest in it. The upshot was that much of the good work that had been done on behalf of national reconciliation was undone.

In all fairness, one should also say that the issues were not quite as clear-cut as Aristide's critics have claimed: He had, after all, been robbed of three years in office, and there was little doubt that most Haitians wanted him to stay. If his departure fulfilled the letter of the constitution, it nevertheless seemed to violate the *spirit* of democracy, not to mention fairness. In effect, it constituted a partial ratification of the coup of September 1991.

Still, in light of Haiti's history and the deep-seated conflicts that continued to plague it, these developments were disturbing. Aristide's behavior did not inspire confidence. A term extension might have set a dangerous precedent. Even if Aristide himself was committed to democracy (and not everyone was convinced that he was), one could hardly be so sanguine about the democratic instincts of his followers. Some, clearly, hungered more after monumental changes than after democracy. Others were opportunists out for their own personal gain. The potential for corruption and the abuse of power were enormous, and only time would tell whether Lavalasians would be able to withstand the temptations.

In addition to the political culture of elites, one must also factor in the values, attitudes, and behavior of ordinary Haitians. Earlier, it was suggested that there were likely to be differences between the two, and that the displacement of the old ruling class might open a window of opportunity for fundamental change. One must temper this optimism, however, with an appreciation that the masses probably share many of the same propensities toward authoritarianism, class hatred, and so on that have marked the behavior of their exploiters.[11] The danger of revolutionary transformation is that the new ruling class (and, specifically its leaders) may become just as corrupt and brutal as the one that it has replaced.

Second, at this stage at least, the Haitian "revolution" is not really a revolution at all. Rather, there has only been a partial displacement of the old ruling class. What remains is civil society, an entity that, as Fatton pointed out, is not always civil and is full of contradictions: "Rather than constituting a coherent social project, Haitian civil society tends to embody a disorganized plurality of mutually exclusive projects that are not necessarily democratic." Within this uneasy conglomerate are neo-Duvalierists and neoliberals as well as moderate and radical Lavalasians, all "competing for state power and involved in continuous struggles, negotiations, and compromises."[12] The outcome is less likely to be a definitive victory for any one class or sector than a soup reflecting different political subcultures and interests. In short, the break with the past will not be clean.

Third, severe constraints on Haiti's economic development may fatally undermine the country's political development. Part of the popular appeal of democracy lies in the expectation that it will lead to an improvement in people's well-being. But democracy makes no such guarantees; moreover, the neoliberal package imposed on the Aristide and Préval governments will likely prolong the current socioeconomic hardship.

Fourth, if the violence that Haiti has experienced recently should increase and become more politicized, it will further undermine the prospects for democratization. If democracy cannot provide people with security, it will be discredited.

Finally, the transformation of a political culture requires the internalization of new values and attitudes; a superficial embrace is not enough. But such profound changes will take years—indeed decades—to complete. And they are much more than the product of a single wise leader. Education will be critical. Aristide began the process of democratization, but he had little time left in his term of office to implement significant changes. Who is there of comparable stature and commitment to carry on the task? Aristide remains a major force on the political scene, but it is too early in Préval's tenure to ascertain whether Aristide can hold together the centrifugal forces that will continue to pull at Haiti's delicate political fabric.

Fragility is the key word. While progress has been made, Haiti still has an enormous distance to go. Moreover, the road is strewn with obstacles. Notwithstanding Aristide's popularity and Préval's peaceful transition to power, the legitimacy of Haitian political institutions remains very much in doubt. Haitians are accustomed to thinking of the state as a bully—the Kreyòl word *leta* has both meanings—and it will take time and a radically different pattern of government behavior to change that expectation. If Haitians are no longer so apathetic about politics, this is as much a product of their faith in Aristide as anything. For many, he is still a messiah. But whether his charismatic authority will be supplanted by institutional legitimacy remains very much in doubt.

The Economic Substructure of Violence

Behind the values, attitudes, beliefs, and behavior that foster political violence in Haiti are stark economic needs and relationships. While the military-institutional bases of violence have been destroyed, the economic substructure remains largely intact. The critical issues here, both for democracy and political stability, are poverty, inequality, economic growth, and class conflict.

Haiti has long been the poorest country in the Western Hemisphere and one of the poorest in the world, but in recent years its rate of impoverishment has dramatically worsened. Three years of terror, plunder, and neglect, on top of international sanctions, have reduced the per capita income to $250–$260.[13] To make matters worse, the wealth of the country continues to be concentrated in the hands of a relatively small number of people—morally repugnant elites (MREs), a U.S. diplomat once called them—who have traditionally profited from monopolies, a grossly unfair system of taxation, and other mechanisms designed to benefit them at the expense of the vast majority of Haitians. Unless these realities change, there is likely to be renewed violence. Indeed, the only way that the system can be maintained *is* by violence.

That, indeed, always was the function of the Haitian armed forces. Typically, the only state entities regularly present in the countryside were the tax office and the military barracks or post, the one to extract, and the other to enforce the one-way flow of resources from rural areas to Port-au-Prince.[14] Over time, the FADH itself became a major economic institution. In the words of Laguerre, the professional soldier was also an "entrepreneur—kleptocratic, parasitic, and competitive." Haitian officers owned businesses and sold their services. Some operated, in effect, as godfathers, maneuvering indirectly behind the scenes to promote economic dealings through intermediaries.[15] Out in the countryside, 565 rural section chiefs operated as virtual feudal lords. They had their own private militias, imposed fines, collected taxes and bribes, dragooned peasants and workers to labor on their farms, and in general served as judges, jury, and executioners in their areas of jurisdiction. At the bottom of this food chain of violence were the lumpen elements who served as the primary instruments of the terror: rank-and-file soldiers and paramilitary *attachés*, many of whom doubled as police or army regulars. They were so poorly paid that their only recourse was to use their weapons to shake-down ordinary citizens for whatever they could get.

Under the generalized corruption of the regime led by Lieutenant General Raoul Cédras, Brigadier General Philippe Biamby, and Lieutenant Colonel Joseph Michel François, military officers appropriated an increasingly large share of the country's wealth. The armed forces received about 40 percent of the national budget and controlled many state-owned enterprises. The public sector was especially infiltrated by the proxies of François, the Port-au-Prince police chief, who controlled the telephone company, the port, the electricity company, and some basic imports. Narcotics trafficking and contraband operations became widespread. The former, alone, brought in tens of millions of dollars a year, and this bonanza was by no means restricted to the high command. By 1993, discipline had so disintegrated that officers down to the rank of captain had become economic powers in their own rights.[16]

During these years, the merchant-bourgeois and land-owning (*gwandon*) sectors of the elite steadfastly supported the dictatorship and opposed Aristide's return. Powerful military-business alliances dominated much of the country's economic activities, controlling the import of Haiti's four main staples: flour, cement, sugar, and oil. Within the merchant-bourgeois group, three rival conglomerates run by the Mevs, Brandt, and Bigio families competed with one another, with other influential families and businessmen, and with more moderate technocratic-managerial elites associated with the assembly industries, for political influence, oligopsonistic market control, and other opportunities for profit. Some of these leaders had close ties with high-ranking members of the regime. Colonel François, for instance, was on the Mevs's payroll; Cédras was allied with the Brandts.[17]

Today, the military institution is gone but the oligarchy remains. The prospects for economic development and a substantive improvement in living conditions are problematic. The redistribution of economic power in favor of the poor majority does not seem likely. Although Mintz has argued that hardly any beneficial long-term political changes can be accomplished without such a redistribution, this is an explosive issue.[18] More than any other single factor, it was the threat of class warfare that led to the coup that overthrew Aristide in September 1991. A resurrection of that specter would have repolarized Haiti, risked more violence, and frightened away investors. Furthermore, the neoliberal economic policies being imposed on the Haitian government by international donors would seem, on the surface, to preclude such a strategy. Haiti is utterly dependent on foreign aid, and as long as that is the case, its options will be severely constrained. The price of defiance would be very high.

For 200 years, Haiti has been locked into a process of de-development. Peasant productivity today is less than it was in 1843. The agricultural technology that prevailed during the last decades of colonial rule was arguably superior to that used at present.[19] Even if one takes the optimistic view that the predatory state, the primary obstacle to economic development, is no more, the challenges are enormous. The only sector of the economy to show any promise over the past couple of decades, assembly manufacturing for export, lies in ruins, a casualty of military repression and international sanctions. Even if it can be restored, it will not produce more than a small percentage of the jobs that are needed to absorb the rapidly expanding work force, and these jobs would offer a pitifully low wage.[20] At the same time, Haiti lacks the human capital to make a rapid transition to high-growth, more advanced technology industries. In the countryside the peasantry remains trapped in a descending spiral of rapid population growth and accelerating soil erosion that increasingly threatens the very basis of its existence.[21]

In short, the task in Haiti is less a matter of economic recovery or restoration than of starting from scratch: There is very little to build on. There are few functioning institutions; there is little human capital; and there is a long history of waste and corruption.

The Haitian private sector has been scarcely less predatory than the state. In general, its members are not free marketeers. The economic elites have never been particularly interested in investing in Haiti under competitive conditions, and they are especially reluctant to face more efficient foreign competitors. Even now, some of the most powerful families oppose privatization and continue to make huge profits by controlling the import of flour, cement, generators, and other key items.[22] Given Haiti's violent past and uncertain future—the debate over privatization remains nothing short of vitriolic—few are rushing to invest. In the words of one official, "No one in Haiti is going to invest in any substantial way for ten years; they are afraid they will lose their money."[23]

Nor is the outlook for foreign private investment much better. Very little has come into the country since 1994.[24] While this is partly a result of the Haitian government's slowness in instituting privatization and other free-market reforms, the security issue is equally important. If foreigners are not investing when UN troops maintain order, what can be expected once those forces leave and maintaining security becomes more difficult?

Two hundred years of misdevelopment cannot be reversed in five years: One must think in terms of decades. Yet there is no reason to believe that the international community is willing to make such a substantial long-term investment. Indeed, the United States is already beginning to downsize its commitment. After contributing $235 million to the Haitian economy in 1995, the Clinton administration reduced its aid request for 1996 by more than half.[25]

But beyond immediate issues, will the United States and the international community stay the course? If they do not, the results will be predictable: Once the foreigners leave, their development projects will be left to decay. One recalls the fate of the all-weather roads that the Americans left after their first occupation: In 1934, Haiti had 1,200 miles of well-constructed highway; in 1971, the country could claim only 300 miles of surfaced all-weather roadways, including city streets.[26]

The Haitian government is trapped. On the one hand, it must please foreign donors or risk losing the aid that it needs to jump-start the economy and avoid a further sharp decline in living conditions. On the other hand, it must satisfy the aspirations of the poor majority for a better life. Unfortunately, despite its possible economic merits, the USAID-World Bank-IMF prescription will likely lead to more hardship in the short run, and probably in the longer run as well. To the extent that the government bureaucracy is streamlined and state enterprises privatized, for instance, greater unemployment will result. There could be an increase in inequality and more social and political conflict. The legitimacy of both the government and the democratic experiment could be undermined. An economic take-off could become even more problematic.

In light of these concerns, there is little chance of a significant improvement in Haitian living standards in the short run, and the situation could very well get worse. As a result, frustration will undoubtedly intensify, and violence will probably increase. While most of the latter will take the form of common crime, some will be political. There will continue to be a large pool of unemployed Haitians willing and able to hire themselves out as gunmen. That most of the attachés were never disarmed, and only a fraction of the weapons in Haiti were ever confiscated or turned in, led to the rationale for providing former soldiers with job training, so that they would not resort to violence to make a living or attempt to destabilize the government.[27] Not everyone can be retrained, however. There are currently tens of thousands of former attachés who are not included in the program. There are serious doubts about how many jobs will be available for those who do receive training. Opportunities for employment in Haiti are scarce, and the Haitian government is understandably reluctant to give its enemies preferential treatment over its own followers.[28]

Finally, one of the problems with creating a Haitian national police force almost as large as the old FADH is that there may not be enough money for salaries. By Haitian standards, salary levels have been set very high (about U.S. $330 a month) so that officers will not have to resort to corruption to make a living. The government may not be able to meet the payroll in coming years, however; already there have been delays in payment. Whether the international community will provide the necessary support, and for how long, remains to be seen. If the police cannot make ends meet by being honest, they will supplement their incomes by committing extortion or theft, or by selling their services to the highest bidders. Will Haiti's past also be Haiti's future?

Reconciliation and Justice: A Contradiction in Terms?

Heinl and Heinl wrote that "deep in the psyche of Haiti . . . lies a violence that goes beyond violence." Haiti's history is "dominated at every turn by death and terror."[29] Can this self-destructive pattern be broken? Can Haiti finally achieve national reconciliation and justice? Or will it once again slip into a fratricidal cycle of revenge and retaliation?

That Haiti has avoided such conflict thus far has been largely due to the international military and police presence and the efforts of Presidents Aristide and Préval to promote reconciliation among Haitians of all social classes. This reconciliation remains extremely fragile, however, and moreover has been purchased in part at the expense of justice.

The Carter-Cédras agreement providing for the 1994 "intervasion" enabled the top leaders of the old regime to escape the country. Although the U.S.-led multinational force arrested hundreds of alleged criminals and human rights abusers, only twenty-six were turned over to the Haitian government in early 1995. The rest were released because there was a lack of evidence, because there was no functioning judiciary, or because they had been permitted to escape by sympathetic prison officials. At the same time, notorious offenders like Franck Romain, the former Duvalierist mayor of Port-au-Prince, and Emmanuel Constant, the founder of the paramilitary group, Front for the Advancement and Progress of Haiti (FRAPH), were allowed to remain at large or quietly to slip into the Dominican Republic. The result was a growing disillusionment with U.S. and UN peacekeeping operations and official Haitian institutions, and a tendency to exact popular justice in the streets.

As months passed and the Aristide government itself became increasingly the target of criticism, it began to move more aggressively on the justice issue. A National Commission of Truth and Justice was formed to investigate past human rights abuses. A number of people were arrested in connection with a 1987 peasant massacre at Jean-Rabel. François, along with sixteen codefendants, was tried in absentia for the murder of Aristide supporter Antoine Izmery. How far would President Aristide go? The list of human rights violators potentially subject to prosecution was very long.

In this respect, the Haitian government also was trapped. Caught between the left, which wants an aggressive pursuit of justice, and the right, which mortally fears such a development, it will have to perform a delicate balancing act. A failure to satisfy the former will undermine one of the government's traditional bases of support while feeding an instinct for revenge that could very well lead to more political assassinations and mob violence. On the other hand, a too vigorous pursuit of justice might have the same effect while so frightening the economic elite as to shatter its fragile support for (or tolerance of) the government and perhaps provoke a violent response from the right. The rampage that followed Aristide's speech urging the disarmament of those thought to be responsible for the growing incidences of political assassination provides a cautionary example of how volatile the situation remains and how easily violence from one side can trigger violence from the other.

The Haitian National Police: Bellwether for Stability?

In spite of all of this, Haiti may overcome the legacy of its past. Certainly, progress has been made. The FADH, the central institution of the predatory state, has been dismantled. All that is left are several hundred or so former military personnel who were part of the recently dissolved Interim Public Security Force and who are now being absorbed into the Haitian National Police (HNP). At the same time, FRAPH and the army's other paramilitary appendages have been disbanded. Without the FADH to organize and empower them, such groups will find it harder to reemerge and regain their former potency.

Clearly, too, the creation of the Haitian National Police has provided a major opportunity to foster political stability and democracy. At minimum, the HNP should serve as a deterrent to any former FADH or attaché who might be thinking about launching a comeback. A serious effort has been made to create an apolitical, civilian police force capable of dealing with internal security and criminal problems. Although it is too early to render judgment, preliminary reports have been mostly favorable: "Rigorous and impartial recruitment standards and procedures [have been] developed and have produced young and well-motivated recruits." Initially, at least, they were enthusiastically received by the populace.[30]

Even so, critical problems remain. The new police are sorely lacking in experience at all levels. In recent months, charges of incompetence and human rights abuse have increased, seriously eroding public support for and confidence in the institution. Uncertainty continues about the trustworthiness of the former members of the FADH who are being brought into the HNP, especially those in the second-echelon ranks of the command structure. Furthermore, questions remain regarding how many police the Haitian government will be able to maintain at current salary scales; whether foreign aid for such purposes will be forthcoming and for how long; whether officers will be paid regularly and promptly without the kind of bureaucratic delays that have marked the process in the past; and whether they will have the cars, radios, uniforms, and other equipment that they will need to do their jobs in a competent, professional manner. By the same token, the credibility and legitimacy of the HNP are likely to be tested by the continued weakness of the judicial and penal systems. If the courts do not function, or if they cannot keep pace with the number of arrests, then the police may be tempted to take the powers of judgment and punishment into their own hands (through extrajudicial executions, for instance). That, in turn, would undermine the rule of law before it has a chance to take hold.

Nor is it clear how many police will be needed. As matters now stand, the HNP should be able to provide a minimum level of urban security but not much more, and it cannot hope to control rural areas. Haiti will almost certainly need more police than the 5,000 to 7,000 that are currently being planned. (The U.S. Atlantic Command believes that approximately 7,000 to 12,000 security personnel will be required, with 9,000 considered necessary to provide a marginal degree of security.) In the "fog of peace," it is impossible to know what dangers lie ahead. As the FADH and its paramilitary allies have been disbanded, many former soldiers and attachés have turned to crime.[31] Others have sought to organize as pressure groups and have engaged in protests, some of them violent. There is evidence, too, of growing paramilitary hit-squad activity. Such problems are likely to increase after the UN peacekeepers leave, and it remains to be seen whether the HNP will be up to the task of maintaining law and order.

Things Fall Apart: Five Scenarios

In short, the moment of truth is still to come. There is a very real danger—if not a probability—that sooner or later things will fall apart. The following scenarios are suggestive of what could go wrong:

The "Woodwork" Hypothesis

After the departure of the UN peacekeepers, former FADH and paramilitary personnel would reemerge from hiding in Haiti and the Dominican Republic, where they had been stockpiling arms and biding their time, waiting for the chance to regain power. The country would be plunged into civil war.

This is the most widely feared scenario, but it is also—at least in the form presented above—overrated. For one thing, there is serious doubt as to whether any large arms stockpiles exist. U.S. troops received numerous tips of such caches following the September 1994 intervention, but were never able to locate any. Colonel Mark Boyatt, who commanded the U.S. Special Forces in Haiti, believes that they do not exist.[32] Beyond this, any resurgent FADH-macoute army would require leadership, organization, and popular support, which do not exist. Even if leadership and organization could be developed and arms could be obtained (and the latter, certainly, would not be difficult), there is no sea in which these fish could swim. The populace is no longer cowed; it would provide little shelter, intelligence, or other support for such an army. On the contrary, it would almost certainly strongly resist a Duvalierist restoration.

Moreover, it seems unlikely, in the short run, that the United States or the UN would allow such a development. Each has too much at stake to let the situation fall apart so fast. For President Clinton, it would be a political embarrassment, at the very least. Haiti represents one of his few foreign policy "successes." Haiti's return to chaos would reopen the immigration problem, creating a headache for President Clinton in his second term.

Antigovernment conspiracies will undoubtedly emerge—they are endemic—and gunmen will likely come out of hiding. Terrorism aimed at probing the government's defenses will most likely increase as well. This is the real danger implied by the woodwork hypothesis. It would not require a large or well-organized force to create incidents that might trigger an overreaction, which in turn could spark more mob violence and do incalculable damage to the legitimacy of the government, to national reconciliation, and to democratization.

The Jacobinization of the Police

Another, more medium- or long-term possibility, is that the HNP might become politicized by radical elements in Lavalas and turned into an instrument of terror, class warfare, and revenge. In this scenario the police would, in effect, become the functional equivalent of the old military, but would be under the control of the radical left rather than the right.

This was certainly a possibility under Aristide and may well still be possible under Préval, should he and Aristide decide to revert to the kind of direct democracy that seemed to be developing during the latter's initial period in office. Although many observers today argue that the radical Lavalas political and socioeconomic program is all but dead, political and class conflicts in Haiti remain so volatile and the historical record so dismal that the resurrection of the project in the form of a Jacobin dictatorship cannot be discounted. One should remember that dictators are not always military men. (Witness the Duvaliers.)

There have been other incidents: An unsuccessful attempt in early 1995 to place several hundred unvetted men in the Interim Public Security Force, for instance, was initially interpreted by American officials as a move by Aristide to take political control of the military. While most U.S. officials eventually concluded that the episode was the product of a lower-level conspiracy and incompetence rather than a high-level government effort to subvert or take over the institution, other developments have since resurrected the concern over politicization. The attempted appointment of a former FADH medical officer and alleged human rights violator as head of the HNP (rejected by parliament) and the incorporation of hundreds of former military members into the police have done nothing to bolster public confidence. At the same time, there has been growing suspicion, even within the Clinton administration, that Haitian security forces have been involved in political assassinations. In one case the Haitian government even impeded FBI efforts to investigate the killing.[33]

A major issue, of course, has been Aristide himself. Who is the real Aristide—the unstable demagogue portrayed by the CIA or the pragmatic statesman who seemed to be emerging in the months following his restoration? That question cannot yet be answered. What can be said, however, is that the political culture, the class antagonisms, the desire for revenge, the likelihood of continuing political and social violence, the enduring economic disaster and the frustrations that it is generating, and Haiti's deteriorated relations with its international sponsors (especially the United States) make some degree of state or state-sanctioned violence likely in the years ahead. As long as the state can manipulate the composition of the police and the system of economic rewards under which they operate, the HNP will be susceptible to political abuse.

The Mob

A third scenario, which might be independent of or closely related to the first two, involves massive mob violence directed against the Haitian oligarchy, former military and paramilitary elements, leaders of the political opposition, and common criminals. There is still an enormous amount of suppressed tension in Haiti. Natural desires for justice and revenge for the human rights abuses of the old regime have been largely frustrated by the absence of functioning police, judicial and penal systems, and the reluctance of UN peacekeepers to seek out and arrest past human rights violators. While massive violence has been generally avoided (thanks to public restraint, the leadership of Presidents Aristide and Préval, and the presence of international peacekeepers), many isolated instances of vigilante justice have occurred. There is a very real danger that this violence could grow much worse after the UN peacekeepers leave, especially if crime continues to increase, the military and macoutes reemerge, and the left seeks to mobilize the masses to defend the government or wage class war.

The Rise of the New Macoutes

With the economy depressed and tens of thousands of former military and paramilitary unemployed, some of these alienated and armed elements have turned to crime. Many of the robberies and shootings that have been taking place are believed to be the work of former police attachés, some of whom are hiring out their services as assassins. Such killings have become commonplace, and a number appear to have been political.[34] Among the most notorious of the latter were the hit-squad murders of Mireille Durocher-Bertin, a prominent Aristide critic and defender of the Cédras dictatorship, and former Brigadier General Henri Max Mayard. Since a number of other former military officers, wealthy businessmen, and associates of the old regime have also been assassinated, there has been speculation among U.S. military intelligence officers that some in the Aristide camp were engaged in a preemptive campaign to destroy the enemy (or at least its potential leaders) before the UN forces left and the enemy had a chance to launch an attack of its own.[35]

Very little hard evidence supports this theory, however. While the government (or elements within it) is the most obvious suspect—Interior Minister Mondésir Beaubrun (since replaced) was even accused of masterminding the Durocher-Bertin murder—there are certainly other possibilities.[36] Some of these killings may have been drug related. Some may be the work of disgruntled former soldiers who have not received benefits to which they feel entitled. Some may have been provocations by the right, designed to undermine public confidence in the government's intentions and ability to maintain order and to destroy its international support. Nor have all those targeted been members or supporters of the dictatorship; some were Aristide partisans or at least foes of the Cédras regime.[37]

What can be said for certain is that there is a very large potential for things to get worse. There are too many guns around, and the police have neither the manpower, the vehicles, nor the experience to patrol the whole country. Already, former soldiers have formed groups such as the Rally of Military Dismissed Without Reasons to press for stipends, jobs, and other compensation for their lost careers. Disruptive protests have been held. Shadowy groups, apparently linked to the Rally and elements in the now-defunct Interim Public Security Force and to such Aristide foes as former President Prosper Avril, have organized conspiracies and conducted assassinations. Criminal gangs, such as the so-called Red Army in Cité Soleil, are sowing fear and anger in the slums, attacking police and inciting mob violence.

Meanwhile, the oligarchy, which has increasingly become a target of the crime wave that has shaken the country, has bolstered its private security forces. These organizations have grown in number and size since Aristide's return, and some are better armed than the HNP.[38] The danger is that these groups have the potential for acting as private armies and death squads. (Some may already be engaged in such activities.) There also is a concern that the oligarchy may provide financial and other support to violent groups and that former FADH officers who are brought into the HNP might link up with former colleagues and attachés on the outside.

By the same token, there is also some concern about the presidential security force, which was chosen on the basis of loyalty rather than professionalism or merit. It is this group of several dozen bodyguards, the inner circle within the larger outer circle of palace guards, that U.S. officials suspected of conducting political killings.[39] Papa Doc, it may be recalled, used his presidential guard to help neutralize the FADH, elevating the guard to the status of a military department. Indeed, the guard became the most powerful military unit in Port-au-Prince.

A Bonapartist Restoration

Finally, remilitarization and politicization could occur along traditional lines with the HNP becoming the functional equivalent of the old FADH. While in the short run a coup seems unlikely (although not impossible if the wrong people gain control of the police), in the longer term, deeply rooted values, attitudes, and habits may well reassert themselves. A certain amount of corruption and brutality are almost inevitable. Moreover, if Haiti fails to develop strong democratic institutions, the police/military may be tempted to step into the vacuum. This would most likely occur during periods of intensified political or class conflict, especially if such interventions were supported by or at the behest of conservative or reactionary elements in the business and political sectors. The pattern might be similar to the gradual militarization of politics that occurred after the departure of the U.S. Marines in 1934.[40]

Conclusions and Recommendations

The United States and UN need to be sensitized to these potential developments and devise long-range plans to avoid them. Otherwise the tactical successes that have been enjoyed so far may presently turn into strategic failures.

The most obvious requirement is for a continuing international security presence. The UN peacekeeping mission can be reduced, but some substantial presence will be needed until at least 1997. A smaller presence will be needed for several more years, that is, until the HNP and the judicial system are functioning effectively. Without it, the entire experiment could collapse. In addition, a rapid response force should be formed to back up the Haitian government as circumstances require. Ideally, the United States should be involved in all of these operations to bolster their credibility.

At the same time, there must be ongoing foreign monitoring and training of the Haitian police. To expect the HNP to be professionalized and capable of maintaining law and order after only four months in training and a year or two of experience is probably unrealistic, particularly in light of the enormous challenges that it will face and the resource constraints under which it will operate.

The United States has agreed to give the police not only basic training but also advanced instruction in evidence gathering and analysis, crowd control, and other specialized skills over a period of five years. In addition, foreign civilian police advisors will be needed to provide hands-on mentoring and backup in the field and to serve as role models for their Haitian counterparts. Particular attention needs to be paid to continuing to improve the HNP's leadership at all levels.

The police will need more officers, weapons, vehicles, and equipment. Continuing efforts at professionalization designed to instill respect for human rights and constitutional rights are critical. Toward this end, most of the former military should be replaced by personnel not tainted by their association with the FADH. A structure of accountability capable of effectively dealing with police abuses must be created. The HNP's model should be community-based policing, in which the use of firearms is a last option. While heavier weapons may be needed to deal with emergency situations, such arms must be closely controlled and limited to specially trained backup units.

In the final analysis, however, these needs are only part of a much larger equation. Without functioning courts and prisons, security will remain an illusion. While progress has been made in these areas, much needs to be done. Similarly, security cannot be attained so long as Haiti remains economically prostrate. The economic substructure of violence must be chipped away, or it will undermine any efforts that are made to establish political stability and democracy.

A nation cannot be built in one year or even five; Haiti needs a substantial, ongoing international commitment for the foreseeable future. Unless the country's foreign sponsors are willing to stay the course, everything that is being accomplished now will be wasted. In effect, Haitians will have been set up to fail.

That has implications. The central lesson of the recent U.S. experience with Haiti is that half-way efforts lead to half-way, ineffective, and sometimes counterproductive results.[41] In the current instance, Washington defined success in such narrow terms (the restoration of Aristide and the creation of conditions that would allow for a U.S. exit), that it could hardly fail. The difficult and painful issues were ignored. Under such circumstances, the danger facing the United States and the international community is that they will have raised Haitian expectations to astronomical heights, only to dash them through an unwillingness to do what is necessary.

Notes

1. See, especially, Robert I. Rotberg, *Haiti: The Politics of Squalor* (Boston, 1971); Michel-Rolph Trouillot, *Haiti: State Against Nation* (New York, 1990); Michel S. Laguerre, *The Military and Society in Haiti* (Knoxville, 1993); Mats Lundahl, *Politics or Markets? Essays on Haitian Underdevelopment* (London, 1992).

2. This was not always the case. In the 1960s and 1970s, political culture studies were attacked by the left, and for a while went out of fashion. More recently, however, there has been a renaissance. Indeed, no less an authority than Harry Eckstein has argued that political culture may be one of the two "still viable general approaches to political theory and explanation proposed since the early fifties to replace the long-dominant formal-legalism of the field—the other being political rational choice theory." See "A Culturalist Theory of Political Change,"*American Political Science Review*, LXXXII (1988), 789. For a recent overview and sampling of the literature, see Larry Diamond (ed.), *Political Culture and Democracy in Developing Countries* (Boulder, CO, 1993).

3. See, for example, Donald E. Schulz and Gabriel Marcella, *Reconciling the Irreconcilable: The Troubled Outlook for U.S. Policy toward Haiti* (Carlisle, PA, 1994), 7–17; Robert Heinl and Nancy Heinl, *Written in Blood: The Story of the Haitian People, 1492–1971* (Boston, 1978), 6; Lawrence Harrison, "Voodoo Politics," *Atlantic Monthly* (June 1993), 105–107; Rotberg, *Haiti*, 17–24. The best general treatment of the subject to appear in recent years is Trouillot's *Haiti: State Against Nation*. On the social underpinnings of the political culture, see James G. Leyburn, *The Haitian People* (New Haven, 1966).

4. Harrison, "Voodoo Politics," 106. Generalizations like these are by their very nature unfair. Some members of the elite do share Western beliefs in democracy, equality, and so on. But they are not typical of their class.

5. Leyburn, *Haitian People*, 287–288.

6. Rotberg, *Haiti*, 18; See, for example, Jacques Roumain's classic novel of rural Haiti, *Gouverneurs de la rosée* (Paris, 1944).

7. Anthony Maingot, *Grasping the Nettle: A "National Liberation" Option for Haiti* (Miami, 1994), 2. Michel-Rolph Trouillot has noted that while collective action in Haiti is rare at the national level because of the stigma of illegitimacy attached to politics and political institutions this is much less true at local levels.

8. On these developments, see especially Robert E. Maguire, "From Outsiders to Insiders: Emerging Leadership and Political Change in Haiti," paper prepared for the conference The Political and Economic Reconstruction of Haiti, Mayagüez, Puerto Rico, September 23, 1995.

9. Foreign Broadcast Information Service (FBIS), *Daily Report: Latin America*, November 1995, 14.

10. Ibid., November 27 and 29, 1995.

11. Again, it is an open question as to which aspects of the dominant political culture the masses share, and to what degree. For instance, many Haitian scholars argue that the peasantry has been less violent than the middle and upper classes. Whether this has been because ofdifferent values and attitudes or other factors (for example, a lack of opportunity and weapons) remains unclear.

12. Robert Fatton, "From Predatory Rule to Accountable Governance," paper prepared for the conference The Political and Economic Reconstruction of Haiti, 2.

13. Inter-American Development Bank, *Emergency Economic Recovery Program: Haiti*, report of the joint mission (November 7–20, 1994) (Washington, D.C., 1995), 28; International Monetary Fund, *Haiti—Recent Developments*, SM/95/43 (Washington, DC., 1995), 2.

14. Maguire, "From Outsiders to Insiders," 9.

15. Michel S. Laguerre, "Business and Corruption," *California Management Review*, XXXVI (1994), 94–95.

16. Schulz and Marcella, *Reconciling the Irreconcilable*, 14–15.

17. Other influential families who supported the dictatorship included the Acras, Madsens, Duforts, Elyzees, Khawlys, Lissades, Feurys, Mourras, and Moscosos. Other business supporters included Gerard Cassis, George Sassine, Reynold Bonnefil, Raymond Roy, Bernard Craan, and Lionel Turnier.

18. Sidney W. Mintz, "Can Haiti Change?" *Foreign Affairs*, LXXIV (January-February 1995), 86

19. Trouillot, *Haiti: State Against Nation*, 84; Mats Lundahl, "The Haitian Dilemma Reexamined: Lessons from the Past in Light of Some New Economic Theory," paper prepared for the conference The Political and Economic Reconstruction of Haiti, 5.

20. At its peak in 1990 the assembly sector accounted only for about 46,000 jobs in a labor force of 3.5 million. By the end of 1994, however, operations had virtually ceased. In late 1995 it employed about 10,000 workers. Don Bohning, "Intervention in Haiti Slowly Restoring Peace," *Miami Herald*, September 16, 1995.

21. Lundahl, "Haitian Dilemma," 28–29.

22. Larry Rohter, "Privatization Starts Feud in Haiti," *New York Times*, October 19, 1995.

23. Pierre-Richard Leroy, principal advisor to the Ministry of Economy and Finances, in a conversation with the author, September 22, 1995.

24. Bohning, "Intervention in Haiti."

25. Larry Rohter, "The Suspense Isn't Over in Haiti," *New York Times*, October 15, 1995.

26. Heinl and Heinl, *Written in Blood*, 3.

27. According to John Merrill, the deputy director of the OSD Haiti Task Force, only about 30,000 or so of the roughly 175,000 guns in Haiti were ever seized. Comments at the conference The Political and Economic Reconstruction of Haiti.

28. Quoted in Rachel Neild, et al., *Policing Haiti: Preliminary Report on the New Civilian Security Force* (Washington, D.C., 1995), 36.

29. Heinl and Heinl, *Written in Blood*, 6.

30. Neild et al., *Policing Haiti*, 22, 29–30.

31. To borrow Fishel's classic play on Clausewitz, in John T. Fishel, *The Fog of Peace: Planning and Executing the Restoration of Panama* (Carlisle, PA, 1992).

32. Conversation with Colonel Mark Boyatt, September 22, 1995. Nevertheless, there continues to be great concern about this possibility. There have even been claims that some U.S. Special Forces soldiers helped FADH troops and attachés stash their weapons to avoid confiscation. While it is conceivable that such collaboration may have occurred in a few isolated instances, these reports have not been verified and are suspect. See Douglas Farah and Dana Priest, "Haiti Says U.S. Troops May Have Helped Forces," *Washington Post*, December 8, 1995.

33. Neild et al., *Report on Latin America*, 16–17; Human Rights Watch/Americas and National Coalition for Haitian Refugees, *Haiti: Security Compromised; Recycled Haitian Soldiers on Police Front Line*, VII (1995), 7–9; Douglas Farah, "U.S. Exercises Its Influence on Aristide," *Washington Post*, February 22, 1995; Thomas W. Lippmann, "U.S. Accused of 'Stonewalling' on Haitian Murders," *Washington Post*, December 23, 1995; Lippmann, "U.S. Officials Say Haitians Stymied FBI," *Washington Post*, January 5, 1996.

34. Some U.S. military intelligence sources have estimated that there have been over eighty political killings since October 1994. In contrast, the American embassy has tried to minimize the problem, contending that only a relative handful of assassinations have been political. In turn, the International Civilian Mission, which monitors the human rights situation, reported that there had been twenty commando-style killings since Aristide's return. But there have been others since then; as of April 1996 the number had probably surpassed thirty. See Robert D. Novak, "A Shooting in Haiti," *Washington Post*, October 12, 1995; Sandra Marquez, "Leaked Report Shows Internal U.S. Discord Over Haiti Policy," *Miami Herald*, August 17, 1995.

35. Robert D. Novak, "Downward Spiral in Haiti," *Washington Post*, August 10, 1995.

36. Larry Rohter, "U.S. Suspicions Over Killing May Mar Clinton's Haiti Trip," *New York Times*, March 31, 1995.

37. Letter of Colin Granderson, head of the OAS/UN International Civilian Mission in Haiti, in *Washington Post*, November 3, 1995. The most obvious case was that of Jean-Hubert Feuillé, Aristide's cousin and friend. Another victim was Eric Lamothe, a member of the National Front for Change and Democracy, which supported Aristide's bid for the presidency in 1990. See "Pro-Aristide Lawmaker Is Found Shot to Death," *Miami Herald*, March 4, 1995.

38. Conversation with Boyatt, September 22, 1995.

39. From a knowledgeable U.S. military source to the author.

40. In the two decades that followed, the FADH evolved from a political mediator to a guardian and, eventually, a political ruler before being purged and subordinated by the Duvalier regime. See Laguerre, *Military and Society in Haiti*, 84–104.

41. On this theme, see especially Schulz and Marcella, *Reconciling the Irreconcilable*, 17–49.

CHAPTER FIVE

A Popular Democratic Revolution in a Predemocratic Society: The Case of Haiti

Robert Pastor

IN 1791, stirred by the spirit of the French Revolution, Haitian slaves rose up and defeated Napoleon and the greatest army of the time. In 1804, proclaiming Haiti the world's first black republic, Haitians rid themselves of colonialism, but not of oppression. Haiti's new leaders exploited the people and transformed the richest colony in the Caribbean into the poorest country. A peaceful, democratic process never took hold. Instead, a succession of civil wars and brutal dictators devastated the country. Only the pride of the country's birth helped Haitians to withstand 200 years of abject poverty, international isolation, and brutal dictatorship, culminating in the twenty-eight year Duvalier dynasty.

Haiti's long struggle for liberation entered its most recent phase on February 7, 1986, when Jean-Claude ("Baby Doc") Duvalier fled to France. From then, until the inauguration of René Préval as president, ten years to the day after Duvalier's departure, Haiti had nine elections. The first, in November 1987, was aborted by paramilitary thugs who murdered thirty-four voters. The second, in January 1988, and the fourth, five years later, were manipulated by the military, and only 10 to 15 percent of the people voted. Under the democratically elected presidency of Jean-Bertrand Aristide, legislative and municipal elections were held on June 25, 1995, and reruns and runoffs were held on August 13, September 17, and October 8. In these cases as well as the presidential election on December 17, most of the political parties protested the election and rejected the results. In the ten years since the end of the Duvalier dynasty, only one of nine elections was acknowledged by all parties and international observers as being free and fair: That presidential election occurred on December 16, 1990.

In that election, a young, multilingual priest named Jean-Bertrand Aristide entered the race at the last moment against eleven other presidential candidates. With a compelling slogan, *lavalas* (flood), Aristide catalyzed a movement that earned him two-thirds of the vote. Aristide's election represented a popular democratic revolution, the up-ending of a power pyramid that had ruled the country for 200 years. Suddenly, the great mass of poor people had their leader in the presidency, and the elite found themselves with their faces pressed up against the palace windows trying to read lips that could decide their fate.

Democracy, de Tocqueville wrote 150 years ago, requires an assertive middle class. In Haiti, there is a very thin buffer between the impoverished masses and the elite. Social scientists have catalogued national attributes that are most commonly associated with consolidated democracies; Haiti possesses none of them.[1] It is the poorest country in the Western Hemisphere ($340 annual per capita income), with the smallest middle class and the highest rate of illiteracy (70 percent). Political parties are little more than the personal vehicles of their leaders, and more than sixty parties were registered for the 1995 elections. Rumors, arbitrary decisions, and targeted violence have been the currency of Haitian politics.

The administrative capacity of the country is weak—where it exists— and it probably could not conduct a credible election without massive international support. Even with such aid, its elections have been flawed. When political suspicions combine with technical incapacity, the prospects for a free and fair election, let alone a functioning democracy, are limited. Until the people of Haiti develop an educational system that can instruct the vast majority of its people, and until the economy can sprout a middle class and an administrative elite, democracy will be problematic in Haiti.

The parliamentary elections of June 25, 1995 were the first ones held under a democratic government. More than 2,000 legislative and municipal offices were at stake, and twenty-seven political parties competed. The elections were nothing less than an administrative disaster, with an insecure vote count. Virtually all the political parties except the Plateforme Politique Lavalas (PPL), which was associated with the government, condemned the election and called for its annulment even before the results were announced.

Can Haiti be democratic? Yes is the short answer. It is possible, but it is very difficult, and the path to democracy will be convoluted. This should come as no surprise. Haiti has never followed a conventional path. Two hundred years ago, Haiti became a kind of political Galapagos island, evolving its own unique political and spiritual forms.

Still, since 1987 progress has been made. In assessing the current situation and future prospects in Haiti, this chapter reviews the rise, exile, and return of Aristide (1990–94); examines the security situation in Haiti since his return; surveys the political and electoral process in 1995 and the transition to President Préval; and identifies the current and future obstacles to democratic consolidation.

The Rise, Exile, and Return of Aristide

When Jean-Claude Duvalier fled Haiti, the military remained in charge. After trying unsuccessfully to manipulate the electoral process, the army grudgingly allowed a free election in 1990. This did not happen by accident, and the lessons of that election were either forgotten or not learned by the time of the 1995 elections.

In 1990 Ertha Pascal-Trouillot, the provisional president, invited the UN, the OAS, and the Council of Freely Elected Heads of Government, chaired by former U.S. president Jimmy Carter, to observe the electoral process in order to ensure that all parties would accept it as fair. The UN and the OAS advised the Provisional Elections Council (CEP) on how to conduct the elections. The council collaborated with the National Democratic Institute for International Affairs (NDI) and sent numerous prestigious delegations to observe the electoral process. Although the OAS and UN were initially uninterested in conducting a quick count (a random sample of results), the council and NDI convinced them to use their resources to do so, and that permitted a reliable, rapid prediction of the final results of the presidential election before the actual counting had concluded.

At the same time, Carter and his colleagues, including former prime minister Michael Manley of Jamaica and former prime minister George Price of Belize, worked with the opposition parties to distill their complaints and helped the government and the CEP to fashion fair responses.

These efforts increased confidence in the electoral process. In addition, the council, through its incumbent members, lobbied the UN to send security observers to monitor the Haitian military and prevent a recurrence of the 1987 violence.

On December 16, 1990, some 63 percent of the eligible voters participated, and 67.5 percent of those voted for Jean-Bertrand Aristide as president. A quick count and the international monitors proved crucial in persuading all of the candidates to accept the results within a day of the election, although the real count was not completed until weeks later.

Weber identified three ways by which authority may gain legitimacy: traditional (handed down by kings); rational-legal (by a constitution and free elections); and charismatic (by faith in a leader of divine worth or extraordinary talent).[2] Democratic governments rely on rational-legal authority and on the separation between the source of authority (the people) and the agent of authority (the government). If governments fail to fulfill their promises, the people, as the ultimate source of authority, elect new governments.

Although Aristide was elected by the people, the bond that connected him to the masses was of a religious and charismatic kind. This was evident when the masses rose up to protest the attempted coup against him in January 1991, and it was confirmed on the day of his inauguration in 1991, as the people chanted, "Thank you God, for sending Titi [Aristide]."

But Aristide was human, not divine, and his popularity, while great, was not invariable. He was slow to assemble a government. Despite pledges by the international community to provide $1.2 billion in aid, those funds sat idle while the new government stumbled, instead of forging and implementing an economic plan. Barely seven months after Aristide's joyous inauguration, there was silence when the military overthrew him. And three years of brutal repression followed.

When he later reflected on what had gone wrong, Aristide acknowledged that perhaps he had won the election by too wide a margin.[3] He therefore had little incentive to compromise, and he showed too little respect for the independence of the parliament. One of his mistakes was replacing General Herard Abraham, the commander in chief of the army, with General Raoul Cedras. Abraham, a skillful political actor, had secured the election and stopped the military coup led by Roger Lafontant in January 1991.

In exile, Aristide marshaled international support for his return. The OAS condemned the coup, imposed sanctions on the military regime, and sent mediating teams, but to no effect. President George Bush supported these efforts, but was unwilling to put any muscle behind them. His principal concern was the flow of Haitian refugees to Florida. After he decided to send Haitian refugees back to Haiti without a hearing, the refugee crisis disappeared, and the pressure for him to restore Aristide to power also diminished. Candidate Bill Clinton criticized Bush's refugee policy, but in office as president adopted it. Clinton gained Aristide's support for this policy by promising to restore him to power.

It took eighteen months for President Clinton to come to grips with the implications of that promise. In July 1994 the United States persuaded the UN Security Council to approve a resolution calling on member states to use force to compel the Haitian military to accept Aristide's return. On September 15 President Clinton warned the Haitian military to leave power immediately. Although he said that all diplomatic options had been exhausted, on the very next day he asked Jimmy Carter, Senator Sam Nunn, and General Colin Powell to fly to Haiti to negotiate the departure of the Haitian military leaders.

The Carter team succeeded in gaining the agreement of the provisional government for the entry into Haiti of a large multinational force led by the United States. On September 19, the day after the agreement was signed, 20,000 U.S. troops arrived to create a secure climate that permitted Aristide's return on October 15. Aristide had his second chance.

The Security Context

The mission of the multinational force (MNF) that arrived in Haiti was to produce a secure environment for the consolidation of democracy. The size of the MNF declined rapidly from 20,000 troops in September to 8,414 troops (of which 5,818 were from the United States) in January 1995. On March 31, 1995, the MNF transferred its responsibility to the UN Military Mission (UNMIH). At that time, there were 6,000 troops, half of whom were from the United States. In addition, there were 780 international police monitors (IPM), whose job was to monitor human rights violations and train the new Haitian police force. The UN troops were supposed to remain until the new president was inaugurated on February 7, 1996. (Later, their mandate was extended until the end of February.)

At the time of the entry of the MNF, the Haitian armed forces (FADH) reportedly numbered 7,100 troops. A count of the FADH after the MNF entry revealed only 5,800 soldiers. The others either had disappeared or had existed only on paper, with their salaries diverted to various officers. The UN presence immediately produced significant reductions in the number of human rights violations and permitted an atmosphere in which Haitians felt free to express their resentment against the FADH for its long history of repression. Reports of crime increased, but this increase was due to the fact that people felt free to make such reports, and many reported crimes that had occurred during the previous three years. Also, the elite could no longer rely on the military for protection against criminals. Despite the reported rise in crime, UN statistics showed that the incidence of crime in Port-au-Prince was much lower than that in Detroit, a city of comparable size and population.

From his return to Haiti through December 1994, President Aristide said he would preserve the army but reduce it to a force of 1,500 members. This was consistent with both the agreement negotiated by Carter, Nunn, and Powell, and approved by Presidents Clinton and Aristide, and with the constitution of 1987. The government and MNF set up screening committees to purge those soldiers who had been engaged in human rights violations. By December, however, there were increasing signs that Aristide wanted to dismantle the army, a point he finally acknowledged in conversations in February 1995. In late April 1995 Aristide disbanded the last remnants of the army and called for a constitutional amendment to erase it as an institution.

Without an army, the new police would be the only Haitian security force. The International Police Academy began four-month courses in late January 1995 to train a permanent police. Because of the large pool of applicants, the recruits were advanced in education and experience. Although the impressive backgrounds of the new recruits represented a positive sign of quality, it was also a point of concern that so many of them were very well educated by Haiti's standards, not very well paid, and extremely ambitious. The Haitian government initially planned to train a police force of 3,500, but that had been based on the continued existence of an army. Several months after Aristide's plans to dismantle the military became known, the United States proposed an increase in the numbers in the new police force to about 6,800. The new recruits were trained in Haiti and the United States.

In the fall of 1995, as Haiti began to prepare for the presidential elections, some of the new members of the Haitian police were involved in a series of attacks on the population. The country's anxiety was exacerbated by the knowledge that U.S. troops would leave by February 1996, and Aristide showed no inclination to ask the UN to extend their mandate.

Only after the inauguration of René Préval as president in February 1996 did Haiti make a formal request to extend the UN presence, but by that time the People's Republic of China had decided to block a UN vote on Haiti because it was piqued over Haiti's relationship with Taiwan. Barely days before the withdrawal, China permitted an extension until June 30 of 1,200 troops, which was a much smaller presence than originally anticipated. U.S. forces withdrew, but Canadians filled the vacuum, pledging an additional 700 troops.

Haiti's dictators have always used their security forces to maintain power. The central challenge under the new, democratic government is to create a nonpoliticized security force that is subordinate to the legitimately elected civilian leaders and obedient to the rule of law. This goal will be hard to attain, but without it a civil democracy in Haiti is impossible.

While the UN remains in Haiti, most Haitians feel relatively secure, but long before its anticipated withdrawal, both the rich and the poor were secretly trying to control the new security force. The longer the UN stays and the more it supervises and trains the new police, the more likely it is that Haiti's democracy will survive.

The Political and Electoral Context: An Uncertain Transition

After his return to power, Aristide stressed the importance of reconciliation, the need for his country to bind the wounds and move forward together to build a democratic Haiti. He assembled a multiparty government, reached out to the private sector, and met periodically with leaders of all the political parties to discuss his economic program and the best means for establishing the Elections Commission.

Many of Aristide's followers were confused or concerned about the degree to which he extended himself to their enemies, and he responded to their concerns by increasingly speaking out for justice and the need to hold accountable those responsible for human rights violations. The division in the country was so deep that the use of the words "reconciliation" and "justice" generated contrasting responses from the two major groups within the country: "Reconciliation" angered many of Aristide's followers, while "justice" sent ripples of fear through the traditional elite. The Truth Commission that he established was intended to balance the need for justice with that of reconciliation.

Human rights violations declined markedly after Aristide's return to power, but there were at least twenty serious political assassinations, and no cases were brought to justice. The U.S. Congress was concerned about this failure; however, despite the seriousness of those crimes, most Haitians felt more secure in 1995 than they had at any earlier time in their nation's history.

Aristide appointed Leslie Delatour, a well-respected economist, as president of the central bank, and proposed an economic program that elicited both praise from the international community and a reaffirmation of pledges of $1.2 billion from donor governments and the multilateral development banks.

Besides providing emergency food assistance, the government seems to have had as its priorities in the area of economic development: (1) developing a plan that would attract international support and offer the best chance for sustainable development; (2) clearing Haiti's arrears owed to the international development banks so as to permit the country to receive new loans for development; (3) enhancing the technical and administrative expertise necessary for implementing development projects; (4) establishing a stable macroeconomic foundation to resist inflation; (5) reducing trade barriers and the power of the monopolies; and (6) privatizing inefficient state corporations, especially the utilities and the telephone company.

These were, and remain under Préval's administration, the correct priorities. If the current government achieves these goals, then Haiti will be on a secure road to development. Unfortunately, these priorities do not translate into jobs or visible development in the short term; Haitians may eventually run low on patience before they see tangible returns. Regrettably, Aristide failed to explain to the Haitian people how these priorities would relate to the future development of the country. This encouraged a climate of scapegoating that undermined these very same objectives.

For example, the controversy on privatization seemed related to old ideological preconceptions but also to legitimate concerns of loss of control and jobs. The failure by President Aristide to explain the program led to an unproductive delay and inhibited private and foreign investment. Since it was part of the initial development plan, donors questioned the president's commitment, and his prime minister, Smarck

Michel, resigned when he realized that President Aristide did not support his own development plan. The United States suspended aid, as did some of the other donors.

Aristide never explained his reluctance to privatize. The most likely reason was that some of his supporters in Lavalas were opposed to it. Aristide had only a few months left before the end of his term, and one would have expected that to be an appropriate time for him to have implemented an unpopular but responsible decision. He may, however, have wanted to maintain Haitians' support because he did not, in fact, want to leave office.

The uncertainty of Aristide's commitment to the constitution's single-term requirement lingered throughout the year of his return despite his public pledge to President Clinton to honor the constitution.

Aristide deserves substantial credit for moving Haitian politics in a tolerant and democratic direction, but his greatest single failure was the chaotic way that he handled the electoral process during 1995. At the time, skeptics saw his vacillation as a sign that he was trying to stay in power. Others saw Haiti's weak administrative capacity as the cause of the flawed electoral process.

Parliamentary elections were supposed to be conducted within a few months of Aristide's return, and so he spent some time consulting with political parties about the membership of the new Provisional Elections Council (CEP). In the end, his consultations did not seem to bear on the final selection of the members. When the new CEP was announced at the end of 1994, most of the parties felt that Aristide had chosen primarily Lavalas supporters.

The CEP proved to be extremely disorganized and completely unresponsive to the complaints of the parties. By the election on June 25, three political parties boycotted the polls, and many of the twenty-seven parties that participated in the election distrusted the process and the CEP and were skeptical that the election would be fair.

Because of repeated delays in registering voters and approving candidates, the actual campaign was compressed, and very few Haitians knew the issues, parties, or candidates. The return of Aristide had transformed Haitian politics. The masses were much better organized than at any previous time, though a small percentage of the population voted. The elite became apathetic and hardly participated.

The main political struggle shifted to within the family of those who had supported Aristide's election in 1990. Some supporters appropriated his slogan, *lavalas*, and secured the president's endorsement. Another group of supporters, led by Evans Paul, mayor of Port-au-Prince, used Aristide's 1990 campaign vehicle, the National Front for Democratic Convergence (FNCD). Two other parties that served in Aristide's government, KONAKOM and PANPRA, ran independently but soon viewed themselves as part of the opposition.

The OAS initially claimed that 50 percent of the electorate had voted, and they attributed this lower percentage to the complexity of the election and a history of centralizing power around a single leader. But the final data indicate that only 30 percent of registered voters participated in the first round of elections for the Senate, and 32 percent for the Assembly. Fourteen percent voted in the runoffs (tables 5-1 and 5-2). While one cannot be certain of the reason for the low turnout, the compressed campaign and the uncertainty of the election probably played important roles.[4] Still, although there were some violent incidents, the 1995 elections were the most secure in the country's history. The presence of a UN military mission and the absence of a Haitian army were the main factors permitting a peaceful election. A large number of party poll watchers was an encouraging sign of the beginning of a civil society. Most election officials seemed dedicated, but they were poorly trained.

Nonetheless, the level of irregularities was so high, and the vote count so insecure that virtually all of the parties except Lavalas condemned the legislative elections, called for annulment, and threatened boycotts if their concerns were not addressed. President Aristide met with opposition leaders, but they could not agree on which parts of the election should be accepted and which parts should be rerun.

On July 12, the CEP finally released some of the election results, showing Lavalas winning most of the Senate and Assembly seats. The FNCD came in second and KONAKOM third, but many of the individual contests needed to be rerun or have runoffs. Of the eighty-four main mayoral elections, Lavalas won sixty-four, including the one for Port-au-Prince.

One positive consequence of the flawed June election was that the major opposition parties united and prepared a reasonable set of requests for reforming the electoral process. The U.S. government publicly encouraged these parties to participate and privately tried to persuade the Aristide government to be flexible. Yet Aristide and the CEP showed no signs of wanting to respond to these requests. The OAS, the UN, and the U.S. missions then downplayed the defects of the June election and urged the contending parties to move on to the runoffs.

Table 5-1. *Haitian Parliamentary Elections, Senate Results, by District, June–September 1995*

Department	Candidate	Political party	First round[a]					Runoff elections (Sept. 17, 1995)				
			Voters registered	Votes cast	Votes received	Percent of votes cast	Votes as percent of registered	Voters registered	Votes cast	Votes received	Percent of votes cast	Votes as percent of registered
West												
1st senator	Joseph Emmanuel	Lavalas	1,202,822	334,456	212,714	64	28 / 18	1,202,822	186,249			15
2d senator	J.R. Sabalat	Lavalas/IND			133,782	40	11			144,033	77	12
	Turneb Delpe	FNCD			43,479	13	4			42,216	23	4
South												
1st senator	Jean G. Laguerre	Lavalas	339,712	118,410	61,585	52	35 / 18					
2d senator	Paul Denis	Lavalas			60,625	51	18					
	Louis Dejoie II	PAIN			14,209	12	4					
Northeast												
1st senator	Jean Claude Daniel	Lavalas	126,295	40,498	24,380	60	32 / 19					
2d senator	Lucien Pierre Louis	Lavalas			23,637	58	19					
Northwest												
1st senator	Elie Plancher	Lavalas	69,171	58,247	33,201	57	84 / 48	69,171	45,692			66
2d senator	Rhode H. Jadotte	Lavalas			27,959	48	40			29,986	66	43
	F. Pierre Louis	PROP			9,320	16	13			15,706	34	23
Grande Anse												
1st senator	Edgard Leblanc	Lavalas	362,275	91,812	50,956	56	25 / 14					
2d senator	J. Maxime Roumer	Lavalas			49,723	54	14					

	Candidate	Party										
North			384,183	106,926			28					
1st senator	Renaud Bernadin	Lavalas			73,886	69	19					
2d senator	Mehu M. Garcon	Lavalas			69,782	65	18					
Southeast			208,565	73,488			35	208,565	49,130			24
1st senator	Irvelt Chery	Lavalas			35,023	48	17			41,160	83	20
	Rosemond Pradel	KONAKOM			11,023	15	5			8,685	17	4
2d senator	Jean Jeudy	Lavalas			34,539	47	17			39,537	81	19
	Faustin Caille	FNCD			10,288	14	5			8,878	18	4
Center			255,301	79,367			31	255,301	44,753			18
1st senator	Roger Sajous[b]	Lavalas			32,309	41	13			31,735	71	12
	Marino Etienne	FNCD			17,460	22	7			13,540	30	5
2d senator	Yvon Toussaint[b]	Lavalas								33,391	75	13
	J.F. Jean Louis	FNCD								10,840	24	4
Artibonite			424,615	118,484			28	424,615	148,920			35
1st senator	Samuel Madestin	Lavalas			51,419	43	12			128,623	85	30
	Serge Desroches	FNCD			16,588	14	4			19,348	13	5
2d senator	Jean Macdonald	Lavalas			40,285	34	9			107,738	72	25
	Samuel Milord	FNCD				12				42,130	28	10
Total			3,372,939	1,021,688			30	3,372,939	474,744			14

Sources: Provisional Electoral Council (CEP), the OAS, and Department of State reports.

a. Includes both the elections of June 25, 1995, and rerun held on August 13.

b. Discrepancy as to who is the winner. The U.S. Department of State reports Roger Sajous as the winner, but the OAS indicates that Toussant received more votes.

Table 5-2. *Haitian Parliamentary Elections, Deputy Results, by Department, June 25, 1995*

Department	Voter eligibility	Registered voters	Percent of population registered	Votes cast	Percent of registered voters who voted	Candidates registered
West	1,404,372	1,202,822	86	282,525	23	175
South[a]	323,400	339,712	105	135,650	40	90
Northeast	166,301	126,295	76	47,133	37	43
Northwest	198,480	69,171	35	57,833	84	40
Grande Anse[a]	316,800	362,275	114	119,679	33	79
North	391,619	384,183	98	103,343	27	69
Southeast	271,083	208,565	77	93,035	45	53
Center[a]	242,000	255,301	105	89,122	35	57
Artibonite	509,265	424,615	83	153,570	36	116
Total	3,823,320	3,372,939	88	1,081,890	32	722

Source: Provisional Electoral Council.

a. These departments show a higher number of registered voters than those eligible. Two explanations may resolve this discrepancy: the number of eligible voters proved to be higher than expected or the number of registration cards distributed exceeded the number of eligible voters.

At that point, on July 17, the Carter Center released a report that I had written on the election. I described in some detail the flaws in the election and offered specific recommendations on reforming the process. Unless the opposition were brought into the process, the outcome would be unstable. The report generated considerable controversy. I wrote:

The best that could be said of the irregularities is that they did not appear to be a part of a centralized or coordinated effort. Indeed, it is probably more accurate to state that Haiti's problem was that no one seemed to be in control. . . . Some in the international community would close their eyes to this travesty, but that would be unfair to the Haitian people, who together with the political parties, are the ultimate judges of the election. . . . The international community should insist that the political parties' concerns be effectively addressed. [5]

The opposition had been discouraged by the attitude of both the Haitian and the U.S. governments, but many people expressed hope that the report would lead to another round of negotiations. Serge Gilles, leader of the National Progressive Revolutionary party said, "The Carter report proves there are still democrats who will defend the integrity of the democratic process."[6] The report had some positive effects. President Clinton sent Deputy Secretary of State Strobe Talbott to Haiti, and, on the eve of his arrival, Anselmé Rémy, president of the CEP, resigned, and another member of the CEP was removed.

Instead of appointing new members to the CEP who were acceptable to the opposition, however, Aristide appointed figures that were viewed as even more biased in favor of Lavalas. Talbott tried to persuade Aristide to accept a formula for bringing the opposition into the electoral process, but Aristide rejected any change. His aides said that the president could not accept an electoral formula drawn up by the State Department. The use of a non-governmental organization as an intermediary might have been more successful, although it is quite possible that Aristide was committed to controlling the CEP.

The CEP postponed the reruns several times, finally holding them on August 13; the runoff was held on September 17. Additional elections were needed on October 8 and 15.[7] The voter turnout declined markedly, perhaps due to the opposition boycotts. It was a sign of eroding electoral legitimacy. To the opposition, the Haitian and U.S. governments seemed dedicated to seducing some opposition leaders to run in the elections even though their parties had insisted that no one would run. This was a very discouraging turn of events because democracy requires strong parties, and the perception that this was occurring weakened party legitimacy.

In the end, Lavalas won 102 of 133 mayorships (78 percent). It won all of the Senate races, giving the party a majority in that body, and 66, or 80 percent, of the 83 Assembly seats.

By the fall of 1995 the cries for Aristide to remain in power for three more years—the time that he had spent in exile—began to reach a crescendo. He had promised Clinton that he would leave office in February, but he did not discourage those who pressed for him to stay. His opponents feared that the new Lavalas parliament would change the constitution to permit Aristide to extend his mandate.

At the same time, politically related violence increased. On October 3 General Max Mayard was assassinated; two weeks later, the home of former PANPRA deputy Duly Brutus was attacked by a mob. The CEP moved glacially to prepare for the presidential elections. Finally, on November 6 it announced an electoral calendar. The next day, two Lavalas deputies were attacked; one, a cousin of Aristide's, was murdered. At the funeral on November 11, Aristide gave an impassioned speech, calling on his followers to take the law into their own hands and disarm the regime's opponents. A wave of violence swept across the country.

On November 20, the beginning of the official campaign, Aristide called for a "national dialogue" to begin four days later to address a range of issues. On November 23, Anthony Lake, President Clinton's national security advisor, met with Aristide in Port-au-Prince to remind him of his pledge not to seek reelection. Despite this meeting, Aristide the next day addressed a crowd of Lavalas supporters—other parties were impeded from participating—and told them that he would not turn his back on those who wanted him to remain in office for three more years.

Evans Paul, a close ally of Aristide until the June 1995 elections, accused Lavalas of trying to create a climate of insecurity. While waiting for Aristide's decision, the other candidates hardly campaigned. The U.S. government reiterated its understanding that Aristide would not run, and on November 30, Aristide confirmed that decision in an interview with the *New York Times*. But he waited until two days before the December 17 election to endorse the Lavalas candidate, René Préval, who won with 88 percent of the vote. The turnout, however, was only 28 percent.

Current and Future Obstacles to Democratic Consolidation

The transfer of power from Aristide to Préval on February 7, 1996, was a historic moment, the first such transfer in Haitian history. But it also provided a moment to reassess the leadership of Aristide and to assess the current and future obstacles to Haiti's democratic consolidation.

Aristide's continued popularity was evident by the overwhelming vote that Préval, his designated heir, received from the population. But a closer analysis suggests that only about 25 percent of registered voters (88 percent of the 28 percent who participated) voted. We are less certain what to make of the other 75 percent. About half of them voted for Aristide the first time; they may have become apathetic toward or discouraged by the candidates, Aristide's retirement, or the chaotic electoral process, or they may have chosen to follow the opposition's call for a boycott.[8]

Whatever the cause of the low turnout, the election can hardly be considered a mandate for Préval. Préval's government rests on a shaky foundation. First of all, he hardly campaigned. Second, the process was not fair; the opposition parties that boycotted the elections had legitimate complaints that were never addressed satisfactorily. Third, Préval remains in the shadow of the towering figure of Aristide, and given the latter's performance in 1995, it is questionable whether Aristide will use his power for the purposes of helping to build democracy.

What seems remarkable about the events of 1995 is how little Aristide used his power. He vacillated and never made the big decisions that awaited his leadership: privatization and a development plan; elections; party building; jobs and reforestation; and the extension of the UN's security presence. He had a full chest of political capital, but he never used any of it. In a year and at a time when his country desperately needed direction, Aristide provided little.

What is equally surprising, but encouraging, is that despite the flawed mandate of both the parliament and the new president both demonstrated a seriousness and a decisiveness in their first months in office. The parliament rejected Aristide's appointment of a new police chief and evaluated the other appointments with some professionalism. Préval grasped the most difficult issues at the very beginning and showed a willingness to make unpopular decisions. He immediately requested an extension of the UN military presence, and he made many speeches to persuade his followers that privatization was in the nation's interests, despite growing signs that Aristide would oppose it.

Still, as one steps back from the personalities, it is not untoward to ask whether democracy is possible in a country with such low levels of economic development and such high rates of illiteracy. It is no coincidence that consolidated and successful democracies are found in developed countries. Conducting a free and fair election is a complicated administrative exercise that requires a certain level of trust.

Haiti's administrative capacity is so low that the elections in 1990 and 1995 were permeated by serious technical irregularities despite considerable help from the international community. These problems could be reduced over time if Haitian elections officials remained in their jobs and learned from their mistakes, but the problems will not disappear until Haiti's level of development is raised.

Why did the election in 1990 succeed and the elections of 1995 fail? The level of technical irregularities in both was roughly comparable; the difference was that the level of suspicion was reduced significantly in 1990 by the active mediation of trusted interlocutors working with Haitian political leaders, the CEP, and the government. This was absent in 1995 because Aristide did not invite and would not permit outside mediation. The OAS, the UN, and the United States (the Three) tried to mediate, but did not try very hard. The Talbott missions confirmed previous experience that the mediator should not be a government that has a direct stake and wide-ranging interests in a country. When Aristide did not respond to the legitimate complaints of the opposition, the Three simply gave up and tried to put the best face on the electoral process. This was a short-sighted strategy that will return to haunt Haitians.

The current situation in Haiti has an artificial quality due to the presence of UN forces. All of the old sources of power are waiting for the UN to depart. When that happens, the new police will be the only organized force for peace in the country. This institution has had so little experience that it will be vulnerable to being captured politically by either the new government or the old elite.

Returning to Haiti with Jimmy Carter and Colin Powell in February 1995, Senator Sam Nunn said, "The international community has a one-year plan for a 10-year challenge."[9] Democracy in Haiti can be preserved only if the new police force remains professional and accountable to the rule of law. That can happen only if it undergoes an appropriately lengthy training period under international supervision. The UN needs to remain for several more years. President Clinton was right to put the full force of the United States behind efforts to restore Aristide to power. He was right to invest in democracy in Haiti. Washington would be making a huge mistake if it abandoned Haiti because of temporary setbacks.

The international community and Haiti formed a remarkable partnership in the summer of 1990 to reinforce the democratic process. Haiti finally had a government that could permit it to respond positively to its historic double challenge, to respect the rights of all its people and to steer the country into the hemisphere's democratic mainstream. To remain on course, Haiti needs to shed much of its historical burden, and the international community needs to provide continuous support. If one uses Haiti's past 200 years as a basis for evaluating its current government, one can be optimistic that Haiti has taken a large step out of its past.

Notes

1. For a good update and analysis of the prerequisites of democracy, see Seymour Martin Lipset, "The Social Requisites of Democracy Revisited," *American Sociological Review* LIX (1994), 1–22.

2. Max Weber, *Essays in Sociology*, translated by H. H. Gerth and C. Wright Mills (New York, 1962).

3. He made this statement at two conferences at the Carter Center, Atlanta, Georgia, on January 14–17, 1992, and September 20–21, 1993.

4. For a complete analysis of the election, see Robert Pastor, "Mission to Haiti, #3: Elections for Parliament and Municipalities" (Atlanta, 1995); Organization of American States, *Final Report of the OAS Electoral Observation Mission to the Legislative and Municipal Elections in Haiti* (Washington, D.C., 1996); International Republican Institute, *Haiti: IRI Assessment of the June 25, August 13, and September 17, 1995 Legislative and Municipal Elections in Haiti* (Washington, D.C., 11 October 1995).

5. The report was discussed in Steven Greenhouse, "Election Monitor Assails Haitian Vote for Widespread Fraud," *New York Times*, July 21, 1995, A5; idem., "In Haiti, Democracy Still Flounders," New York Times, July 24, 1995.

6. "Carter Center Cites Flaws in June Voting," *Atlanta Journal-Constitution*, July 22, 1995.

7. Organization of American States, *Final Report*, 1.

8. For a commentary on the meaning of the low voter turnout, see International Republican Institute, *Haiti: Election Observation Report, December 17, 1995* (Washington, D.C., 1996), ch. 9.

9. Carter Center of Emory University, "Mission to Haiti, #2, 23–26 February 1995" (Atlanta, 1995), 10.

CHAPTER SIX

The Rise, Fall, and Resurrection of President Aristide

Robert Fatton Jr.

THIS CHAPTER analyzes the process of democratization that has marked the recent history of Haiti. It begins with the 1986 fall of the predatory Jean-Claude "Baby Doc" Duvalier dictatorship, and studies the subsequent rise, collapse, and "resurrection" of the freely elected populist regime of Jean-Bertrand Aristide. It suggests that the transition from authoritarianism to populism was a function of the ascendancy of civil society, and, in particular, the Lavalas movement; it contends, however, that the old balance of class power as well as the vital repressive organs of the Duvalierist state survived the departure of Jean-Claude Duvalier and caused the redictatorialization of Haitian society.

The 1991 coup that overthrew President Aristide reflected the persisting capacity of the Haitian ruling class to unleash the most brutal violence against those forces that threatened to make the change of regime become a change of state. Moreover, this chapter argues that only force could dislodge the coup leaders and their allies. The American military intervention that restored Aristide to his office in 1994 demonstrated once more that violence remained the decisive element in Haitian politics; it represented the only viable means of ending redictatorialization.

The intervention, however, has had contradictory consequences; while it resuscitated the difficult process of democratization and facilitated the relative emasculation of the repressive organs of the state, it protected the old balance of class power and set out constraining parameters for economic transformation. The result was a change of regime rather than the creation of a new state. Nevertheless, such a change of regime may have generated wider popular struggles presaging profound alterations in the nature of the state. Thus, in spite of severe social and material constraints stemming from the existing domestic balances of class power and the external patterns of acute dependence, the future of Haitian society is not foreclosed. In making their history, human beings open up surprising alternatives at unexpected moments; they engender protean politics that defies the binding structures of previous outcomes. A real democratization of Haitian society is thus still possible, even if the existing constellation of forces makes it unlikely.

Predatory Rule

Haiti's political history from the revolutionary period through independence in 1804 to the post-Duvalier era reflects the predatory nature of successive elites who have refused to ground their rule in a meaningful system of accountability. These elites have controlled the state for their exclusive benefit, using it to extract resources from the poor majority. The predatory character of these elites symbolizes more their own class interests than some inherent Haitian cultural norm.[1]

The huge divide separating the elite from the masses has transformed Haiti into two worlds.[2] The first world, comprising the wealthy, French-speaking, and cosmopolitan minority, displays an utter disdain for the masses and sees politics as a zero-sum game. Most mulatto or light-skinned individuals belong to this world. It is antidemocratic and completely excludes the second world from its privileges. The second world comprises *le peuple* and represents the vast majority of the population. It is overwhelmingly peasant, illiterate, poor, and black. The destitution of this second world is pervasive. According to United Nations estimates, 74 percent of Haiti's population lives in absolute poverty, life expectancy at birth is fifty-five years, and the mortality rate for infants under the age of five is 130 per 1000.[3] Not surprisingly, Haitians refer to people of the second world as *san non*, those who "have no name."

These two worlds do not exist in mutual isolation. In fact, the first and second worlds are related; they are the opposite faces of the same coin. The second world is defined in relation to the elite; it is dependent on it and subject to it. At the same time, the first world's wealth and status derive from its control and taxation of the poor majority.[4] The first and second worlds are thus bound together in an unequal but interdependent relationship that has generated an enormous gap between the haves and the have-nots. According to conservative estimates, the wealthiest 1 percent of the population monopolizes 44 percent of the national revenue.[5]

The dichotomic structure of Haitian society is also reflected in acute color consciousness.[6] The conflict of color, or the rift between brown and black, exacerbates social tensions. The line that divides Haitians most, however, is not color but class. The line of class expresses the fact that, while the first and second worlds are thoroughly intertwined in an exploitive material web, elites seek a total moral and psychological dissociation from le peuple, whom they have dehumanized into meek and servile creatures. Armed with an acute sense of cultural superiority, the elites are conscious of their privileged status in the social order and are bent on defending it. They assume an adversarial position toward subordinate classes, whom they regard with scorn and fear. By dissociating themselves from le peuple through their language, religion, education, and etiquette, the elites seek to validate their elevated position and their claims to natural rights of governance.

Cultural differences are thus important in Haiti. They separate the French-speaking, wealthy, Catholic minority from the Kreyòl-speaking, poor *vodouisant* majority. They accentuate racial distinctions dividing mulatto from black. But deep, common cultural qualities exist as well. Paradoxically, these commonalities may have been the unintended result of the American occupation that lasted from 1915 to 1934. The occupiers' racism shortened somewhat the cultural distance between the bourgeoisie and the masses; albeit slowly and piecemeal, the elite incorporated into its Europeanized world view the peasants' indigenized African heritage. A common culture began to crystallize, however much divided by class. Expressed in the universal use of Kreyòl, and in music, food, dance, and artistic taste, it helped bridge the gap separating elites from subordinates. In fact, all Haitians have amalgamated European and American contributions to their distinctively African civilization.

Nothing illustrates this amalgamation better than Vodun (Voodoo). In Vodun, Catholicism is joined with Haitianized African religions to form an integrated system of beliefs and rituals. As one peasant put it, "One has to be a Catholic to serve the *loa* (Vodun spirits)." For most Haitians, Vodun is a way of life that provides them with a haven from the harsh realities of poverty and powerlessness. It gives meaning to existence and sanctions the popular quest for a better world.

Vodun has an exploitative side, however. *Houngans* (male priests) and *mambos* (female priestesses) can request from their disciples sacrifices in the form of money and food, and can use their spiritual authority to legitimize a repressive social order. Vodun became so closely associated with the Duvalier regime that once Duvalier fled, many houngans and mambos were killed in the ensuing popular uprising. On the other hand, Vodun can be a liberating force; it clearly played an essential role in the war of independence by uniting the slaves in a viable army that eventually defeated the master classes. Thus, Vodun is a complex and contradictory system of belief whose plasticity is evidenced in its secular functions as well as in its continuously evolving pantheon of loas.[7] Interweaving indigenous beliefs with Christian eschatology, Vodun creates a sense of national identity and solidarity by cultivating communities of shared values and aspirations.[8]

What truly divides Haitians is neither culture nor color. However much weight is assigned to cultural and color differences within Haiti, the reality is that those differences correspond generally to relations of power and class, and seldom transcend class considerations. To this extent, class appurtenance goes a long way in determining one's color. This is well captured in the Haitian Kreyòle proverb: "Neg rich sé mulat, mulat pov sé noua" (A rich black is a mulatto, a poor mulatto is a black).

The issue of color has, nevertheless, played a significant role in Haitian politics. It has been manipulated by politicians in search of power, and it has helped to hide the reality that both mulatto and black elites have behaved with similar contempt for the poor black majority.[9] Thus, for example, the darkening, as it were, of the upper sectors that occurred under President François ("Papa Doc") Duvalier's regime did not translate into any meaningful improvement in the life of the second world.

"Black power" in this instance was a cover that masked the ascendancy of a black bourgeoisie who lorded it over the poor majority. Moreover, the growth of a black bourgeoisie under Duvalier's brutal rule did not lead to the direct disempowerment of the mulatto elite. While it was forced to relinquish its political hegemony over the black majority, the mulatto minority managed to keep a firm hold on the economy. In fact, an uneasy compromise materialized whereby the brown minority continued to dominate the private sector while the black bourgeoisie took control of the state as a means to enrich itself. That compromise found its ultimate expression when Jean-Claude ("Baby Doc") Duvalier abandoned his father's *noiriste* policies and married Michèle Bennett, a mulatto. This union between mulatto and black elites was resented by the Duvalierist old guard and contributed to the erosion of Baby Doc's political base.[10]

The growing economic crisis of the early 1980s further undermined the president's popularity. The relatively open, technocratic project of *Jean-Claudisme* exhausted itself as liberalization terminated in repression and as economic growth came to a halt due to massive corruption and state predation. Yet this liberalization of the late 1970s contributed to the emergence of an increasingly assertive civil society.[11] Many NGOs challenged the abuses of *Duvalierisme* and began calling for social justice and human rights. Prominent among these organizations was the radical wing of the Catholic Church, known as *ti legliz* (Little Church), which articulated within a theology of liberation a devastating public critique of *macoutisme*.[12] Macoutisme came to symbolize everything that was wrong with Haiti: class exploitation, arbitrary political rule, corruption, and state violence. For ti legliz and the vast majority of Haitians, real change demanded a massive social, political, and economic transformation, a revolution that would overturn almost three decades of Duvalierist domination.

The Rise and Fall of Jean-Bertrand Aristide

Amid growing popular discontent and protest, and increasing international isolation, Baby Doc fled the country in early 1986. His departure, prompted by popular opposition, should not be confused with a revolution.[13] It is true that some macoutes were *déchouké* (uprooted) and that, in a referendum, an overwhelming majority of Haitians voted for a democratic constitution. The new constitution provided multiple checks and balances to prevent the reemergence of the presidential monarchism that had so characterized Haiti's political history. Under the new system, parliamentary authority was dramatically expanded and the presidency was sharply limited. The president had to share some of his power with a prime minister, who in turn had to be chosen from the ranks of the majority party of the National Assembly. Moreover, the president could no longer manipulate the command structures of the military; the chief of the army now had to win the approval of the National Assembly. Thus, Haiti's new constitution was intended to block the rise of any form of personal rule, but as Aristide's regime would soon discover, it could also prove a formidable obstacle to the radical restructuring of society.[14] The constitution, with all its checks and balances, tended to produce a stultifying immobilism that favored the status quo of the dominant classes.

It was this status quo that an increasingly vibrant civil society sought to challenge. Haitian civil society at this time comprised a multiplicity of private groups intent on curbing the predatory reach of the state. It continued to encompass conservative, populist, and radical organizations, but soon came to be dominated by a movement named Lavalas, a Kreyòl word for the flood, symbolizing the huge power of the nascent and loosely structured mass movement of destitutes. It was Lavalas that carried Aristide, a radical advocate of ti legliz, to the presidency in free elections in 1990, with 67 percent of the vote. As Aristide defined it, Lavalas was not just a "collection of a variety of movements and political parties." Lavalas was "much, much more: a river with many sources, a flood that would sweep away all the dross, all the after-effects of a shameful past."[15]

In Aristide's eyes, Lavalas was the united movement of the poor, for as he put it in a message delivered in late 1988, "Alone, we are weak. Together, we are strong. Together, we are the flood."[16] Lavalas was the revolutionary flood that would sweep away all the vestiges of Duvalierisme as well as the parasitic and exploitative bourgeoisie. "Let that flood descend!" Aristide declared. "And then God will descend and put down the mighty and send them away, And He will raise up the lowly and place them on high."[17]

Aristide's prophetic vision was not shared by all, however. He knew that old macoutes, the military, and a segment of the bourgeoisie would oppose his call for social solidarity and an equitable redistribution of wealth. Once in power, Aristide could not but face these harsh realities.[18]

In spite of his multiple condemnations of imperialist and capitalist exploitation, his economic policies remained extremely pragmatic; at most, they entailed a commitment to social democracy and the World Bank's vision of basic needs. He always appealed to the cooperation of what he called the "nationalist bourgeoisie" and accepted the necessity of dealing with international financial organizations.

Aristide acquiesced in a program of structural adjustment designed by the World Bank and the International Monetary Fund, two institutions he had previously denounced as vile capitalist instruments that "suck Haiti's blood." Given the predatory nature of the Duvalierist inheritance, the urban poor and the peasantry would be likely to fare better as a result of the imposition of fiscal restraints and the policy of privatization. The absence of a redistributive welfare state would thus facilitate the imposition of structural adjustment. Only Duvalierist businessmen who pillaged the national treasury and public sector employees who had benefited from a niggardly prebend could oppose such adjustment.[19]

Haiti's desperate material situation and profound dependence on external economic forces left Aristide with few alternatives. He was thus fully cognizant that his radical rhetoric had limits. "I never ceased disputing the value of believing in miracles. . . . We cannot do everything or provide everything tomorrow; we will simply try to move from destitution to poverty," he said.[20]

Such a modest project constituted a revolutionary vision in a predatory society such as Haiti's. Aristide's vision encompassed three fundamental ideas: "dignity, transparent simplicity, and participation," which were symbolized in Lavalas's main electoral slogan: *"Chanje Leta: ba li koulè revandikasyon pèp-la"* ("We have to change the state: we will give it the colors of the people's demands").[21] The political implementation of that project was at odds with the constitutional constraints of liberal democracy, which limited the executive power of the Lavalasian president and ultimately protected the privilege of the privileged.[22]

Neither Aristide nor the forces he represented were enemies of democracy; on the contrary, Aristide's brief first presidency marked the freest and most hopeful period of Haiti's political history. Even so, the Lavalasian conception of democracy departed from the liberal representative democracy that the constitution of 1987 enshrined. What Aristide desired was something else: "The democracy to be built should be in the image of Lavalas: participatory, uncomplicated, and in permanent motion."[23] The parliamentary structures of governance to which Aristide had reluctantly granted legitimacy, were, paradoxically, a constant problem for Lavalas' revolutionary project.[24] Ultimately, déchoukaj and parliamentarism proved incompatible.

Such incompatibility was accentuated further by acute material scarcity that limited severely the capacity of the political system to deliver resources with which to co-opt and integrate social actors into a more accountable public realm. This is not to argue that liberal democracy is impossible in poor countries, but rather that wealth, insofar as it provides rulers with expansive material means, facilitates their difficult maneuvering down the complicated road to democratization.[25] Poverty is a formidable constraint on democratic governance, but not an absolute obstacle. Shin has pointed out:

The establishment of a viable democracy in a nation is no longer seen as the product of higher levels of modernization, illustrated by its wealth, bourgeois class structure, tolerant cultural values, and economic independence from external actors. Instead, it is seen more as a product of strategic interactions and arrangements among political elites, conscious choices among various types of democratic constitutions, and electoral and party systems.[26]

The implantation and consolidation of democracy is increasingly perceived as a matter of political crafting and constitutional engineering.[27] In the view of many observers, however, Aristide had little sympathy for such crafting and engineering. He failed to institutionalize a "political society" that could have mediated conflicts and minimized political deadlock. As the constitutionally regulated realm in which political forces organize themselves as effective blocs to conquer state power and achieve their objectives, political society represents an essential ingredient of any long-lasting democracy. Stepan has explained:

A full democratic transition must involve political society, and the composition and consolidation of a democratic polity must entail serious thought and action about those core institutions of a democratic political society – political parties, elections, electoral rules, political leadership, intraparty alliances, and legislatures—through which civil society can constitute itself politically to select and monitor democratic government.[28]

Aristide, however, believed that he could do without political society. In fact, he had a certain contempt for both consolidated political organs and rules and intraparty alliances.[29]

Structure, Choice, and Political Crafting

Aristide's visceral neglect of political society was deeply embedded in his prophetic presidential style. Many observers have argued that this was partially responsible for his overthrow in 1991. Aristide, they suggest, ruled as if he had never been elected president of the republic; he governed, rather, as a leader of the opposition with a wild and unnecessarily antagonistic rhetoric. He lacked the attributes that would have moved his opponents into his own orbit and would have situated them into his own programmatic strategy of social change. He was a prophet who had yet to acquire the agility and cunning of a Machiavellian prince.[30] Aristide's incapacity to go beyond his own political base precipitated his downfall. In this reading of Aristide's journey into exile, structural constraints and the obdurate opposition of the bourgeoisie are not seen as determining the outcome.[31]

While it is true that politics can be protean, choices that really do matter and represent historical alternatives can be nullified by the structure of power and the balance of class forces. It is one thing to argue that political leaders have multiple choices; it is another to assume that those choices constitute fundamental and plausible options. In 1991, when the power of the dominant classes still rested on brute military force and that of their subordinates on rhetoric, Aristide had little choice. It is true that his prophetic style may have deepened the profound alienation between the popular forces and the elites, but nothing suggests that the elites would have responded positively to a more "princely" demeanor. The dominant classes despised Aristide. They engaged in plotting maneuvers immediately after his elections, and they never entertained the idea of compromise; only a total surrender would have satisfied them.[32]

A consensus for a radical transformation of Haitian society was thus impossible, given that the stark demarcation of class had historically generated a politics of ferocious struggle rather than civil compromise. Hence, in 1991 the available options were too limited. In the process of crafting Haitian democracy, "the realm of the possible, the plausible, indeed, the probable, [could not] be expanded."[33] Aristide's behavior was immaterial; the coup was inevitable.

Similarly, it is highly unlikely that a different constitutional system could have prevented the coup. Whether Aristide headed a presidentialist or parliamentarian regime was irrelevant; the balance of class forces and the Lavalasian program prevented the type of deadlock-breaking compromises that parliamentarism entails, and debilitated the effective imperial rule of presidentialism.[34] The semipresidentialist regime of Aristide acquired the vices of both presidentialism and parliamentarism. The president sought to bypass the National Assembly by imposing his program through popular mass mobilization, while parliament sank into political immobilism under the paralyzing divisions of class, ideology, and personality. In short, the design of institutions played only a very marginal role in the making of a Haitian democracy, given the balance of class forces and the praetorian role of the military as the last redoubt of the dominant classes's power. The question was, would the Haitian ruling class be prepared to accept electoral defeat and relinquish its hegemony to radical populist forces without resorting to a preemptive coup? The overthrow of Aristide in 1991 clearly demonstrated that the ruling class contemplated nothing of the sort. Neither style of presidential leadership nor institutional choices prevented, or will prevent, the bourgeoisie and its allies from violating and destroying constitutional frameworks once they perceive that their fundamental interest has been endangered. This is the hard lesson of the recent Haitian experience.

It is clear that the military and the bourgeoisie felt increasingly threatened by Aristide's appeals for popular justice. They feared a social explosion that would end their own domination. The coup symbolized not their alleged defense of the constitution, but rather their determined resistance to fundamental change. When, two days before the coup, Aristide made his famous "Père Lebrun" speech in which he rhetorically extolled in front of a huge crowd the virtues of necklacing his macoute enemies, he had already lost the battle.[35] His speech was a desperate attempt to prevent the army and the bourgeoisie from striking down Lavalas. Rather than articulating a clear strategy of revolutionary violence, Aristide's wild rhetoric represented a last-ditch attempt to intimidate those who had been busy planning his overthrow.[36] As he later explained: "I was using words to answer bullets."[37] Indeed, rumors of an impending coup, and the preparations for the coup itself, long preceded the "Père Lebrun" speech.

Hence, while the speech came to haunt Aristide's exile, it had little to do with the coup itself. It became, however, a useful pretext for ushering in military rule and for legitimizing the constitutionality of class privilege and abuse.

The coup demonstrated beyond doubt that the old structures of power remained resilient: The army resisted civilian control, old macoutes and Duvalierists were still influential, and the elites maintained their utter contempt for le peuple. What was striking about the immediate post-Duvalier era and Aristide's continued presidency was not the déchoukaj of the old state, but rather its persistence under new forms. The regime may have changed, but the ancient structures of class power endured.

The balance of class power bodes poorly for a radical transformation of Haitian society. Indeed, the question was and still is whether, given the entrenched class division and the constraints imposed by a liberal democracy and external sources of power, the Lavalasian project was at all realizable. Ironically, the conditions surrounding Aristide's return may have signaled the end of the project itself.

The American Restoration of Aristide's Presidency: The Vicissitudes of the Second Coming

The U.S.-led restoration of Aristide's presidency in 1994 clearly dampened his populist appeal and emasculated his social-democratic agenda.[38] It forced him to accept the inclusion of old opponents in his new "enlarged" government of national reconciliation. It was the fear of such a fate that explained Aristide's ambivalence and vacillating attitude toward an American military intervention. In the end, however, Aristide had no choice.[39] Indeed, his return was totally dependent on the exercise of American power, over which he had no control.[40]

Despite its huge ambiguities and contradictions, the American intervention was the only means of ending the military dictatorship. Paradoxically, the intervention tilted the balance of class forces politically toward Lavalas. It facilitated the total emasculation of the army and compelled the Haitian elites to accept Aristide as president. Neither new institutions nor drastic changes of heart could have led to such an outcome. The decisive and determining moment in Haitian politics remained the brute force of arms, even if on this occasion, it originated from without.

While the American intervention strengthened Lavalas politically, it diluted completely its social-democratic economic platform. The intervention inevitably deradicalized Aristide, transforming him from an anti-capitalist prophet into a staunch American ally committed to the virtues of the market. He became the Machiavellian prince, but a prince partially *déplumé*, whose failure to bring the opposition into accepting his initial social-democratic project compelled him to adopt a conservative program of structural adjustment. The major contradiction now facing Haitian society is the coexistence of left-wing politics with right-wing economics; it is a contradiction that is not likely to survive for long. If the experiences of other revolutionary regimes are taken seriously, economic reality will eventually prevail and establish the harsh realities of the market.[41]

A sense of economic fairness and efficiency is, however, difficult to foster in the midst of profound structural adjustment. By promoting market rationality, and simultaneously transforming property relations, structural adjustment generates urban discontent and plunges societies into the uncertainties of polarized instability. Under such conditions, Haitian governments are likely to retreat from the process of economic reform altogether. Confronted with renewed challenges from above and below, they may be forced to choose between either abandoning structural adjustment or relapsing into authoritarianism in order to impose it. The consequences of structural adjustment are thus likely to have gravely debilitating effects on the consolidation of Haitian democracy.[42] Adjustment could ultimately destabilize many future Haitian administrations.[43] The economic exigencies of the economy in Haiti could thus compound the vicissitudes of democratic consolidation and stimulate a transition to a new dictatorship. The temptation of authoritarian rule and the descent into chaos always remain threats to the democratic process.

The American occupation of Haiti succeeded in restoring Aristide to power and preventing, at least temporarily, the country's descent into hell. It ultimately also paved the way for René Préval to succeed him. It opened up the social space necessary to rebuild a popular civil society brutally squelched under the junta.[44] It offered the people a chance to reestablish and consolidate fragile democratic structures while emasculating those institutions that had historically kept the overwhelming majority destitute. Indeed, the virtual abolition of the armed forces was Aristide's single most important contribution to the empowerment of le peuple. Without it, the threat of coups would still hang like a sword of Damocles over Haiti, and the despotic power of the bourgeoisie would remain unrestrained. Finally, the American intervention created the possibility of struggling for a more equitable pattern of economic development.

Such hopes, however, should not mask the enormous obstacles confronting those who seek to construct a more democratic and egalitarian Haitian society. Haiti still hovers on the verge of political catastrophe; it faces economic ruin, ecological destruction, and the mass starvation of the poor. The ruling class, while bewildered and confused by the American occupation, has not surrendered; on the contrary, it is capable of blocking any strategy of development that it deems antagonistic to its interests.[45]

Promises of massive international assistance do not guarantee economic growth, let alone social equity. In fact, Aristide and Préval's conversion to the magic of the market and privatization may generate more inequalities and undermine their popular support.[46] The return to electoral politics and the partial disarmament of the repressive organs of the state are not sufficiently institutionalized to ensure the success of democratic consolidation.

The Aristide administration's moral dilemma of seeking national reconciliation, while at the same time establishing the rule of law, has remained a Gordian knot.[47] A prompt return to social normalcy means accepting the presence of unpunished torturers and murderers; it is a presence that may buy temporary peace but that may ultimately portend future victims. Moreover, armed macoutes could take advantage of the withdrawal of UN troops and their replacement by the ill-prepared Haitian police to unleash a new cycle of violence and unbalance the precarious stability of President Préval's regime. The new police could also become a Trojan horse for the old predatory coalition since its commanding officer positions have been assigned to many members of the "discredited and brutal Haitian army."[48]

The future is thus full of uncertainties, even if the conflict of classes has been momentarily subdued by the presence of foreign troops, Aristide's transformation from radical priest into presidential conciliator, and Préval's succession. It is a conflict, however, that is likely to reemerge once the persistent realities of ostentatious wealth amid acute poverty dampen the euphoria of peace. But will the specter of a hellish war of all against all prove capable of permanently assuaging the obdurate antagonisms of class? Or will it merely cause a temporary, deceptive calm before the flood? Only time will tell. For the moment, ambiguous signs of economic recovery and democratic renaissance coexist with morbid symptoms of political opportunism, mass misery, and criminal delinquency.

The American intervention opened the possibility of another pathway—albeit narrow and uncertain—to an alternative way of life freed from the legacy of authoritarianism, injustice, and destitution. It heightened the reality that the old ways of producing, organizing, and governing were dead, and new forms were struggling to be born. Thus, in spite of its ambiguities and paradoxes, the U.S. occupation has offered Haitians the opportunity to enter what Brecht once described as "the time of struggles between the new and the old."[49] We must wait to see whether the promise of the new will implant its seeds and flourish or degenerate into the ugly vulgarities of the old.

Conclusions

The democratization of Haiti was fundamentally dependent on the balance of class forces; neither institutions nor political statecraft could have prevented the overthrow of President Aristide. In spite of its huge popular following, Lavalas was poorly structured and only had the weapon of rhetoric with which to confront the dominant classes. They controlled the force of arms which they were determined to use. Not surprisingly, the restoration of Aristide demanded another moment of brute military intervention, albeit of foreign origin; without it, the junta and the dominant classes would have never relinquished power.

The American occupation was full of contradictions; while it has reinvigorated the political fortunes of Lavalas and emasculated the armed power of the dominant classes, it has thoroughly deradicalized the economic project of Aristide's regime. The balance of class forces has been relatively equalized, but it is indeed a very relative equality. At most, it implies the demilitarization of the predators and their allies, but by no means does it portend fundamental structural changes. With the peaceful transition of power from Aristide to Préval, the process of changing regimes electorally may now be on firmer foundation than at any previous time in Haiti's history, but the transformation, let alone the democratization of the state, remains a fragile project in the making.

Notes

1. See Alex Dupuy, *Haiti in the World Economy* (Boulder, 1989); Michel-Rolph Trouillot, *Haiti: State Against Nation* (New York, 1990); idem., "Haiti's Nightmare and the Lessons of History," *North American Congress on Latin America*, XXVII (1994), 46–51. For an extreme instance of the cultural explanation of Haiti's underdevelopment, see Lawrence E. Harrison, "Voodoo Politics," *Atlantic Monthly*, CCLXXI (June 1993), 101–107.

2. See Brian Weinstein and Aaron Segal, *Haiti: The Failure of Politics* (New York, 1992), 4–13.

3. United Nations Development Program, *Human Development Report 1993* (New York, 1993), 142, 157, 171.

4. Mats Lundahl, *Peasants and Poverty: A Study of Haiti* (London, 1979).

5. Dupuy, *Haiti*, 184.

6. David Nicholls, *From Dessalines to Duvalier: Race, Colour and National Independence in Haiti* (New Brunswick, 1996), xxxii–xxxiii, 67–238. See also Micheline Labelle, *Idéologie de Couleur et Classes Sociales en Haïti* (Montréal, 1978), 185–313.

7. See Wade Davis, *Passage of Darkness: The Ethnobiology of the Haitian Zombie* (Chapel Hill, 1988); Alfred Métraux, with new introduction by Sidney Mintz, *Voodoo in Haiti* (New York, 1972); Michel S. Laguerre, *Voodoo and Politics in Haiti* (London, 1990).

8. Métraux, *Voodoo in Haiti,* 42–43.

9. See Labelle, *Idéologie de Couleur,* 62–63.

10. See Michel S. Laguerre, *The Military and Society in Haiti* (Knoxville, 1993), 120–122; James Ferguson, *Papa Doc, Baby Doc: Haiti and the Duvaliers* (New York, 1987), 72–73, 86–87.

11. See Laguerre, *Military and Society,* 122–123; Martin-Luc Bonnardot and Gilles Danroc, *La Chute de la Maison Duvalier: 28 Novembre 1985-7 Fevrier 1986* (Paris, 1989), 11–150.

12. Macoutisme refers to the system of terror imposed by François Duvalier. The term derives from the Kreyòl *tonton macoute,* which means "the bogeyman" in Haitian popular folktales; the tonton macoute was the name given to the brutal paramilitary force created by Duvalier. See Laguerre, *Military and Society,* 114–117; Trouillot, *State Against Nation,* 152–156.

13. As Trouillot put it in his important *State Against Nation,* "what Haitians witnessed on 7 February 1986, was not the disorderly escape of an 'entire leadership' pushed out by popular resistance . . . but a transmission of power, orchestrated with absolute order— albeit against the background of a popular uprising" (225).

14. See Haïti Solidarité Internationale, *Haïti 1990: Quelle Démocratie?* (Port-au-Prince, 1990), 118–119.

15. Jean-Bertrand Aristide, *Aristide, An Autobiography* (New York, 1993), 126.

16. Jean-Bertrand Aristide, *In the Parish of the Poor* (New York, 1991), 104.

17. Ibid.

18. See Claude Moïse and Emile Ollivier, *Repenser Haïti* (Montréal, 1992), 137–192.

19. Alex Dupuy, "A Neo-Liberal Model for Post-Duvalier Haiti," unpublished ms. (1995), 21. See also Leslie Delatour, *Propositions pour le Progrès* (Port-au-Prince, 1990).

20. Aristide, *Autobiography,* 128.

21. Ibid., 21.

22. See Moïse and Ollivier, *Repenser Haïti,* 149–174.

23. Aristide, *Autobiography,* 126.

24. See Kim Ives, "The Lavalas Alliance Propels Aristide to Power," *North American Congress on Latin America,* XXVII (1994), 18–19; Marx V. Aristide and Laurie Richardson, "Haiti's Popular Resistance," *North American Congress on Latin America,* XXVII (1994), 34–35.

Aristide's last-minute decision to run for the presidency reflected, on the one hand, his partial acknowledgment that he could become the vehicle of an "electoral *déchoucaj,*" and on the other the desire of progressive and reformist forces headed by the National Front for Change and Democracy (FNCD) to replace their uninspiring candidate, Victor Benoit, by a more charismatic and popular leader. Both Aristide and the FNCD were united in their opposition to Marc Bazin, who represented American-supported conservative forces, and to the macoute Roger Lafontant.

25. Seymour Martin Lipset emphasized a long time ago the correlation between wealth and democracy, arguing essentially that without material abundance brought about by bourgeois industrial development, democracy was impossible. See "Some Social Requisites of Democracy: Economic Development and Political Legitimacy," *American Political Science Review*, LIII (1959), 69–106.

26. Doh Chull Shin, "On the Third Wave of Democratization: A Synthesis and Evaluation of Recent Theory and Research," *World Politics*, XLVII (1994), 138–139.

27. Guiseppe Di Palma, *To Craft Democracies* (Berkeley, 1990).

28. Alfred Stepan, *Rethinking Military Politics* (Princeton, 1988), 4.

29. Alex Dupuy, "The Prophet Armed: Jean-Bertrand Aristide's Liberation-Theology and Politics," unpublished ms. (1995), 25.

30. Dupuy, "Prophet Armed." See also Franklin Midy, "Qui êtes-vous, Père Aristide?" *Haiti en Marche* (October 26–November 2, 1988); "Aristide: Entre le Prophète et le Prince," *Haiti en Marche* (December 26, 1990–January 1, 1991).

31. Youssef Cohen, *Radicals, Reformers, and Reactionaries* (Chicago, 1994), 119–120.

32. In an attempt to prevent Aristide from becoming president, Lafontant, a notorious Duvalierist and macoute, launched a coup on January 6, 1991, against the provisional government of Pascal Trouillot. The coup failed when thousands of Aristide's supporters poured into the streets of Port-au-Prince and forced the army to abort the coup. Aristide became president on February 7, 1991.

33. Di Palma, *To Craft Democracies*, 6.

34. Alfred Stepan and Cindy Skach, "Constitutional Frameworks and Democratic Consolidation," *World Politics*, XLVII (1993), 1–22.

35. The expression, "Père Lebrun," originated from a tire commercial, in which the salesman, Père Lebrun, would put his head through the tires. Aristide's speech was at once surprisingly conciliatory and wildly threatening. He began his address by imploring the bourgeoisie to "cooperate by using [its] money . . . to create work opportunities . . . so more people can get jobs. If you do not do so, I feel sorry for you. Really I do. It will not be my fault because this money you have is not really yours. You acquired it through criminal activity. You made it by plundering, by embezzling. . . . You made it under oppressive regimes . . . under a corrupt system. . . . Today, seven months after 7 February, on a day ending in seven, I give one last chance. I ask you to take this chance, because you will not have two or three more chances, only one. Otherwise, it will not be good for you." Aristide then proceeded to make a plea to legislators to "work together with the people," and he reminded civil servants that "diverting state money is stealing, and thieves do not deserve to stay in public administration." Soon after, however, encouraged by the loud cheers of the Lavalasian crowd, he called metaphorically for the unleashing of Père Lebrun against all macoutes. To tens of thousands of supporters he declared, "You are watching all Macoute activities throughout the country. We are watching and praying. If we catch one, do not fail to give him what he deserves. What a nice tool! What a nice instrument! What a nice device! It is a pretty one. It is elegant, attractive, splendorous, graceful, and dazzling. It smells good. Wherever you go, you feel like smelling it. It is provided by the Constitution, which bans Macoutes from the political scene." Quoted in Mark Danner, "The Fall of the Prophet," *NewYork Review of Books* (December 2, 1993), 52.

152 ROBERT FATTON JR.

February 7 has a symbolic quality in Haitian politics: it marks the date of Jean-Claude Duvalier's departure in 1986 and the date of Aristide's installation as president in 1991.

36. See Moïse and Ollivier, *Repenser Haïti*, 157–160.

37. See Joelle Attinger and Michael Kramer's interview of Aristide, "It's Not If I Go Back, but When," *Time*, (November 1, 1993), 28.

38. For the story of the complicated and ambiguous events leading to the peaceful American occupation of Haiti, see Kate Doyle, "Hollow Diplomacy in Haiti," *World Policy Journal*, XI (1994), 53–55; Ian Martin, "Haiti: Mangled Multilateralism," *Foreign Policy*, XCV (1994), 80–85.

39. In a letter to Boutros Boutros-Ghali, UN secretary-general, Aristide ultimately agreed to an American-led military intervention by calling for "swift and determined action" to restore himself to power. The letter supported UN resolution 940, which authorized "the use of all necessary means" to topple the military junta. See *AP@clarinet*, 29 July 1994.

40. Aristide's relations with the United States have always been ambivalent. During his "first" presidency, he attacked American imperialism and capitalism; his exile in Washington, however, and his American-led return to Haiti transformed him into a staunch ally of the Clinton administration. In fact, Aristide called Clinton his twin brother. The United States has always been ambivalent about the power shift that Aristide's election symbolized. It had traditionally supported the elite and the army.

41. Jorge G. Castaneda, *Utopia Unarmed* (New York, 1994). Economists advocating structural adjustment are in positions of power both in the government and international institutions. They also behave with the missionary zeal of Christian fundamentalists. Anyone questioning or challenging their world view is immediately branded an ideologue incapable of understanding the science of economics. See Adam Przeworski, *Sustainable Democracy* (New York, 1995), viii–ix.

42. See "Privatization: What the Haitian People Can Expect," *Haiti Info*, III (February 25, 1995).

43. Adam Przeworski, *Democracy and the Market* (New York, 1991), 189, explains the paradoxes of the release from authoritarianism in conditions of dire material scarcity.

44. Human rights observers have estimated that at least 3,000 people were murdered by the military or their auxiliaries. In addition, some 300,000 people went into hiding, fearing the violence of the junta.

45. The Haitian elites as well as the military were convinced that the external forces advocating the reinstatement of Aristide had neither the will nor the power to impose his return. Their conviction was further strengthened when the USS *Harlan County*, sent in accordance with the Governors Island agreement, failed to dock in Haiti in October 1993. Fearing a violent confrontation with army-backed thugs, the *Harlan County*, carrying nearly 200 American troops on a noncombatant mission to prepare the island for Aristide's return, backed out of Haitian waters.

Emmanuel Constant, the leader of the paramilitary group Front for the Advancement and Progress of Haiti (FRAPH) and main organizer of the resistance to the Harlan County declared, "My people kept wanting to run away. But I took the gamble and urged them to stay. Then the Americans pulled out! We were astonished. That was the day FRAPH was actually born. Before, everyone said we were crazy, suicidal, that we would all be burned if Aristide returned. But now we know he is never going to return." Martin, "Haiti," 72–73.

46. Michel-Rolph Trouillot, "Aristide's Challenge," *New York Review of Books*, XLI (November 3, 1994), 39–40.

47. National Coalition for Haitian Refugees, *No Greater Priority: Judicial Reform in Haiti* (New York, 1995).

48. William G. O'Neill, "Building a New Haitian Police Force and Justice System," *Haiti Insight*, VI (October-November 1995), 8.

49. Bertolt Brecht, John Willett, and Ralph Manheim (eds.) *Poems 1913–1956*, (New York, 1979), 424.

CHAPTER SEVEN

From Outsiders to Insiders: Grassroots Leadership and Political Change

Robert E. Maguire

IN THE MUNICIPAL and parliamentary elections held in Haiti between June and September 1995, candidates affiliated with President Jean-Bertrand Aristide's Lavalas political movement were overwhelmingly voted into local and national elective offices throughout the country.[1] The magnitude of the Lavalas victory in the national Chamber of Deputies and in the Senate was indicative of the countrywide sweep. In the former, Lavalas affiliates won sixty-six of seventy-nine races decided; in the latter, they won seventeen of eighteen positions.[2]

Candidates affiliated with Lavalas were similarly swept into municipal offices. Most of the country's 133 three-member mayoral councils and its 564 three-member communal section councils were won by partisans of the Lavalas political movement.[3]

With few exceptions, Haiti's newly elected public officials were political unknowns to the world outside the communities from which they were elected. Only three incumbents, for example, were returned to the Chamber of Deputies. Within their communities, however, these emerging political leaders charged with guiding the country toward a brighter future, were not unknown. There, their reputations as leaders, civic activists, and agents of change, preceded them. This chapter traces the emergence of those new political leaders, their mandates for political change, and their promise as a guiding force for a democratic future for Haiti.

Decentralization

"Yes, we have heard them clearly and we understand the people's desire for decentralization. This government will ensure that a fair share of the resources from the countryside that come to Port-au-Prince are returned to the countryside." These remarks, made in mid-1991 by an official of the Aristide government, reflected the optimism among leaders and members of community-based grassroots organizations throughout Haiti following the ouster of Jean-Claude ("Baby Doc") Duvalier that decentralization would be a top priority of the new Haitian government.[4] Despite little, if any, progress toward decentralization during the post-1986 years of successive, military-led or dominated governments, great hope emerged from within the grassroots sector that advances along that line could, in fact, be made.

The official's remarks, while encouraging in that decentralization was recognized as a need and goal of the new government, were at the same time disconcerting. Even as part of a populist, reform-minded government, the official continued to view Port-au-Prince, and the government that occupied the presidential palace there, as the tail that would wag the rest of Haiti.

Many members of grassroots organizations, however, certainly saw things differently. For them, decentralization meant that for the first time in Haiti's history, the dog would wag the tail. Or in less metaphorical terms, the state would respond to, and be fully accountable to, the nation. Further, the nation would actually determine the shape and political posture of the state. It appeared that the stage was set for a lively period of debate and negotiation over the ways and means of achieving effective political and economic decentralization.

Tragically, before that debate could advance, the September 1991 military coup d'etat occurred, and authoritarian recidivism reigned. State-sponsored predation once again ravaged the population until September 1994, when the UN-sanctioned multinational military force intervened. As of mid-1996, those indefatigable voices that had begun calling for economic and political decentralization in 1986 are being heard again. The debate has reopened. The extent to which grassroots voices will find—or create—resonance within the national government in Port-au-Prince will be seen only over time. The stated policies of the Aristide government, even before its restoration to power in October 1994, underscored a preoccupation with these issues. The more recent policies of

President René Préval have begun to move beyond preoccupation to the implementation of decentralized government programs.[5]

Whereas in 1986, those voices emanated from beyond the corridors of government, today they are also heard from within the halls of government; now it is elected officials, at both municipal and national levels, who convey this message. This emergence of new political leadership from the bottom up should fundamentally alter the way government in Haiti responds to the will of the people, to whom it must be accountable. How, not if, decentralization occurs is a critical issue for those now holding public positions and accepting the challenge to make government work to benefit the commonwealth.

Predation

Following 1986, those active in community-based organizations seeking fundamental social, economic, and political change in Haiti identified economic and political decentralization as a top priority. After all, for generations the three-quarters or more of Haiti's population that is composed of rural-based small-scale producers, entrepreneurs, and their families, generally referred to as peasants, had witnessed the painful results of centralization within what has become widely cited as a predatory state.[6]

For decades, rural producers and entrepreneurs had seen both their surpluses and that which they produce to ensure basic survival taken from them by individuals affiliated with state-supported or sanctioned mechanisms of predation. As such, they had come to view the state as nothing more than an obstacle to their well-being. Indeed, in view of the fact that the only state entities regularly present and functioning in rural communities had been the tax office and a military installation—one to extract, the other to impose—is it any surprise that, for Haitian peasants, the Kreyòl word for state (leta) has also become that used to identify a bully?[7]

My grassroots informants of 1986 had also witnessed the one-way flow of resources into Port-au-Prince and knew of the grotesquely disproportionate expenditure of public revenue there, often on "zombie" state employees and on phantom state services for which these rural dwellers had been heavily taxed.[8] When leaders and members of community-based organizations spoke of decentralization during that period, certainly they envisaged from the public sector something largely unprecedented: state investment of public resources in rural areas, not primarily to keep the lines of extraction and control open but rather to improve the lives of those living there. As critical as decentralization was, they sought *demakoutization*, or the demise of state mechanisms of plunder and control, along with vastly enhanced means for local, autonomous control over resources by those who generated them for investments to address local needs.

Confronting Powerlessness and Inferiority

Haiti's state-sanctioned system of predation had long been a masterfully insidious one that led its victims to believe they were powerless, inferior, and somehow completely to blame for their own condition. Whereas some commentators have characterized the behavioral comportment of victims of predation as a case of cultural inferiority or fatalism or both, others have viewed peasant social behavior in Haiti as a manifestation of "crab antics."[9] Crabs in a barrel constantly pull at each other so that as one crab begins to rise above the rest, it is immediately pulled back down into the morass at the bottom. A popular Kreyòl expression, "dog-eat-dog" (*chen manje chen*), also suggests this behavioral pattern.

In rejecting explanations that blame the victim, Trouillot viewed the persistent poverty of Haiti's rural population as an outcome of the historical relations between the nation and the state. Haiti's prevalent system of surplus extraction, he stated, had been organized over time such that "wealth could be pumped out of the peasantry without the urbanites ever coming into contact, or even seeing, them. The nation met its masters only through intermediaries, and only at points of exchange." As a result of this arrangement, he continued,

the peasantry never directly confronted the system's ultimate beneficiaries—the top state officeholders and, above all, the merchant bourgeoisie. Hence, even though the peasants might have wondered about the causes of their poverty, they knew few individuals on whom to place the blame. Indeed, they were more likely to accuse a fellow villager of worsening their lives than an exporter or an official they had never met.[10]

By the 1970s, Haiti's rural producers and entrepreneurs had begun to become more adept at identifying external causes of their poverty. At the root of this change was their exposure first to analyses that helped them understand the structure of the political economy, and then to programs encouraging them to address problems through both self-help initiatives and mobilization to affect political change. Much of this achievement came about through the work of grassroots leadership training and community action programs affiliated with, or sponsored by, the Catholic Church.

Influenced by the Freirian concept of conscientization, and encouraged by regional bishops' meetings in Medellin, Colombia, in 1968 and in Puebla, Mexico, in 1979, which had mandated the church's active involvement in addressing the social and economic needs of the poor, church leaders, particularly the growing numbers of Haitian clergy and religious lay leaders of modest backgrounds increasingly active in the church, began working under the premise that social, economic, and political change could come from the bottom up. Hence, the *ti legliz* movement of grassroots groups was begun within the church. Activists within the institution also developed a hypothesis that community-based agents of change, or *animatè*, could catalyze local grassroots development groups as structures for community mobilization and action. Leadership training and community development programs such as that sponsored by the Holy Cross Priests in Haiti's northern region put the hypothesis into action.[11]

By 1991 this hypothesis was clearly borne out when, as a result of these efforts, hundreds of *animatè* in Haiti had developed such a successful track record of community mobilization that the country was cited as being one of only a handful of nations worldwide where "evidence of grassroots groups' increasing political importance is available."[12] Also by 1991 an estimated 2 million Haitians out of a population of 7 million belonged to, or were affiliated with, these grassroots groups.[13]

The path toward this achievement had been fraught with obstacles, however. The key to the success of those endeavoring to bring about change was to engender both in themselves and in those with whom they associated a sense that "they are somebody." Initially, achieving this goal proved elusive in a context in which the state began conditioning the rural poor from birth to think of themselves as nobodies. In Haiti, people born in cities and towns received birth certificates identifying them as *citoyen;* the certificates of those born in the countryside were marked *paysan.* The implications in terms of class status were clear.[14]

Haiti existed as a bifurcated society. On the one hand was the officialdom of the state; on the other, the tolerated masses of the nation. Critical elements of the *paysan* culture and world view, including language (Kreyòl), religion (Vodun), conjugal arrangements (*plasaj*), and medical treatment from a herbal doctor (*Doktè Fey*) were not official expressions of the society. Rather, they were merely tolerated. French, Catholicism, formal marriage, and Western medicine, respectively, were promoted by the state as official, and hence legitimate, cultural mores.[15] Peasants had become the *moun andeyo,* the people on the outside, to those controlling the society. The *citoyen,* elites of the cities and towns, reinforced this dichotomy by ensuring that peasants were locked out of any meaningful participation in the political process.

The moun andeyo, in their contacts beyond their intimate world, literally kept their heads bowed, feigning docility and masking their thoughts and comportment to avoid conflict with those who held power over them. In this context, getting people to sit together, share problems and common experiences, and determine that they could, through their own concerted actions, effect change in their lives was an almost overwhelming task confronting animatè in their initial stages of work.[16]

Further challenging those endeavoring to produce change was the fact that they confronted an official environment extremely hostile toward them. Essential to the strategy of those seeking to maintain the status quo of a powerless population was to keep that population ignorant, off balance, and disaggregate. Peasants who organized groups that sought to understand and improve their social and economic status were uniformly viewed by those in power as both impertinent and threatening. Grassroots groups discussing state-sponsored predation as a system of extraction (called *pese-souse,* or "squeeze-suck") directed at them, impinged on the comfort zone of those living off the system. Poor rural producers and entrepreneurs who began actively applying the well-known proverb "the mule works for the benefit of the horse" to their condition and social-economic relationships within the predatory system sounded an alarm among those reaping the benefits of peasant labor.

Hence, state-sponsored or sanctioned actions, ranging from extortion and intimidation to arrest, physical abuse, and imprisonment, that sought to undermine and sabotage grassroots organizations and their endeavors were so common that it seemed as if Haiti's grassroots actors were caught in their own Sisyphusean syndrome. In the same way that this mythical Greek figure had been condemned to push a stone up a hill throughout eternity, Haitian grassroots leaders and members of community organizations seemed condemned to having their own stone pushed back to the bottom of the hill whenever they began to push it upward.

To counteract these obstacles, Haiti's grassroots leaders and groups adopted a strategy, practiced widely throughout the country's history, of resistance through elusiveness (mawonaj): When exposed to external threats, leaders and groups retreated from view, staying in relative seclusion until it was safe to reemerge. This practice would serve them well, not just during their early days of organization, but into the future. Using mawonaj, Haiti's evolving grassroots movement survived under Duvalier and later under the rapacious military led by Generals Henri Namphy, Prosper Avril, and, finally, Raoul Cedras and his cohorts.

Removing the Muzzle

It was when Baby Doc Duvalier left Haiti and the muzzle came off that Haiti's grassroots leaders and groups truly emerged. With the predatory state initially demonstrating weakness in its ability to maintain control, established grassroots groups quickly abandoned mawonaj and surged forward, raising their voices and promoting programs designed to confront and resolve fundamental problems that kept them poor, isolated, and locked out of the political process. Membership of existing groups grew and hundreds of new community associations formed, adding their voices to the post-Duvalier call for fundamental social, economic, and political reform. Not long after the demise of Baby Doc Duvalier, one could drop a pencil anywhere on a map of Haiti and, where the point made its mark, identify at least one organized group in its vicinity.

Haiti's grassroots organizations surged forward on two fronts: initiating programs aimed at improving the social and economic status of Haitians, and participating in efforts aimed at improving the political standing of poor Haitians. Typical of the former were the plethora of initiatives by small-farmer associations in grain storage and marketing that appeared. They were aimed at improving producer and community food security while increasing revenue through greater producer control beyond the farm gate. The latter was characterized in the immediate post-Duvalier years by widespread participation in education and training initiatives, such as the Catholic Church's short-lived national literacy program, Misyon Alfa, and by grassroots mobilization to vote in the constitutional referendum of 1987. Ultimately, this mobilization at the grass-roots level played a critically important role in electing Aristide to the office of the president in December 1990.[17]

Leading the surge was a cadre of new-generation community-based civic leaders, including the animatè, whose experience, stature in their communities, and analytical sophistication continued to grow. Working from within their communities and among their peers, these individuals performed key roles in helping community groups to harness resources for local development projects. This included serving as intermediaries between grassroots groups and city-based non-governmental organizations and international donors, and presenting and negotiating proposals for project funding. Animatè took leadership positions in literacy programs and organized sessions to study the constitution.

By and large, these civic activists endeavored to affect political change as outsiders, working from their non-governmental bases. Because of their long-standing distrust of the state and the need for common sense and caution at a time when the future of democratic processes was far from certain, this emerging generation of leaders from the grassroots excluded themselves from direct involvement in what passed for political parties in post-Duvalier Haiti and refused consideration for political posts.

Although the muzzle had come off in 1986, in succeeding years the ultimate outcome of what had become an ebb-and-flow struggle between those seeking true reform and those accepting only cosmetic change and a return to, and maintenance of, the status quo was far from clear. As neo-Duvalierist forces fought to reassert themselves, they aimed their efforts at those leading the struggle against them. In large numbers, those targets were the catalysts and leaders of community-based organizations mobilized for change. During successive post-Duvalier periods of military rule, grassroots leaders and organization members confronted intimidation, violence, and abuse of power that was often more severe than that experienced previously simply because the muzzle had come off and their voices had been raised.

As has been well documented by Haitian and international human rights monitors, this was particularly the case following the September 1991 coup.[18] During the coup and over the following three years, military and paramilitary violence was directed as much against the leaders of community-based organizations as it was against members of the Aristide government. As a result, grassroots leaders and groups were forced underground, their voices seemingly silenced. The recidivists leading and supporting the coup, it appeared, had succeeded in refitting the muzzle, disaggregating groups, driving their leaders into hiding, and reinstituting predation at will.

As events since late 1995 have shown, however, predictions of the demise of Haiti's new generation of grassroots leaders and of grassroots organizations during the coup were premature. Although their ranks had certainly thinned over those difficult years, as international forces began to secure a lawful environment in Haiti and the muzzle again came off, grassroots groups thought to be destroyed or fragmented by the military, along with grassroots leaders thought to be cowed by the violence and intimidation against them, surfaced again. As they reappeared, they brought stories of how they had survived the darkest hours of the coup.

The stories were remarkable. They demonstrate impressive determination and resilience on the part of these leaders, and their ability to retool and call on strategies of resourcefulness and passive resistance to ensure their survival, and to move forward when the coast cleared. Other stories included instances of leaders from diverse communities throughout Haiti living in hiding in Port-au-Prince and organizing ad hoc leadership associations among themselves for purposes of maintaining morale and continuing their analysis and education. Many people engaged in these efforts realized that in order to ensure that the reforms they sought were enacted and sustained, they would have to engage the political system directly.

Locked Out No Longer

In Haiti's elections of December 1990, most eyes were on what had always been the ultimate, if not exclusive, prize of Haitian politics: the presidency.[19] Although parliamentary and municipal posts were also at stake, voters cared little about those "minor" races. This was especially noticeable in the run-off elections held five weeks after Aristide's victory, when voter turnouts did not exceed even half of what they had for the "main event." The keen focus on the presidential race and the corresponding limited attention paid by most voters to the other races resulted in two important outcomes.

First, few of Haiti's new generation of community-based grassroots leaders became involved in the 1990 elections either as political party activists or as candidates. While most of them lent their full support to Aristide's late-blooming presidential candidacy (he had declared himself on the final day of registration), only two months before the elections, they tended to remain outsiders, aloof from political parties, including that which embraced Aristide. Even if grassroots activists had wanted to run once Aristide had declared his candidacy, his late entry into the race prevented them from entering the elections even later and supporting him as candidates. Focusing almost exclusively on the presidency, grassroots leaders and voters betrayed their own nascent understanding of parliamentary government as reorganized under the constitution of 1987 and misread the vital importance of the parliamentary and municipal races.

Haiti's experience with bottom-up democracy, in which all citizens can choose those who will govern them from among their peers, has been extremely limited. Since the nineteenth century, candidates for elective office in Haiti have tended to come from among urban-based elites who organized limited-constituency political parties. Frequently, urban-based parties chose candidates for rural districts from among absentee rural land owners who resided in cities. Given restrictive gender and property ownership covenants, registered voters represented an elite group as well. Indeed, in the 1880s Port-au-Prince had fewer than 1,000 qualified voters. Seats in Haiti's Senate could be won with as few as 100 votes.

By the 1990 election, constitutionally guaranteed universal suffrage for those eighteen years of age and older had broadened the electorate considerably. Political parties, however, in spite of attempts by some to broaden their base, remained by and large exclusive, urban-based entities intent on brokering elections. Their candidates were still often absentees sent out from the city or, at best, locally based *citadin* (elites) determined to exclude the lowly *paysan* from meaningful political participation and to conduct political business as usual. Regardless of their origin, these candidates by and large represented Haiti's tiny classe politique, which had conducted state business for generations and had miserably failed to recognize the legitimate aspirations for change expressed by the Haitian nation following the demise of Baby Doc.

Given this track record of Haiti's political establishment, it is no surprise that voter enthusiasm in 1990 toward most political insiders—the parties and candidates who mirrored their nineteenth-century counterparts—was limited. This sentiment, combined with Aristide's late entry in the race and the resultant disproportional focus by most voters on the presidency, resulted in the second outcome: the irony of traditional candidates of traditional parties gaining a majority share of parliamentary and municipal seats in the 1990 elections.

As symbolized by the joy that swept the country in the aftermath of Aristide's election, his supporters, comprising an overwhelming majority of the population, felt little need to concern themselves with the fact that the President would have to govern in conjunction with a parliament that largely opposed him and sought to play out politics as usual. The immediately strained relations between the executive and legislative branches, thoroughly documented in such contemporary sources as *Haiti en Marche* and *Haiti Observateur*, devolved into innuendo, acrimony, and conflict. This not only hindered the executive's ability to enact reforms, but also fed into the anti-Aristide frenzy building among the military and its allies and contributed significantly to extending the duration of Aristide's exile after the coup.

For Aristide's supporters, especially those political outsiders whose positions of leadership in non-governmental organizations pushing for change translated into a miserable life under military rule, parliamentarian alliance and support (real or perceived) of the coup leaders brought home an important lesson in participatory elective politics. Each office is a prize of some importance, be it president, parliamentarian, mayor, or village councilor. Results of that lesson learned were played out in Haiti in the past year, particularly during the parliamentary and municipal elections that commenced on June 25, 1995.

From Outsiders to Insiders

A fundamental change in the nature of political participation in Haiti began to occur with Aristide's first administration. In essence, it shifted many rural-based, grassroots leaders and community activists away from their previous position of eschewing participation as candidates in elective politics to a position of direct involvement, first as candidates for municipal and national posts, and now as public officials. As such, they are moving away from being political outsiders trying to influence change to being active players working for change from the inside. The shift is apparent beyond elective politics.

It also includes the entry of civic activists and non-governmental organization leaders into government through their nomination to appointed positions within government. Particularly since October 1994, when the Aristide government was restored to power, and more recently since Préval assumed the presidency, a considerable number of political appointments and posts have gone to individuals who have been affiliated with, or at a minimum openly sympathetic toward, grassroots movements and, as such, have been willing to work closely with the newly elected national and municipal officials. One way or the other, the moun andeyo are increasingly engaging and guiding Haiti's nascent democratic political process.

For many grassroots leaders, this shift to becoming directly engaged in what most had previously abhorred, regardless of the lessons learned from the 1990 exercise, did not come easily or automatically. In the immediate aftermath of the UN intervention and the restoration of the Aristide government, grassroots leaders gave priority to issues of personal and institutional security. Most foresaw that their involvement in helping to pick up the economic pieces in their devastated communities would also have a top priority. They expressed a need to resuscitate community-based organizations.[20] As a newly elected deputy in the Haitian parliament said, "We have to strengthen our economic position to be ready to withstand a return to mawonaj if that is necessary."

As animatè and other civic activists returned to their homes and their positions of leadership, and became increasingly convinced that issues of personal security could be eclipsed, at least for the moment, by other, more pressing needs, many found themselves confronting a dilemma they had not completely anticipated. Grassroots groups, with one eye on Haiti's economic recovery but with another eye on political reality, encouraged leaders from among their own ranks to seek elective office. Among their reasons was their belief that the election to office by their peers would be a key factor in ensuring that the macoute had less chance to return.

Sizing up both the needs and the chances for their success in the elective arena, a significant number of local activists decided to become involved in politics.[21] All over Haiti, experienced community leaders and activists, encouraged by their neighbors and their colleagues in community civic associations, came forward by June 1995 as candidates for members of village councils, city halls, and the parliament. In some constituencies, they formed tickets (cartels) with other grassroots activists. While most candidates and tickets became affiliated with the Lavalas Political Platform (Plateforme Politique Lavalas, or PPL), a three-party coalition, some joined the newly emergent Popular Organizations Power

Movement (Pouvwa Rassableman Oganizasyon Popile, or PROP), or were associated with the National Front for Democratic Convergence (Front National pour la Convergence Democratique, or FNCD) or the National Congress of Democratic Movements (Komite Nasyonal Kongre Mouvman Demokratik, or KONAKOM). Still others ran as independents, despite the fact that registration fees for independent candidates were as much as ten times those of candidates running under political party banners.

As candidates from and of the moun andeyo, these political newcomers viewed their rural roots as a distinct advantage in Haiti's changing political configuration. Today, a significant majority of registered voters are those who until recently were considered simply moun andeyo. As the results summarized in the introduction to this chapter indicate, the voices of these previously disenfranchised voters were heard loudest as the votes were counted.[22]

As the new, nontraditional candidates of Haitian politics campaigned among their neighbors, they emphasized issues of decentralization, local autonomous control over resources, government-to-citizen accountability, and the need for Port-au-Prince to respond to, and invest in, the needs of the countryside. Some of those who were candidates for national office spoke of the need to open offices in their districts and return home regularly to monitor their constituent's pulses, a significant modification from the behavior of their political predecessors. In general, as new insiders, they promised to incorporate their positions into reinventing government and, for the first time in Haiti's history, to fashion a state that had a genuine contract of service with the people of the nation.

Now that these nonconventional Haitian politicians have been swept into office, they are beginning to organize themselves to manage the political affairs of the country, and of the localities they represent.[23] The considerable challenge now is to make and sustain a break from the predatory politics of the past, to resist the temptations of power, and to make good on their promises for state accountability and decentralization of power. In essence, doing so translates into building new, bottom-up political institutions that ensure that government in Haiti responds to, and serves, the nation. As they undertake their work, their neighbors back home—those who voted them into office—will be watching them, very closely.

Notes

1. At the time of the elections, the Lavalas political movement was formally represented by the Plateforme Politique Lavalas (PPL), a coalition of three political parties: Mouvement d'Organisation dy Pays (MOP); Organisation Politique Lavalas (OPL); and Pati Louvri Baryè (PLB). Many Aristide-affiliated candidates for elective office, however, ran under the simple designation of Lavalas.

2. Of the seventeen newly elected deputies not affiliated with Lavalas, five were independents with Lavalas leanings and one was affiliated with a small political party that has since become affiliated with the PPL. Races for four remaining seats in the eighty-three member Chamber of Deputies were held simultaneously with the December 7, 1995 presidential elections. The lone senator elected in 1995 who was not formally affiliated with Lavalas was a Lavalas-leaning independent. Nine of the twenty-seven senate seats were held by incumbents elected for six-year terms in December 1990. A fifth seat in the Chamber of Deputies that became open because of the assassination of Lavalas Deputy Jean-Hubert Feuille, was also filled in a by-election. All five open seats in the Chamber were won by candidates identified as Lavalas.

3. An indication of the magnitude of the Lavalas victory in municipal races was evident during a meeting of the country's 133 newly elected mayors held in Port-au-Prince in mid-October 1995. At that meeting, nearly all the mayors identified themselves as Lavalas. Interviews in Port-au-Prince, November 1995.

4. See Robert Maguire, "Standing Tall: Balanced Development in Haiti," *Grass-roots Development*, X (1986), 8–11.

5. The Social and Economic Reconstruction Plan presented in August 1994 by the Aristide government to international financial institutions emphasized elements of decentralization. Aristide's discourse since returning to Haiti in October 1994 echoed that emphasis. Program initiatives and disbursements emanating from the Prime Minister's Office, the World Bank, the Fonds d'Assistance Economique et Sociale (FAES) program funded by the Inter-American Development Bank, and international donors have placed a priority on rebuilding the rural infrastructure. Préval's government has begun to physically move agronomists from the capital to the countryside, and has pledged that municipal governments will receive central government funding for local development programs.

6. See Maguire, "Defanging the Predatory State," *Hemisphere*, VII (1995), 14–16.

7. See Michel-Rolph Trouillot, "Haiti's Nightmare and the Lessons of History," *North American Congress on Latin America*, XXVII (January–February 1994), 46–51.

8. Several statistics widely cited during the Duvalier years were that 80 percent of all government expenditures were made in Port-au-Prince, whereas 80 percent of government revenues came from the provinces. In recent years another statistic—that government ministries spend more than 90 percent of their budgets on salaries—has also been circulated widely. Incipient reforms initiated by the Préval administration are beginning to lower these percentages in favor of investment in the countryside and in government ministry expenditure on programs, not personnel.

9. For an example of this perspective, see the work of Lawrence Harrison, including his "Voodoo Politics," *Atlantic Monthly*, CCLXXI (June 1993), 101–107.

10. Trouillot, *Haiti: State Against Nation: The Origins and Legacy of Duvalierism* (New York, 1990), 81, 86.

11. The efforts of the Holy Cross Priests were undertaken under the auspices of l'Institut Diocésain d'Education des Adultes. This program is examined in Maguire, *Bottom-Up Development in Haiti* (Rosslyn, VA, 1981), 46. This monograph was reprinted in 1995 as occasional paper 5, Institute of Haitian Studies, University of Kansas. See also Paulo Freire, *Pedagogy of the Oppressed*. (New York, 1970).

12. Alan B. Durning, "People, Power, and Development," *Foreign Policy*, LXXVI (Fall, 1989), 80.

13. I have traced these developments in *Bottom-Up Development*; Maguire, "Haiti's Emerging Peasant Movement," *Cimarrón*, II (Winter 1990), 28–44; Maguire,"The Grassroots Movements," in Georges Fauriol (ed.), *Haitian Frustrations: Dilemmas for U.S. Policy* (Washington, 1995), 145–150.

14. In July 1995 the Aristide government issued an executive order discontinuing this practice.

15. See Maguire, *Bottom-Up Development*, 12–13.

16. A fictionalized account of a peasant member of a community group by Roland Lamy, "A Haitian Peasant's Dilemma," *Journal of the Inter-American Foundation*, V (1981), 15–20, beautifully illustrates this point.

17. A more detailed description and analysis of these developments is provided in Maguire, "Food Crop Storage and Marketing in Haiti," in Renée Prendergast and H. W. Singer (eds.), *Development Perspectives for the 1990s* (London, 1991), 146–159; Maguire, "The Peasantry and Political Change in Haiti," *Caribbean Affairs*, IV (April–June 1991), 1–18.

18. See, for example, Americas Watch and the National Coalition for Haitian Refugees, *Silencing A People: The Destruction of Civil Society in Haiti* (New York, 1993), 136.

19. Some of this section is taken from Maguire, "Haiti's Grass-Roots Democracy," *Miami Herald*, June 25, 1995, 1C.

20. These comments are based largely on a series of ongoing interviews with grassroots development leaders and representatives of Haitian NGOs commencing in November 1994. See also, Larry Rohter, "Rooting Up Fears, Haiti's Farmers Fill the Silos," *New York Times*, February 3, 1995, A6.

21. Unfortunately, since to my knowledge there is not yet an organization or institute in Haiti that performs systematic data gathering and objective political analysis of municipaland village councils, concrete data on the number of civic activists and community leaders who have sought and won elected posts nationwide is not easily available. Such a Haitian organization or institute is needed. Findings here are based on my experience with various grassroots groups and their leaders, review of candidate lists, and postcoup fieldwork conducted as recently as June 1996.

22. According to the figures of Haiti's Provisional Election Council (CEP), 3 million eligible voters registered for these elections. According to the Organization of American States, voter turnout in the June 1995 initial round of voting, reported by department, ran between 35 and 65 percent. Turnouts diminished progressively in

the runoff elections. Voter confusion, widely documented logistical ineptitude, and deficient organization by the CEP were in large part to blame for inhibiting a higher turnout. Even if voters had fully understood the process and the CEP's management had been flawless, however, it seems safe to surmise that the results would not have been different.

23. Field research conducted in November 1995 and January 1996 indicated that newly elected public officials began creating political blocks and coalition groups shortly following their election. These emerging groupings were based on geographic and issue-specific factors. One example was the creation of a regional forum of mayors in the northern part of the country to meet, discuss common problems, and define common positions and approaches to confronting them.

CHAPTER EIGHT

The Role of the Diaspora in Haitian Politics

Michel S. Laguerre

THE HAITIAN political system has emerged with a new social identity as a part of a social field that encompasses the activities of the diaspora as well as those of the Haitian state. The Haitian diaspora in the United States and elsewhere has become an integral part of the transnational Haitian political field and has influenced in various ways the behavior of the Haitian political system.

This chapter analyzes the transnational political field that links the diaspora to the homeland, the transnational circuit of social mobility, and informal transnational practices as they influence the local Haitian political reality.

Transnational Political Field

The transnational political field means a system in which the political process of the nation state encompasses actors who live inside and as well as those who live outside its legal and territorial boundaries.[1] Moreover, it refers to the content, process, and outcome of both formal and informal transnational political practices. Traditionally, transnational politics has been carried out mostly between states: It is normally viewed as the result of interactions among formal actors in which the rules of international diplomacy prevail. I define the transnational political field more broadly, as an open arena in which elected and nonelected individuals, with or without the explicit knowledge of the state, and sometimes acting against official state policies, engage in formal and informal political practices for the purpose of influencing the everyday policies and politics of another state. Transnational informal political transactions are carried out at the state, regional, and local levels, engaging actors from the homeland and from the diaspora, and encompassing their networks of relationships.

Since the collapse of the Jean-Claude ("Baby Doc") Duvalier administration in Haiti in 1986, Haitian-Americans have, in various ways, influenced the course of national politics in Haiti, either directly through their active participation in national political practices or indirectly from their bases of operation in New York, Miami, Boston, or Chicago. These efforts have been carried out both by individual practitioners and by grassroots groups. Here it is important to delineate this system of practice by identifying its modalities.

Individual and Group Practices

The transnational political field is the framework within which the activities of political actors that transcend national boundaries take place as they reinvent the rules of the game. This is an arena wherein individuals and groups are engaged in the business of opening up the national political space and maintaining an active network of relationships for the purpose of carrying out their political goals. Because the transnational political field operates inside at least two political systems, it links them together in various ways through the agency of formal and informal actors. I show how these processes develop and become routinized, thereby linking people from at least two different nations to each other or allowing the same individual to operate in two different states.

It is important to stress that among Haitians, individual practices in homeland politics take various forms. Among the most productive are those that involve direct interaction with the Haitian electorate and the political establishment. Also productive are actions that are carried out in the United States by the diaspora on behalf of the Haitian government or the Haitian people at large.

Haitian politicians are very well aware of the strength of the diaspora and have sought to tap into its human and financial resources. During the election of 1990, they campaigned actively across the diaspora, and in their political platforms they defined the role that they expected the diaspora to play in the development of their country. It has become evident that any presidential candidate who does not enjoy the backing of a large segment of the diaspora will have enormous difficulty winning in the general elections.

The financial resources of the diaspora are an important asset that helps defray the electoral expenses of presidential candidates. These expenses can be costly. In the past, members of the Haitian elite provided much of the necessary funds, but they also controlled the apparatus of government.

In an effort to establish a democratic system of governance in Haiti, politicians can no longer rely exclusively on the bourgeoisie to finance their campaigns. That is why the role of the diaspora in this particular political sector is fundamental. The diaspora is able to support its candidates and thereby to displace, or at least compete with, the traditional elite's control over the political process.

The diaspora also lends its technical skills to political candidates. These human resources cannot be easily matched in Haiti. In past presidential campaigns, members of the diaspora prepared radio and television advertisements for their preferred candidates. Some campaign speeches were written abroad, and even those prepared in Port-au-Prince benefited from the input of the diaspora. Into these speeches the diaspora injected its own democratic vision of society.

Some members of the diaspora even took leaves of absence from their jobs so that they could return to Haiti and help run the presidential campaigns of their candidates during both the 1990 and the 1995 campaigns. They brought with them their technical and organizational skills, their money, and their time.

Since the Haitians in the diaspora send remittances back home, its members influence the votes of their relatives and friends. They use the telephone to advise people on which candidates to vote for. The advice sent with the remittance check is usually sought and appreciated by friends and relatives since the senders often have better access than do people living in Haiti to accurate information pertaining to the backgrounds of candidates.

During the embargo period that followed the overthrow of the Aristide regime, the underground resistance movement in Haiti communicated regularly with the diaspora, informing it about the situation at home and receiving information about developments abroad. All of that was carried out through media that the de facto government could not control: fax and telephone and, to a lesser extent, audio and video cassettes. Faxes received in Haiti were duplicated and distributed among members of the resistance.

During this same period, correspondents for Haitian radio programs in New York, Miami, and Boston broadcast their reports every evening directly from their hiding places in Haiti. By providing accurate analyses of the local situation through their local contacts, and sometimes with the help of foreign journalists, they kept alive the interests of the diaspora in Haitian matters.

The diaspora also participates in island politics by contacting congressmen and formal voluntary and grassroots organizations for favors on behalf of Haiti. Members of the diaspora have been able to introduce their presidential candidates to U.S. politicians and members of Congress. In this way, one might say that there is an embryonic and acephalous Haitian lobby in the United States made up of both Haitian-Americans and their sympathizers. In the recent past, various attempts have been made to establish a Haitian political action committee to lobby and influence congressional policies toward Haiti. Some members of the diaspora have enlisted American grassroots groups in organizing protests on behalf of Haitian refugees, raising funds for the cause, and bringing grassroots leaders living in Haiti to the United States to network with American activists and sympathizers and to inform the American public about their activities. In cities where Haitian-Americans are numerous, they have been able to speak out against human rights abuses in Haiti and to interest other people in Haitian causes.

Several political groups and non-governmental organizations in New York City serve as subsidiaries of the headquarters of their operations in Port-au-Prince. As such, they raise funds to be channelled to Haiti and are consulted in the headquarters' decision-making processes. They meet both financial and organizational needs of the headquarters and enlist support for its projects among members of the diasporic community.

Diasporic newspapers are widely read in Haiti and contribute immensely to the national debate in terms of shaping society's views of candidates for electoral office. At times they are able to undo a politician's prospects or to help place another politician ahead of his competitors.

The diaspora has organized several protests, often at the UN Plaza or in front of the White House, in the hope of changing the course of action in Haiti. Before 1986 they carried out these protests in front of the Haitian consulates in New York, Boston, and Miami in an effort to undermine the image of the Duvalierist administration. The protests were usually meant either to embarrass the party in office or to make such a strong call for action that the party would come up with more acceptable policies.

These examples show the transnationality of Haitian politics: how actions taken in Haiti have repercussions in the diaspora, and how the diaspora has helped shape policies vis-à-vis Haiti (and, more directly, the outcome of certain policies) because of the influence that it exerts on the electoral process, policy formation, politics in general, and policy implementation in particular. All of this takes place mostly in the informal arena since diasporans are not elected officials or officially assigned agents of the Haitian government. During his term in office, Aristide began to establish a formal structure linking the government apparatus to the diaspora. President Préval has continued these efforts.

The Extraterritorial Tenth Department

The diaspora was conceptualized by the first Aristide administration as an extraterritorial unit of the republic, existing for the most part overseas.[2] Although the diaspora is viewed as an extension and part of the nation, there are many issues still to be resolved before this informal relationship can be placed on a solid legal footing.

The diaspora as the tenth department comprises Haitian immigrants living in the United States, Canada, France, and other countries. It is modeled on the political administrative division of the Haitian territory, where each departement is subdivided into arrondissements. The metaphor of the *dixième département* collapses all of these disparate immigrant sites into a single diasporic site. The diaspora, conceived of as a full-fledged department, is also divided into arrondissements, with California, for example, as one of them. In a sense, by this arrangement the Haitian government was inscribing its own geographical map on the U.S. landscape. In placing Haitian-American settlements as the main element of the makeup of the map, one obtains a reading of the U.S. mainland quite different from that of the mainstream American society: It is a social and political map, not a legal and physical one.

Because various tentacles of the Haitian diaspora reached across the

United States, a central committee was established by Aristide's administration to coordinate the activities of the tenth department in regard to the return of Aristide to Port-au-Prince to complete his term in office. A grassroots leader was selected for each region. This structure created a number of problems for the official representatives of the Haitian government in particular and the diasporic community in general.

These appointed leaders were not elected by their respective local communities. In some areas their status as official representatives of the community was challenged by grassroots community leaders who had control over a larger constituency. Since some of these local organizations had been constituted prior to the conceptualization of the tenth department as an administrative concept, some resisted cooptation and preferred to continue their traditional linkage to specific regions of Haiti.

The relations of the appointed activist leaders to the government of Port-au-Prince have yet to be settled fully. These relations can only be informal, since the activist leaders are not on the government's payrolls. In the late 1980s the Office for Diaspora Affairs functioned under the aegis of the Ministry of Foreign Affairs. However, during the first Aristide presidency, the person in charge of the diaspora was attached to the Office of the President and not to the Ministry of Foreign Affairs, but was not known to be a government employee. Currently, the Ministry of Diasporic Affairs (Ministère des Haitiens Vivant à l'Etranger) is the official unit responsible for the coordination of the relations of the diaspora with the government of Haiti.

It is worth noting that the diaspora's vision of the transition to democracy in Haiti has not always coincided with that of the homeland government. Moreover, the diaspora has considerable resources, and because there are large settlements of Haitians in the United States, Canada, the Bahamas, the Dominican Republic, and France (including its overseas Caribbean territories), the diaspora is now seeking a dual citizenship status for its members.

The relations of the representatives of the tenth department to the official representatives overseas of the Haitian government (ambassador and consular officers) still need to be clarified. The frequent direct contacts between diaspora leaders and U.S. officials at times undermine the effectiveness of the diplomatic corps; they create a sustained tension between the latter and the former and, consequently, confusion among the resident population. Clear guidelines must be set so that the jurisdictional path of each entity can be defined.

The fundraising capacity of the diaspora is a critical factor that accounts for its strength vis-à-vis Haiti. In addition to financing the electoral campaigns of Marc Bazin and Jean-Bertrand Aristide in the elections of 1990, it raised approximately $250,000 to finance projects of the new government. Its resources can strengthen one side of the political spectrum at the expense of the other. Whether the central committee coordinating the activities of the diaspora is seen as an independent voluntary association, an overseas leg of a political party, or part of the government in office will determine the level of participation of the people or the survival of the organization.

Whether the structure of relations between the tenth department and Haiti is formalized or not, the diaspora will continue to remain a key player in the conduct of Haitian politics because of its resources and access to U.S. politicians and officeholders. Through their informal diplomacy, members of the diaspora will continue to pressure Congress for a change in American foreign policy on Haiti. In fact, the diaspora currently provides a strategic link between American policy-makers and shapers and the Haitian government. In other words, the diaspora at times plays a brokering and lobbying role on behalf of the civilian Haitian population and government.

In dealing with the Haitian government, the U.S. administration and members of Congress increasingly seek the advice of Haitian Americans concerning U.S. policies on Haiti. This is so not only because the diaspora continues its lobbying efforts, but also because the Haitian communities in New York, Miami, and Boston represent blocs of votes to be delivered on election day. Aristide's high profile during his exile in Washington no doubt partly resulted from the leading role played by Haitian Americans in contacting their congressmen, organizing public protests in alliance with grassroots organizations, and inviting Aristide to speak in their respective communities.

The Transnational Circuit of Mobility

The extension of the boundary of the state has become the basis for a new form of social mobility, a mobility that crosses state borders and is inscribed in the transnational field of social interactions. Transnationality allows people to be socially mobile because they can transform themselves into transnational actors. The social mobility of this transnational process mainly entails either emigration to the United States or the return migration of transnational players to Haiti. However, local actors can also act transnationally or can become socially mobile through transnationality, as in the case of individuals who receive remittances from abroad and use those funds to reposition themselves in the hierarchical structure of Haiti. This double process is very much at work today and is one factor that accounts for the dynamic process of the transnational circuit of social mobility.

For some, the return to the homeland is likely to signal upward mobility because local people frequently think that returnees may be better off than those who have never left the island. In contrast, emigration to the United States often leads to downward mobility for middle or upper class Haitians due to their lack of English and their inability to find good jobs.[3]

In the past decade this transnational circuit allowed army officers to emigrate to the United States upon their retirement and to become members of the diaspora. The military maintained a love-hate relationship with the diaspora.[4] Its members loved diasporans for their ingenuity, success abroad, and the financial aid that they sent to Haiti, but they also hated them because civil society relied heavily on the diaspora in its struggle against the military for civilian control; therefore, the diaspora was seen by the military as an oppositional force with which to be reckoned.

In the past two decades many army officers incorporated emigration to the United States into their long-range plans, thus making the army particularly vulnerable as an institution because its officers were tempted to serve as informants for the U.S. government, particularly if they were offered guarantees that they or their families would be allowed subsequently to migrate to the United States. Among the forty-one individuals whose assets were blocked by the Department of Treasury in October 1993, thirty-two were army officers. Nine owned houses in the United States.[5]

Because army service had become a stepping stone toward the United States, the role of the military was compromised; individual career goals took precedence over institutional goals. There is no reason not to believe that members of the new police force will follow a similar path, that is, using migration to the United States as a way to achieve upward mobility for themselves and members of their families.

The Diaspora and Transition to Democracy

The diaspora has become a guarantor for the transition to democracy in Haiti. Civil society has never been able to sustain civilian control over the state for long periods of time. It was the military-business alliance that had been the major obstacle to the transition to democracy: The strength of the military-business coalition always overpowered the capability of the government to remain in office or to exert effective control over the military.[6]

For the first time in the history of the republic, a fourth factor in the conduct of national politics has been added to the army/police, civil society, and the government: the diaspora. In allying itself with civil society and the civilian government against the army and police, the diaspora provided civil society with new ammunition to move the country away from army control and toward democracy and civilian control. (The military as an institution was dismantled in 1995 and replaced by a civilian peace force.)

This new development has had an impact on American politics. It has created opposing tendencies in the decision-making process of the U.S. government. While the Department of Defense and Republican members of Congress usually sided with the military-business coalition, and thereby chose a status quo type of stability, the Clinton White House and the State Department were more in favor of civilian control over the military. The lobbying effort of a vocal contingent of human rights activists, and the gentle pressure exerted by the diaspora on its respective representatives in Congress, have contributed to this fracture in the American body politic. This new transnational factor must be integrated into any analysis of the Haitian political system. Furthermore, the diaspora is now a major force behind civil society.

It is perhaps in the realm of mass media that the influence of the diaspora on Haitian politics is felt the most. Three major newspapers—*Haiti Observateur*, *Haiti Progrès*, and *Haiti en Marche*—are published in the United States. Through their provocative political ideas—at times somewhat inflammatory—and their vast distribution network, they not only compete with the local papers in Haiti, but also contribute to the shaping of political discourse in and on Haiti.

Informal Transnational Processes

One fundamental aspect of the transnational circuit is the informality that permeates the flow of social relations. While formal relations between the United States and Haiti are achieved through official channels, the relationship of the diaspora with the homeland occurs rather on an informal and sometimes ad hoc basis. The informality of these practices is supposed eventually to lead to some formal mode of operation.

Understanding the modalities of the transnational circuit implies some focus on the grammar of informal practices. [7] Informal practices, as they affect this fluid border crossing political field, display the following characteristics.

— They are *experimental*, in the sense that there are no fixed patterns to be followed simply because the experience is novel and is a result of the implantation of offshoot Haitian communities in the United States. A period of trial and error opens this field of practice for experimentation as actors from the homeland and the diaspora adjust to the everyday political reality.

— They are *transitional* in the sense that these practices should lead to a better understanding of the process, to a permanent formal structure, and to a form of stability in the way that the flow of interactions is maintained and nurtured. They should lead both the diaspora and the government to establish the rules of interaction and the forms of cooperation that are needed to make the effort productive.

— They are *multiplex* in the sense that connections are made on an informal basis with various sectors of the homeland and the diaspora with or without the formal acknowledgement of the government and sometimes in opposition to the views of the government.

— They are *multivocal* in the sense that diverse voices are heard and diverse means of communication are used for the purpose of maintaining a flow of informal relations between the homeland and the diaspora.

— They are *underground*, not because they are necessarily illegal or outside the realm of the formal arena, but rather because they do not follow formal channels, or if they follow them, they do it in a somewhat informal way.

— They are *transnational* in the sense that they are border-crossing practices that encompass interactions among individuals living in at least two distinct states and under different legal systems.

Informal practices imbue the life of the informal system as actors circulate in the transnational circuit, or as they maintain ongoing informal communications to keep alive the transnational informal circuit.

Informal Diplomacy

Transnationality has created a new kind of interstate relations whereby individuals and groups cross national boundaries to engage in productive informal interactions and dialogue.[8] The diaspora is a major factor in the opening up of the closed political system in Haiti. By intervening at all government levels, by injecting money in the various sectors of the national economy, and by providing human and financial resources to grassroots and formal voluntary associations, the diaspora has infused the country widely and deeply with its democratic views.

The phrase *informal diplomacy* is used here to contrast it with the official realm of formal diplomacy. While formal diplomacy is conducted by officials from different countries, informal diplomacy is carried out rather by civilians speaking not on behalf of their government but on behalf of themselves or their organizations. This informal diplomacy often collides with formal diplomacy. For example, while the U.S. government was following a policy of appeasement during Aristide's exile in the hope that the Haitian military and the exiled government would find ways to bridge their differences, informal diplomats (local leaders in the diaspora known as *ambassadeurs du béton ou sans cravate*) were struggling, along with Haitian grassroots organizations, for civilian control over the military.

Non-governmental entities do not have a monopoly over informal diplomacy; government agencies are also involved in this practice. Individual ministers of the Haitian government have also contacted the diaspora to release funds for their cherished projects. Campanella accurately notes that "the traditional monopoly of the foreign ministry on external contacts is challenged by non-governmental actors and by the centralized and decentralized state agencies themselves. . . . *Non-governmental associations have taken on an external profile*."[9]

It is a fact that informal diplomacy, an outcome of transnationality, is totally outside the control of both the U.S. and the Haitian governments. It reminds us that globalization is at work through a flow of unregulated relations that transform the immigrant subject into a transnational citizen.[10] Grassroots leaders will continue to use informal diplomacy to guarantee the transition to democracy in Haiti.

Conclusion

Transnationality sheds light on the new orientation of the Haitian political process. Shortly before his 1993 inauguration, President-elect Clinton recorded a radio message addressed not to the government of

Haiti but rather to the Haitian masses, informing them that he was working on the resolution of the Haitian political crisis and advising them not to use leaky sailboats to emigrate to the United States. Similarly, while in Haiti, President Aristide recorded a message in 1991 addressed not to the U.S. government but to the diasporic population in the United States. Each of these national leaders was able to speak to the electorate of the other country by enlarging the transnational arena of traditional diplomacy.

The diaspora brings a new ingredient to the political mix of Haitian society. The diaspora is very much interested in the success of the democratic process, since its own fate is linked to the success of democracy in Haiti. Although there will continue to be more migration from Haiti to the United States than return migration from the United States to Haiti, the transnational Haitian American has developed loyalty to his new country as well as to his homeland. This gives rise to a fragmented bipolar identity that transcends national boundaries and is central to the social construction of the transnational subject.[11]

Because of the border-crossing practices emanating from Haiti and the diaspora, the erosion of traditional Haitian society is in full swing. The models to be emulated are no longer exclusively provided by the local elite, but are rather instilled in the minds of the people by the diaspora, who are trusted as allies by the civilian population. This is why the former members of the army, the elite, and the corrupt elements of society see the people of the diaspora as competitors capable of outdoing and outmaneuvering them in terms of their influence on the direction of Haitian society.

Notes

1. Carolle Charles, "Transnationalism in the Construct of Haitian Migrants' Racial Categories of Identity in New York City," in Nina Glick Schiller and others (eds.), *Towards a Transnational Perspective on Migration* (New York, 1992), 101–123.

2. Jean Jean-Pierre, "The Tenth Department," *North American Congress on Latin America*, XXVII (1994), 41–45.

3. Michel S. Laguerre, *American Odyssey: Haitians in New York City* (Ithaca, 1984).

4. Michel S. Laguerre, *The Military and Society in Haiti* (Knoxville, 1993).

5. *Roundtable on Haiti—October 1993.* Briefing before the House Committee on Foreign Affairs, 103 Cong. 1 sess. (Washington, D.C., 1993), 34–35.

6. Michel S. Laguerre, "Business and Corruption: Framing the Haitian Military Question," *California Management Review*, XXXVI (1994) 89–106. See also Laguerre, "National Security, Narcotics Control, and the Haitian Military," in Jorge Rodriguez Beruff and Humberto Garcia Muniz (eds.), *Security Problems and Policies in the Post-Cold War Caribbean* (New York, 1996), 99–120.

7. Michel S. Laguerre, *The Informal City* (London, 1994), 1–26.

8. Michel S. Laguerre, "Transnational Citizenship," address delivered at the annual meeting of the Sociology of Education Association, February 1995.

9. Miriam L. Campanella, "The Effects of Globalization and Turbulence on Policy-Making Processes," *Government and Opposition*, XXVIII (1993), 200–201.

10. See Glick Schiller, *Towards a Transnational Perspective*, 11–12; Linda Basch et al., *Nations Unbound* (New York, 1994).

11. Basch, *Nations Unbound,* 1–5.

CHAPTER NINE

Alternative Models for Haiti's Economic Reconstruction

Clive Gray

HAITI WILL be condemned to live in a poverty trap so long as leading Haitian intellectuals and politicians believe that their government can and should take the lead in molding the economy's productive apparatus. They should simply observe where that strategy has led in Africa, eastern Europe, and the former Soviet Union, not to mention countries in the Caribbean and Latin America. Haiti's economic situation is so desperate and the administration's capacity to implement anything is so weak that the only possible increases either in production or the associated tax base must come through private investors persuaded that they can make a profit.

The highest priority of the Haitian authorities should be to establish a climate favorable to private economic activity. This means not only offering adequate incentives, including freedom from harassment by corrupt officials, but also resisting the blandishments of operators who say that they will invest if they are given concessions that exclude their competitors.

If the Haitian government succeeds in convincing foreign (and domestic) investors that Haiti is a place where they can make money, there is hope that production can revive sufficiently to lead the economy out of its present trap. Haitians should take heart from the way in which other economies that were once regarded as hopeless have rebounded and found a path to sustained growth. South Korea provides the most striking example. In 1953 at the end of the Korean War, economists regarded South Korea's economy with despair. As late as 1965 South Korean

183

exports totaled a mere $170 million, less than Haiti's total exports in 1979. By that time, however, South Korea's leaders had glimpsed the possibility of using foreign trade as an engine of growth. Thirty years later, exports were nearly $100 billion—from a country poor in natural resources and with a mean distance to foreign markets several times Haiti's distance from its own markets.[1]

An example to which Haitians may more easily relate is that of Uganda, once regarded as one of Africa's most promising economies but brought close to ruin by the megalo-kleptomaniac President Idi Amin (1971–1981). During the 1970s Uganda's exports declined at a rate of 10 percent a year—similar to Haiti's more recent fate. By 1987 Uganda's tax base had all but disappeared, its ratio of revenue to GDP falling to 2.6 percent, even lower than the 4 percent currently estimated for Haiti by Paul Latortue.[2]

However, in 1986 Uganda embarked on a program of structural adjustment. From 1988 to 1995, through increasing monetary and fiscal discipline, liberalization of the business environment, adoption of a flexible, market-oriented exchange rate, and structural reforms in the areas of state enterprise, civil service, army demobilization and financial institutions, Uganda raised its per capita GDP by an average of 3.5 percent annually. By 1994 its ratio of revenue to GDP had recovered to 8 percent.[3]

The Lavalas Model à la Dupuy: Is It a Viable Alternative?

Alex Dupuy contrasts the economic development program, the Lavalas model, proposed by the first Aristide government with the neoliberal model imposed on the second Aristide government by the international financial institutions.[4] This latter model Dupuy describes as reflecting "the class interests of foreign multinational capital and foreign investors, of the multilateral and bilateral aid institutions, and of the Haitian bourgeoisie, in that order." This contrasts with the "people friendly" Lavalas model, which Dupuy terms viable under current conditions.

The Lavalas model "considers the peasant's interests and points of view as primary" and "extends to the rural areas basic services such as health care, a literacy campaign, education, drinking water, as well as road and transportation networks." Unfortunately, Dupuy gives us no figures to indicate either what this model would cost or how it might be financed. His sole reference to tax measures under the Lavalas model is a call for revising or abolishing "the various other methods of directly and indirectly taxing the peasants" (in addition to the *chèfs seksyon* system).

Manufactured Exports as the Engine of Growth

Latortue accurately identifies the export of goods and services as the most promising engine for growth for Haiti. Given the weakness of domestic purchasing power and the degradation of its farm land, Haiti has no choice but to integrate itself into the global economy by attracting investors to develop niches in two world markets, those of light manufactures and tourism.

Haiti's potential for attracting investment in export-oriented light manufacturing has already been demonstrated by the fact that by 1986, notwithstanding the uncertain environment associated with the second Duvalier administration, these exports totaled nearly $370 million (gross of imported inputs).[5] That year, manufacturing accounted for some 84 percent of the country's exports, rising from a negligible level twenty years earlier.[6]

By 1990 a total of 252 export manufacturers in Haiti employed some 46,000 workers, still a minuscule proportion of the Haitian labor force of 3.5 million, but nonetheless a base on which to build.[7] Table 9-1, based on 1991 World Bank figures, suggests the diversity of the products that were being sold to the United States, which absorbed about 95 percent of these goods. Textiles and related products accounted for half the sales; two other categories, electrical machinery and equipment, and baby carriages, toys, and sports goods, accounted for an additional 32 percent of the sales, leaving about 18 percent in fifteen smaller categories and two groupings labeled "Other."

Following the military coup the number of operating enterprises fell to 145 by the end of 1991 and to less than 30 by early 1994, with employment dropping to between 6,000 and 8,000.[8] According to the monthly employment survey conducted by the U.S. embassy, by May 1996 employment was back up to 20,000 and rising rapidly.[9] The government should now give top priority to creating conditions that will restore production in the other plants that were operating as late as 1990 and to attracting new manufacturing operations.

The fact that Haiti may appear to be trapped in a low-income equilibrium or that the majority of jobs in export manufacturing are unskilled should not deter the government from encouraging this sector. The experience of the world's so-called newly industrializing countries has been that as workers gain experience in manufacturing, they also acquire skills, raising their productivity and incomes. Workers would not be queuing up for jobs in Haiti's export industries if the industries did not offer them a better livelihood than they have now or than anything the state is going to be able to offer them out of its own resources.

Table 9-1. *Haiti's Exports of Light Manufactures to the United States,*
Fiscal Year 1988

millions of dollars

Products	Millions of dollars	Percent of total
Products from domestic materials		
Textile yarns, fabric manufactures	16.4	4.5
Paper, paperboard manufactures	3.9	1.1
Brooms, brushes, buttons, umbrellas, canes	3.3	0.9
Cork and wood manufactures	1.3	0.4
Wood furniture and parts	0.8	0.2
Nonmetallic mineral manufactures	0.6	0.2
Manufactures of metals	0.6	0.2
Artworks	0.2	0.1
Other	2.3	0.6
Subtotal	29.5	8.1
Products from imported materials		
Wear apparel, accessories and fur articles	166.3	45.8
Electrical machinery and equipment	75.1	20.7
Baby carriages, toys, sports goods	40.7	11.2
Leather, leather manufactures and dressed furskins	13.6	3.7
Luggage, handbags and the like	9.2	2.5
Professional, scientific and control instruments	5.6	1.5
Articles of rubber or plastic	2.6	0.7
Textile fibers, lace, ribbons	1.6	0.4
Footwear	1.3	0.4
Tools (hand or machine)	1.0	0.3
Musical instruments and records	0.1	0.0
Other	16.4	4.5
Subtotal	333.4	91.9
Total	362.9	100

Source: World Bank (1991, p. 80). The Bank cites the U.S. Department of Commerce and the
IMF as its sources.
Dollar values are f.o.b.

Making Haiti a Free Trade Area

Haiti's relatively high nonwage production costs—unavoidable in the
short run—resulting from the degradation of its infrastructure and persistent political uncertainties make it necessary for the country to offer
the lowest possible costs with respect to production inputs in order to

lure back former export producers and attract new ones. Essentially, this means transforming the whole country into a free trade area. Admittedly, to do so involves sacrificing some existing sources of revenue, which could be offset by concentrating the focus of the customs service on imports of finished consumer goods.

Curbing Wasteful Public Expenditure: State Enterprise Deficits

Given the constraints on Haiti's ability to increase revenue in the near future, the government must increase efforts to curb wasteful expenditures. In particular, deficits of state enterprises must be reduced. As Latortue notes, these deficits are a burden on the national budget; a decade ago the enterprises were positive contributors.

Apart from the weight of these deficits on Haiti's minuscule fiscal resources, managing or supervising management of commercial enterprises is a complex task that heavily burdens the administrative capacity of any public sector. This sector already has more than it can handle in restoring and expanding traditional public services and in taking the steps needed to create an environment conducive to private investment. (Merely greeting prospective investors and deciding which of their inevitable requests for concessions can reasonably be granted is a time-consuming, specialized task.)

If private managers who can eliminate a state enterprise's deficit while meeting import competition and generating tax revenue do not come forward, then it is better to pension off the labor force, sell the enterprise's assets for salvage value, and let traders import the goods in question, subject to excise taxes.

Conclusion

As far as economic policy is concerned, Haiti has three top tasks:

— establish an environment that will stimulate private investors to relaunch the industrial apparatus that made such a promising start during the 1980s;

— reorient the government to remove it from functions for which it is not equipped;

—redirect the government's energies into services to the population and economy that no one else can provide: public safety, management of those components of infrastructure that cannot readily be privatized, and basic social services for low-income groups.

Notes

1. Haitian exports were $185 million in 1979. International Monetary Fund, *International Financial Statistics Yearbook* (Washington, D.C., 1995), 420, 480, 482.

2. World Bank, *African Development Indicators 1994-5* (Washington, D.C., 1995), 191; Paul Latortue, "Toward a Viable Economic Structure in Haiti," unpublished ms. (1995), 18.

3. International Monetary Fund, "Uganda: Back from the Brink and on the Path to Sustained Growth," *IMF Survey* (December 11, 1995).

4. Alex Dupuy, *Haiti in the New World Order: The Limits of the Democratic Revolution* (Boulder, forthcoming).

5. Computed from World Bank, *Haiti: Restoration of Growth and Development* (Washington, D.C., 1991), 80, following indicated data as to share of U.S. in these exports (90 percent in products from domestic materials and 95 percent in products from imported materials).

6. Some Haitian series measure manufactured exports in terms of domestic value added only. Following international convention, I take exports gross of imported inputs. World Bank, *Haiti: Restoration*, 78, 80, indicates that the latter accounted for about 70 percent of gross export value.

7. Number of firms is according to Mats Lundahl, "The Haitian Dilemma Reexamined: Lessons from the Past in the Light of Some New Economic Theory" in this volume, citing Inter-American Development Bank, *Emergency Economic Recovery Program, Haiti*, 36, and International Monetary Fund, "Haiti—Recent Economic Developments," SM/95/43 (1 March 1995), 3. Employment is according to Jennifer L. McCoy, *Haiti: Prospects for Political and Economic Reconstruction*, World Peace Foundation reports 10 (Cambridge, MA, 1995), 9.

8. Lundahl, "Haitian Dilemma Reexamined," 25.

9. Oral communication from Ambassador William Swing, June 20, 1996.

CHAPTER TEN

Priorities in the Economic Reconstruction of Rural Haiti

Anthony V. Catanese

THE STRUCTURE of the Haitian economy is important in the reconstruction of Haiti. Understanding the unique characteristics of both the country and its economy is essential if reconstruction is to reach the many rather than only the few. By reaching the vast majority of Haitians, the government can better ensure the long-term stability and prosperity of the country. Haiti's economic reconstruction must go hand-in-hand with its political reconstruction so that the country eventually has the opportunity to participate in—not just observe—changes occurring in the world economy. Haitians will then want to remain in Haiti and not emigrate.

This chapter suggests steps to be taken during the reconstruction of the Haitian economy if the vast majority of Haitians are to enjoy better lives than they have in the past. Rather than present an exhaustive list of issues, this chapter lists those that are most important to improving the lives of most Haitians. This focusing is particularly important because for the first time in its history, Haiti has the opportunity to undertake major economic reforms within a democratic framework.

Approaches to economic restructuring contrast significantly, however. The prevailing point of view among most economists is that Haiti and Haitians will be better off if scarce resources are primarily focused on the urban assembly industries for export purposes. The opposing view is that such a focusing of resources is ill advised. The disagreement is not about the respective lists of ideas; it has to do with priorities. The prevailing conviction is misdirected; other economic issues should receive priority.

Land Ownership

The issue of land ownership is one about which Haitians have strong feelings. Because of the importance of land ownership with respect to the political and economic reconstruction of Haiti, any policy regarding land ownership must be given serious consideration. Despite heinous examples of official exploitation of peasant farmers' land, this is not a serious national issue that requires immediate attention, because the benefits of a national and highly visible effort at land reform will not be worth the costs. This does not mean that efforts to return misappropriated land to the poor should be abandoned. Nor does it mean that government-owned land should lay fallow. However, the issue of land ownership should not gain political prominence because the resulting economic benefits will not be worth the economic costs.

Land ownership is not an ongoing, contentious issue among most poor rural Haitians. Most Haitians have a permanent arrangement regarding land use or ownership that has evolved over a long time and that is acceptable to them. Most poor rural Haitians own their land. Many others, however, are tenant farmers or sharecroppers on land owned by other Haitians and have a secure, long-term relationship with the landowners. Some Haitians have long-term arrangements (de jure and de facto) allowing them to live on and farm government-owned land; only a few do not know from year to year if they will have land to farm.

The burden of proof will be on those who believe the economic benefits to the rural poor are worth the economic costs the rural poor inevitably will incur. National, departmental, and sectional data are critical. The evidence that land ownership is a serious national problem does not need to be unambiguous but it must be convincing.

Focus on Rural Poverty

A simple guiding principle when allocating new and existing resources should be, "will this allocation reduce rural poverty in Haiti?" Why must there be such a narrow focus? The vast majority of Haitians are rural people, and their economic options are considerably more limited than those of their urban counterparts. For Haiti as a whole to prosper economically, the rural population must prosper.

Urban Haitians are more dependent on the rural economy and on the incomes of relatives in rural areas than is often realized.[1] For example, urban migrants often are supported by relatives who live in rural areas and frequently leave their children with rural relatives while earning a living in the cities. As a result, much urban economic security is derived from rural economic progress.

A prosperous rural population will provide benefits beyond the nonurban areas to the urban population. In contrast, however, a vigorous urban economy will not have comparable spillover benefits to the rural population because it will encourage more migration to urban areas. A continued flow to the urban areas, particularly into Port-au-Prince, will overtax the cities in terms of public services and housing. The attendant negative urban effects will far outweigh their limited benefits. Therefore, invigorating and strengthening the rural economy should be the central focus of reconstructing the Haitian economy.

Real Per Capita Income

Economic progress in Haiti cannot occur unless rural Haitians have economic power over basic goods and services. The national economy depends on economic progress because its macroeconomic recovery requires increased spending by a large number of Haitians, who typically live in rural areas and do not currently earn enough money to buy even basic goods. The international community expects economic progress after spending substantial time and resources on the Haiti embargo and invasion. Unless the average real per capita income rises in rural Haiti and existing economic inequality is reduced, economic improvements will never be realized regardless of democratic political regimes.

Addressing the economic needs of rural Haitians has both an economic and political dimension. A significant economic disparity among key sectors of Haiti's population can hinder economic development and growth. From a domestic political perspective, Haiti's rural population will no longer quietly and conveniently allow the urban elite to ignore its needs and calls for justice. Rural peasant groups, the primary targets of the most recent and unprecedented political cleansing by the ousted military regime, not only survived their ordeal but gained political strength through steadfastness. This successful experience helped to ensure that the rural poor would not continue to be entirely at the mercy of elites and government officials.[2] The rural majority is now better organized than at any other time in the past and is committed to fighting politically for its rights. In fact, for the first time in Haiti's history, rural Haitians have been freely elected to the national assembly, represent the rural perspective, and reside permanently in rural Haiti.

Accurate data about Haiti's per capita real income must be obtained in order to monitor the country's economic progress. Most human development indicators reflect the inability of Haitians to buy goods and services but not as unambiguously as their wretched real annual per capita incomes indicate. This not to say that indicators other than real per capita income should be ignored. Rather, it suggests that the other indicators are less important in measuring Haiti's current economic situation. Specifically, it is important to know the average purchasing power for Haitians and the variations around that average. It is especially important to know those numbers for rural Haiti, particularly at departmental and sectional levels, numbers that do not now exist.

Strengthening Agriculture

New resources should go primarily to the agricultural sector, which is the driving economic force in the current Haitian economy. This may not be so in fifty years, but today it clearly is the major economic engine that will increase per capita wealth and reduce economic inequality. In addition, much of the urban poor population derives its livelihood from agriculture. The exceptions are those whose incomes depend on manufacturing for export, and who, during the best of economic times in Haiti, have represented only a small proportion of the total Haitian population.

The major focus of this agricultural allocation should be on agricultural extension services, credit, storage, education, health services, marketing cooperatives, and nonwood sources of energy.[3] For the most part, those involved in these agricultural endeavors should reside in rural areas and not be absentee agents of structural change. The focus of attention should be the individual farmer on his or her small plot of land.

Deforestation and Reforestation

The single most important environmental issue in Haiti is deforestation.[4] This serious and ongoing environmental concern has been attributed to numerous factors, and although debate continues about possible solutions, the reversal of this devastating condition must be initiated and sustained. The solution must consider both demand and supply. Use of fuelwood—charcoal and firewood—must be discouraged and its production encouraged through a variety of reforestation programs. Encouraging individual farmers to grow fuelwood on private land as a cash crop as well as large-scale plantings on public lands must be sustained and labor intensive.

Targeting the Poor

The poor who are in most need of assistance must be identified and targeted for specific policies and programs.[5] Targeting regions will not work; more differentiation among groups is needed. For example, merely allocating resources to the general northwest area, supposedly the poorest region in Haiti, without giving careful and serious consideration to the individual recipients' economic conditions will not reduce rural poverty to the extent needed for economic growth.

All poor Haitians, rural as well as urban, should be targeted, and careful attention should be given to their respective economic needs. Targeting these needs should be a means to an economic end and not an end in itself; that is, the overall goal should be to increase the real per capita income of all poor Haitians.

Reverse Migration and Emigration

The migration of many Haitians between rural areas and urban Haiti and their emigration out of Haiti is an ongoing concern.[6] If Haitians are to be encouraged to remain in their rural areas, they need to be convinced that their human capital skills will be used productively near their rural domiciles. They will not leave friends and relatives in the rural areas if they can obtain a reasonable return for their labor. Rural migrants have considerably less human capital than their urban counterparts, yet they have the same economic needs.

Only after the government at least in part succeeds in reversing current trends in emigration and migration should it address concerns related to the diaspora. The attention devoted by the government of Haiti to the diaspora, called Haiti's tenth department, should be quite modest. On the one hand, emigrants' remittance of financial capital is important to individual Haitians, injects some spending into the Haitian economy, and should be encouraged. On the other hand, the flow of human capital into Haiti by the diaspora, though well intentioned, will be limited and temporary at best. For example, the country is in critical need of experienced law enforcement officials for its internal security. The diaspora could be a source of such human capital. However, it is unlikely that enough Kreyòl speakers with the requisite skills exist abroad and could be found. Those few may return to their homeland, but probably for only a short time because they and their families have established new lives abroad to which they will want to return. In short, the diaspora's financial and human capital could be a source of economic growth and stability in Haiti but should not be expected to be an important source.

Role of Markets

Most rural Haitians would agree with western economists on the critical prominence of markets.[7] Convincing the nonpoor, particularly the urban policy-makers, of the efficiency and the decentralization of power brought by free markets is the issue.

Haiti's poor have long been the victims of government monopolies; yet convincing urban officials that monopolies largely do not benefit the poor will be difficult. Few poor Haitians have escaped poverty through state-run enterprises. They generally prefer relying on the private sector rather than on the government. In the immediate future, the poor will want and need help from Adam Smith's invisible hand. In spite of this, they will quickly suspect the visible hand of Port-au-Prince.

The current danger in Haiti is that state-run monopolies will be replaced by private monopolies.[8] If this occurs, Haitians will be forced to continue paying exorbitantly high prices for commodities if single suppliers of these commodities go unregulated. Privatization does not mean replacing a gun-toting monopoly with a mufti-suited monopoly. Despite the nature of the monopolist, the economic effects will be the same. Success in privatization will be in competition and not in a different monopolist. Privatization does not preclude a role for the government in economic reconstruction. However, it must focus on those economic issues, such as road building, that will not be addressed by the non-governmental sector. The government can be a bully pulpit focusing on particular issues, but the vast majority of Haitians are deeply suspicious of the central government even when it is in the hands of benevolent Haitians. The world's movement away from government activism in economic affairs in Haiti and toward individual efforts is inexorable and cannot be overruled or even ignored by Haiti.[9]

Short-Term Reliance on Foreign Aid

Haiti cannot rely on foreign aid indefinitely, but in the near future it will be dependent on international donors, particularly the United States and those agencies to which the United States is a major contributor. How long that dependency will continue is uncertain. A detailed plan for reducing that aid gradually and systematically over the next twenty-five years should be developed. For example, a maximum level of foreign aid, as a percentage of Haiti's GDP, should be negotiated and should decline on average over each five-year period to a predetermined and irrevocable percentage.

Such aid should be directed primarily to the rural poor. Its effectiveness can be measured by increases in the real per capita income of the poor and decreases in national income inequality. If both measures improve over predetermined periods of time, then the percentage reduction in foreign aid could be less. In other words, progress against rural poverty and inequality would be rewarded by smaller reductions in foreign aid.

The aid numbers above should reflect all foreign aid, not only major international aid agencies such as the UN, USAID, and the World Bank. This would include aid provided by NGOs and reflect cash and in-kind donations.

Support from NGOs

Contrary to the perception held by many people, one of Haiti's untold international success stories is the extensive and successful use of NGOs to deliver foreign aid. The recent embargo and Haiti's embrace of NGOs in the early 1980s appears to have benefited Haiti's poor. The contention is that NGOs are closer to those in need and were not corrupted by past governments. Many of these NGOs are affiliated with a particular religious denomination and serve local congregations only. Yet others, such as Catholic Relief Services, have served an entire region. The current existence of an umbrella organization of NGOs in Haiti and a decade of experience with NGOs will make this continued focus easier and even more productive. If more aid flows into Haiti, however, the limits and efficiency of these organizations will be tested. The initial assumption should be that the organizations can handle more aid efficiently and equitably. Additional regional and sectional coordinators will be needed to develop a more decentralized administration. However, any increase in their number should be questioned. Their effectiveness should be corroborated against the aid's contribution to alleviating rural poverty and reducing income inequality.

Roles of Government

Domestic leaders in Haiti and major international donors should initiate discussions on the exact roles of the central and regional governments in alleviating rural poverty, increasing real per capita incomes, and reducing income inequality. Various government levels should only assume those economic responsibilities that businesses and individuals will not or cannot assume. Reforestation of public lands and the restoration and development of rural infrastructures are obvious examples.

Lessons from SINS

There is a growing literature on the unique features and histories of small island nation states (SINS), most of which are located in the Pacific Ocean and Caribbean Sea.[10] Some economists believe that the economic lessons learned from larger, less developed countries often do not apply to these smaller island nations. Although it is too early to tell if economists are correct about SINS' uniqueness, much of what they discover about the economic growth of these islands may prove helpful to those working to bring prosperity to Haiti.

There has been practically no reference to this emerging paradigm in the literature on Haiti. The literature on SINS examines issues such as problems arising from these islands' reliance upon tourism as a panacea to underdevelopment and unique environmental concerns related to the fragile environment of islands. The SINS literature also speaks of the human capital brain-drain among these islands, and even suggests that it may be a net benefit (benefits minus costs) to poor island economies.

The Future

The central premise of this chapter is the overwhelming importance of rural Haiti to the economic future of the entire country. Many would disagree with this premise and suggest that Haiti needs to broaden its focus to prepare for the new world order so as to prevent the continuation of its protracted descent into economic obscurity. What needs developing, they argue, is Haiti's urban infrastructure in order to accommodate the inevitable migration of rural populations to its major cities. In addition, the urban population needs to be organized and trained for the export market that is essential for the hard currency required for economic betterment.

In a generic way, there is some truth to the urban-export arguments, but this strategy did not work in Haiti in the 1970s and early 1980s. Instead, the social and physical infrastructure should be developed in the rural towns that are economically dependent on agriculture. These investments and their related amenities should be used to enhance the human capital of the rural population. Smaller regional towns with existing populations of approximately 5,000 should be provided development assistance. Such a strategy supports the emphasis on alleviating rural poverty through agricultural development. It also will reduce the push of the rural population to Port-au-Prince and create a pull of urban human capital skills back to the countryside.

Meeting the short-term economic needs of Haiti's vast majority is essential if there is to be a successful reconstruction of Haiti's economy. Unless these needs are fulfilled within the next twenty years, the twenty-first century in Haiti will be much worse economically than the twentieth century.

Notes

1. It is often reported that one urban assembly-line job in Haiti supports seven other Haitians, and, by implication, unemployed Haitians. The source of that statistic is unknown, and there are no similar figures for rural jobs. As a result, the implication that urban jobs are more valuable than rural jobs is not verifiable.

2. The cynics will argue that, as in the past, rural leaders will abandon their rural constituencies for their personal benefits. While there is evidence that this occurred in the past (and the rural section chiefs provide the most recent example), the present situation is different. It will most likely take at least one generation to revert to the old way of doing business in Haiti.

3. This does not preclude nonagricultural rural activities. However, it does suggest that such activities strengthen agricultural development rather than act as a focal activity.

4. For a summary of Haiti's deforestation and the mainstay of efforts in the last decade to arrest and reverse it, see Anthony V. Catanese and Robert Perlack, "Reforestation in Haiti," *Canadian Journal of Development Studies*, XIV (1993), 59–72. For an analysis of the effect of environmental degradation on Haiti's poor, see Catanese, "Rural Poverty and Environmental Degradation in Haiti," occasional paper, series on the environment and development, Indiana Center on Global Change and World Peace, Indiana University (November 1991).

5. See Anthony V. Catanese, "Identifying the Poor as a Targeted Population: An Inductive Outcome in Rural Haiti," *Journal of Developing Areas*, XXV (1991), 529–540.

6. For a discussion of the history and possible sources of Haiti's domestic and international population movements, see Anthony V. Catanese, "Haiti's Refugees: Political, Economic, Environmental," *Field Staff Reports,* Universities Field Staff International (1990–1991).

7. For a comprehensive survey of Haiti's markets and monopoly power, see Mats Lundahl, *The Haitian Economy: Man, Land and Markets* (New York, 1983); idem., *Politics or Markets: Essays on Haitian Underdevelopment* (New York, 1992).

8. A survey of rural Haitians about the current furor against privatizing the state monopolies would reveal strong support for ending the monopoly power in the affected sectors. For example, rural Haitians have paid double-digit prices every time they need bags of cement to build a commodity storage facility or improve their homes. They know that competition in the cement industry would be beneficial.

9. For a longer-term historical account of Haiti's role in the world economy, see Alex Dupuy, *Haiti in the World Economy: Class, Race, and Underdevelopment since 1700* (Boulder, 1989).

10. For a survey of this literature, see David McKee and Clem Tisdell, *Developmental Issues in Small Island Economies* (New York, 1990).

CHAPTER ELEVEN

No Longer a Pipe Dream?
Justice in Haiti

William G. O'Neill

AMONG HAITI'S many priorities, reforming the legal system is essential. Court reform, recruiting and training new judges and prosecutors, creating a new civilian police force, revamping Haiti's backward prison system, and investigating past human rights violations are fundamental in the delicate transition from dictatorship to democracy. These reforms must proceed in tandem; if police reform, for example, outpaces legal reform, the police will quickly become demoralized and frustrated and may jettison their training and revert to brutal and illegal behavior. Without any basic changes in the ways in which justice is administered, human rights guarantees will remain fragile and the rule of law a pipe dream.

The Duvalier dictatorships and ensuing military regimes intentionally devastated the Haitian justice system. Haiti's best judges and lawyers joined the growing diaspora and often ended up running the judiciaries of the newly independent francophone African states in the 1960s. Since an independent judiciary and an educated populace pose the greatest threats to dictators, Haiti's Ministries of Justice and Education consistently received the least amount of government funding throughout the Duvalier era. Well into the presidency of René Préval, the Duvaliers' legacy is a compliant, corrupt, and incompetent judiciary and an illiteracy rate of 80 percent. The Haitian people, justifiably, have enormous contempt for a legal system that is anything but just.

199

Even after several years of restored democracy, Haiti's justice system barely functions. Moreover, powerful members of Haitian society and the military, and certain wealthy industrialists and landowners, in particular, have long prevented it from delivering justice. The law has instead been used as a weapon to oppress and terrify.

Haitian justice lacks everything: financial resources, materials, competent personnel, independence, stature, and trust. Court facilities are a disgrace; courthouses often are indistinguishable from small shops or run-down residences in Haitian cities and towns. Judges and prosecutors, ill trained and often chosen because of their connections or willingness to comply with their benefactors' demands, have traditionally dispensed justice to the highest bidder or to the most powerful. Until mid-1995, when some training began, no judge or prosecutor in Haiti had received any specialized professional training. Law schools are woefully inadequate and lack such rudimentary necessities as decent classrooms and law libraries; furthermore, cronyism reigns, professors are ill trained, students are ill prepared, and passing grades are bought and sold. Haiti has three functioning law schools.

In late 1993, after the OAS/UN International Civilian Mission had been evacuated from Haiti to the Dominican Republic, Guy Malary, Haiti's justice minister requested that the mission conduct a thorough nationwide assessment of Haiti's justice system to identify its greatest weaknesses (he was gunned down by a paramilitary death squad soon after).[1]

Mission human rights monitors involved in the investigation included experienced lawyers who had observed trials, pretrial hearings, and police work. Throughout their investigation, the observers presented information and concerns to judges and prosecutors regarding specific human rights violations, including evidence of military responsibility for human rights abuses and inhumane prison conditions. These lawyer-observers inquired about developments in criminal investigations in cases brought to the judiciary's attention by the mission. They regularly met with judges, prosecutors, and defense attorneys and attempted to exert pressure on judicial officials to follow proper procedures and fulfill their duties. These officials were encouraged to visit prisons regularly and hold hearings within forty-eight hours of an arrest. Based on this direct experience, the mission's human rights monitors identified problems that plagued the administration of justice throughout Haiti in 1993 and 1994. Among the most serious were the following.

—The armed forces, including the army, police, rural section chiefs (members of the army charged with policing rural areas), attachés (civilian paramilitaries), and members of the armed paramilitary group *Front pour l'Avancement et le Progrès Haïtien* (FRAPH) threatened, beat, and sometimes killed judges, prosecutors, and lawyers. The most egregious example was the execution in broad daylight of Malary. Port-au-Prince Chief Prosecutor Laraque Exantus, who had been named to the prosecutor's office by Malary, was abducted from his home in early February 1994 and never seen again. Exantus was responsible for several sensitive criminal investigations, including the Malary and Antoine Izmery killings.[2] Other lawyers murdered for their efforts to protect human rights and promote the rule of law include Yves Volel (October 1987), Lafontant Joseph (July 1988), and Jacques Philippe (October 1988). Human rights lawyers Camille Leblanc and Paul Yves Joseph had to either go into hiding or avoid appearing in court during especially tense periods of repression. Wealthy absentee landowners hired soldiers or local enforcers to intimidate judges and lawyers representing peasants involved in land disputes. Judges and prosecutors admitted that they were too afraid to issue arrest warrants or investigate cases involving the military, paramilitary groups, or certain civilian supporters of the military.

—Corruption and extortion thrived at every level of the justice system. The mission investigation revealed that people had paid the police to arrest a rival and that in some instances, prosecutors and judges had demanded payment before opening an investigation or issuing an order. Section chiefs arbitrarily imposed illegal taxes and then threatened to beat or imprison those who refused to pay. Jailers demanded payment before allowing relatives to bring food to a detainee and also extorted money from desperate prisoners to avoid beatings or even worse treatment. Sometimes families paid for a relative's release from prison.

—Most judges and prosecutors were poorly trained and lacked motivation. Many judges, especially the lowest-level *juges de paix* (justices of the peace), had never been to law school, had received no specialized training to be judges, and had shown scant interest in receiving such training. In 1990 the UN Special Expert on Haiti, himself an eminent French jurist, offered to look into training possibilities in Europe for Haitian judges. The head of the Haitian Supreme Court rejected the offer, saying that Haitian judges already knew all that they needed to know to fulfill their duties. A 1995 survey by USAID showed that many justices of the peace did not know how to read or write.

— Courts lacked the most basic materials necessary to function. Most had no electricity or phones. Copy machines, computers, and fax machines were not available. Many judges and prosecutors did not even own the texts essential to their work: the *Civil Code*, the *Code of Criminal Procedure*, and the *Penal Code*. One judge who sat on the Commerce Court did not have a copy of the Commercial Code; when asked how he decided cases, he shrugged and said he did the best he could. Record keeping was in complete disarray, with barely legible orders and decisions on frayed paper, some dating more than ten years back, tacked to courthouse walls and doors.

— Most Haitians viewed with well-deserved scorn and contempt most lawyers, judges, and virtually anyone connected with the justice system. People avoided contact with the system unless it is was their last resort. The courts were expensive, corrupt, and largely mysterious, since all of the laws were written in French and most of the proceedings were conducted in French, a language most Haitians can barely understand and only a wealthy elite can speak or read. Haitians tried to resolve disputes on their own, in some instances in inventive and acceptable ways appropriate to a country with deep poverty and high illiteracy, and in others in deplorable ways best described as vigilante justice.

— The most powerful sectors of Haitian society—the wealthiest families, government officials, and most of all the entire military apparatus—enjoyed virtual impunity. Soldiers were never prosecuted in civilian courts for abuses committed against civilians despite the constitutional requirement that these cases be heard in civil courts.[3] This impunity fueled the cycle of violence and the population's cynicism about Haitian justice.

— Haiti had never had a professional police force. Until January 1995 the police were members of the armed forces who had received no specialized police training. Members were rotated in and out of the police and army; in some cases an officer literally had two uniforms hanging in a closet and would select the appropriate one, police blue or military khaki, depending on the month or the assignment. Haiti's police did not walk the beat, investigate crimes, or carry out other normal policing tasks. Rather, they functioned by beating people, riding in trucks carrying high-caliber weapons and grenades, and shooting first and asking questions later—and then only to interrogate the person about his or her presumed political opinions or activities. The police were for hire by the rich and influential; they also would make arbitrary arrests in response to a wide range of complaints provided by a jealous neighbor, jilted lover, or ambitious farmer who wanted more water from the irrigation canal or a piece of particularly fertile land. The mission's jurists consistently found that law enforcement was intensely political and personal, rarely neutral and objective.

— Although Haitian law stipulated elaborate procedures governing arrests, detention, and prison inspections and monitoring, all of these procedures and protections had been systematically breached. Most arrests were made without a warrant. Based on interviews with hundreds of detainees in most of Haiti's prisons, the mission found that often persons arrested had no idea why they had been detained and that family members often were not notified of their arrests. In many instances, arrests appeared to be abductions; in reality, there is no difference between a warrantless arrest and an abduction. Without a paper trail, those arrested often slipped into the black hole of Haitian detention centers, both official and unofficial. These centers uniformly failed to keep registers required under both Haitian and international law. Unofficial detention centers are illegal; thus prisoners in these centers remained entirely isolated and without any means of contacting the outside world. They could not contact relatives or lawyers, nor could they obtain medical care. During these extended periods of isolation, detainees were at great risk of being beaten, tortured, or killed.

— Conditions in Haitian prisons and detention centers were inhumane and cruel. The prisons, frequently decrepit remnants of garrisons built by the U.S. occupying forces seventy years previously, and with some even dating from the French colonial era, lacked all basic services: electricity, potable water, toilets, and medical supplies. The mission's observers found conditions in the prisons to be particularly deplorable, even considering the fact that the general population in Haiti lived without many of the same necessities. Detainees were kept in overcrowded quarters; most were forced to sleep on the floor unless they could pay for a cot. Women prisoners were not segregated from male prisoners. Sexual abuse was common, and tuberculosis, HIV, and other viral diseases were rampant. Children and adolescents were kept with adults. Haitian law requires a separate facility for youthful offenders, but the law, as with many issues relating to rights, existed purely on paper. A Haitian proverb aptly summarizes the attitude toward the legal system: "Law is paper, bayonets are steel."[4]

The Current Situation

Some of the conditions highlighted in the 1994 mission report have since been addressed by both the Aristide and Préval administrations. Upon his return in October 1994 President Aristide fired the hated rural section chiefs and abolished their positions. The Haitian military was dismantled. Paramilitary death squads and FRAPH have largely gone underground. Unsolved killings persist, most notably the March 1995 murder of Mireille Durocher-Bertin, a lawyer and fervent supporter of the 1981 coup against Aristide. A number of judges and prosecutors have been fired for incompetence or corruption, and USAID has held round-table discussions for judges and prosecutors to provide them with the opportunity to discuss their concerns for the first time in their professional careers.

Teams of U.S. lawyers who were also in the U.S. Army Reserves were deployed, along with the U.S.-led multinational forces, to mentor their Haitian counterparts. Known as *conseillers techniques*, they attempted to make an immediate assessment of the legal system and to provide advice based on that assessment. While their mentoring was severely restricted by their inability to speak French or Kreyòl as well as their lack of knowledge of the Napoleonic civil law system, they conducted a useful survey of the material and logistical needs of the courts and the educational level of justices of the peace.

A judicial academy financed by the U.S. Department of Justice and staffed primarily by Haitian practitioners opened in July 1995 to provide interim training to 120 prosecutors and judges. Numerous Haitian prosecutors received a month's training at France's prestigious judge's academy, the Ecole Nationale de la Magistrature, in Bordeaux in June 1995. Justices of the peace received salary increases, and copies of the basic Haitian legal texts and office materials have been distributed to some courts, although many judges and prosecutors still lack these core tools.

By mid-1996, police practices were somewhat improved. After a rigorous selection process, by February 1996, when Aristide turned over the presidency to René Préval, the new police academy had trained approximately 5,000 cadets of the Haitian National Police (HNP). Unofficial detention centers have closed. After receiving training from Kreyòl-speaking French prison experts, 480 interim prison guards and administrators began trying to improve treatment of prisoners.

The Ministry of Justice, with assistance from the OAS/UN International Civilian Mission and the UN Development Program, has provided each prison with a prison registry. A senior prison administrator from the French penitentiary service arrived in August 1995 to oversee training of permanent prison personnel, the upkeep of prison registers, and overall penal reform. The International Committee of the Red Cross began working with the Haitian Ministry of Public Works to rehabilitate seven prisons by fumigating cells, digging water and sewer lines, and installing toilets and showers. A European NGO provided food to prisons until late summer 1995, when the Haitian civilian prison authority took over this task.

In 1995 and 1996 reports of mistreatment of prisoners dramatically decreased. Although several provincial prisons still were slow to segregate prisoners according to age and gender, women and children were separated from adult males in the national penitentiary in Port-au- Prince and moved to Fort National. Despite these improvements, several children under the age of thirteen were reportedly beaten while in detention in June 1995. In December 1995 a dozen prisoners in Port-au-Princes's national penitentiary died from beriberi, a disease caused by a rice diet deficient in vitamin B-1.

Serious problems that remain in the administration of justice, however, continued in 1995 and 1996 to erode the population's patience and undermine their confidence. In March 1995 the OAS/UN Mission reported dozens of summary executions of suspected thieves by angry crowds, especially in or near the principal outdoor markets in Port-au-Prince. The reason most often cited was that the people had no faith that the alleged thieves would be punished under the judicial system, so the population took justice into its own hands. The mission noted a decrease in summary killings during the following few months but an increase in July.

The newly created and trained HNP used deadly force in questionable circumstances in which more moderate responses have been warranted. The police have killed at least a dozen unarmed civilians in Cité Soleil, Cap Haïtien, and Gonaïves. A three-year-old girl was killed by a ricocheting bullet when the police fired at a fleeing robbery suspect. Many members of the HNP have also kept their weapons when off duty, a violation of police rules, and some refuse to wear uniforms. In 1996 there was still a severe dearth of command-level officers with adequate training and management skills.

In many districts, courts still barely function. In many outlying areas, courts are usually closed after noon; frequently they do not open at all.

A severe lack of funds for basic materials and travel continued to hinder the effectiveness of courts throughout the country. Judges often ask complainants to pay for the issue of various judicial orders so as to cover the costs of the paper on which they are written. Other less scrupulous judges have been known to charge for their services in order to supplement their incomes. Some judges cannot afford to buy even a bicycle to ride to work; others must rely on public transportation to cover several districts.

Arrest warrants are frequently issued on the basis of flimsy accusations and are often exceedingly vague. And despite the fact that collective warrants are illegal under Haitian law, they have been issued. In one notorious case in March 1995, the assistant prosecutor for Port-au-Prince issued a single warrant for twelve individuals, alleging terrorist acts as part of a plot to overthrow the government. The warrant contained no details—no specific offenses, dates, or place—nor did it identify which sections of the penal code had been violated.

In August 1995 the OAS/UN Mission issued a press release expressing its concern about Haiti's ongoing failure to follow prescribed legal procedures, thus undermining respect for human rights. The mission urged the Justice Ministry to guarantee due process rights, including the presumption of innocence and the right to a speedy trial before a competent, impartial, and independent tribunal. Despite these efforts, arrest warrants continue to be issued by officials who did not have the requisite legal authority to do so.[5]

Some judges, especially in northern Haiti, refused to issue arrest warrants against reputed members of the paramilitary, the infamous attachés, and former members of the Haitian military, fearing retribution once the international military and police presence end. One judge refused to investigate charges of brutality, including rape, brought against four Haitian soldiers. Despite the fact that the judge knew that under article 267-3 of the 1987 Haitian constitution, civil courts had jurisdiction over members of the military in cases involving alleged acts of violence against civilians, he argued that they did not. His argument merely demonstrates the level of fear that the Haitian military and paramilitary forces still exert over the judiciary in some parts of the country. The people who brought the case to court and the judge who held the initial hearing felt especially threatened and vulnerable. One stated: "We feel that if the situation is ever reversed, we'll be very easy, very public targets of the military." Another questioned, "Should the people take justice into their own hands?" Thus the frustration with the legal system and the impetus to vigilante justice that may result.[6]

The constitutional requirement that every detainee be brought before a judge within forty-eight hours of arrest to determine the legality of the arrest and detention continued to be violated, but much less frequently than under military rule. Delays stem primarily from the unwillingness of some judges to work, poor record keeping in the prisons, and the lack of vehicles to transport detainees to courts or judges to prisons. Whatever the reason, in 1996 detainees' rights were violated. Prisoners rioted in the National Penitentiary on two different occasions in early 1995, in part because many did not know why they had been arrested and many had not been arraigned within forty-eight hours of their arrest. Few persons in Haitian prisons have actually been convicted of crimes; most await charges or trial. Judges compound the overcrowding by sentencing debtors to prison, in violation of international law binding on Haiti.[7]

Public outcry or denunciation (*clameur publique*) still substitutes for criminal investigations and rigorous proof that the accused are criminally responsible. Denunciations, not hard evidence, are frequently the basis for issuing arrest warrants and findings of guilt. Observers from the National Coalition for Haitian Rights monitored a July 1995 criminal court session in Mirebalais where a murder trial had resulted in two convictions based solely on the testimony of the victim's relatives and on public denunciations. The police presented no evidence gathered through investigation.

The absence of a viable police force marks wide swaths of rural Haiti and has a debilitating effect on the legal system. One judge in the northern town of Milot told an international investigator in December 1994, "It's very difficult for the court to function normally. We open the doors of the court, but we don't really function." Another judge in late 1994 in nearby Terrier Rouge noted, "the justice system has come to a halt. We have no one to serve warrants and no way to convoke people before the court. Without any police there is no way to prevent, solve, or prosecute crimes."

Corruption continues to flourish. A field report from the U.S. embassy dated summer 1995 noted that the UN International Police stationed in the southwestern city of Jérémie stated that "local law and practice make it possible for people to convince/bribe some local magistrates to issue arrest warrants for frequently trivial reasons."[8]

Préval's Tasks

Deep structural weaknesses in a justice system cannot be erased overnight. Equally daunting is the challenge of creating a culture of human rights and rule of law in a country that has experienced violence and ruthless authority for so many years. In this period of transition from military dictatorship to democracy, reforms to the Haitian justice system are urgently required. To show that the government intends to break with the past, President Préval's government needs to implement a number of reforms.

The competence and independence of all currently serving prosecutors (the *commissaires du gouvernement*) should be determined. Those deemed unfit to serve should be replaced by recent graduates of Haiti's law schools. New prosecutors should undergo intensive training in the rudiments of criminal investigation and procedure, preferably taught by experienced Haitian lawyers and prosecutors brought from France or other civil-law countries (especially the Kreyòl- speaking French Caribbean territories of Martinique, Guadeloupe, and French Guyana). Curriculum and lesson plans should reflect Haiti's French-based Napoleonic system and take into account the needs of an exceedingly poor, largely illiterate population. International human rights law should be a central component of this training. In addition, specialized expertise available through the UN Division on Crime Prevention and Criminal Justice in Vienna should be sought.

All judges should receive expedited training, preferably from senior Haitian judges. French judges, especially those from the French Caribbean regions, should be encouraged to participate in this training. Training should be provided initially to the justices of the peace, who have by far the most frequent contact with the Haitian population and the least amount of training, and are therefore the most ill equipped for their work. Investigating judges and senior trial and appellate court judges should receive retraining as well. International human rights law should be a central component of this instruction, and relevant expertise should be sought from the UN Human Rights Centre in Geneva, the Division on Crime Prevention and Criminal Justice in Vienna, and the International Commission of Jurists.

Training should take place both at the Ecole de la Magistrature and at the work place. On-the-job training and oversight are essential. Regional seminars for all judicial personnel should be held regularly outside Port-au-Prince to foster collegiality, lessen professional isolation, and provide a crucial forum for airing problems and grievances so that local solutions can be found to local problems.

Salaries should be raised for all judicial officials, including court clerks and bailiffs, to a level commensurate with their education and experience. These officials should be paid regularly and on time.

The government should seek assistance and advice from the UN Development Program, USAID, and other bilateral donors, to improve the Justice Ministry's capacity to manage the courts. Personnel in the Justice Ministry should receive training in modern management and administration, document preservation and retrieval, and personnel management issues. Training in case management and administration, including delegating responsibility, establishing effective channels of communication, and evaluating projects is urgently needed within the Ministry of Justice.

International donors should provide equipment and the supplies necessary to run a court system properly, including copies of the basic legal codes for all judges and prosecutors, pens, paper, legal forms, file cabinets, office furniture, copy machines, fax machines, computers, and vehicles. There must be a balance between efforts to improve the human capacity of the judicial system and improving its physical infrastructure. Judges and prosecutors who have completed weeks of training cannot be expected to maintain a high degree of motivation if they must return to inadequate facilities. Funds to pay salaries on an emergency basis to prosecutors, judges, and Justice Ministry officials should be allocated so that the system can function and Haitians can see that its government is committed to reforming and reinforcing justice.

All police officers should receive additional training regarding the appropriate use of force and firearms. Particular attention should be given to procedures involved in using the minimal amount of force necessary to maintain order or make an arrest. Training in crowd control techniques, mediation, and conflict resolution is also urgently needed. The police inspector general must investigate and punish any breach of discipline and refer to the courts any act that violates Haitian or international law, especially the illegal use of force. Disciplinary proceedings and court hearings on police misconduct must be open to the public in order to reassure Haitians that the police are not above the law, and to send an unequivocal message to the HNP that violating rules will not be tolerated.

Permanent prison personnel—guards, administrators, and inspectors—should be hired and receive accelerated training in effective prison administration. A census of all prisons must be completed, and all unofficial detention centers must remain closed. Ongoing training in maintaining prison registries properly must be provided so that the justice system can readily determine the identity of each prisoner, the reasons for incarceration, the date of entry, and current judicial status. All children in Haitian prisons should be released immediately and appropriate supervised shelter should be found for them. The International Committee of the Red Cross and other agencies with relevant expertise should be sought to train prison personnel to help the Association Penale Nationale (APENA), the new Haitian civilian penal authority, establish monitoring mechanisms and provide necessities such as drinking water, latrines, food, and medicine. APENA should vigorously and publicly investigate all charges of mistreatment of prisoners.

Effective leadership in the police force has become a major problem for the HNP. Recent figures show that only 43 of 185 departmental director and commander positions have been filled. In many areas, recently graduated police cadets are deployed without commanding officers to supervise and provide guidance. Many police commanders have received little formal training, and this has undermined authority, discipline, morale, and professionalism.

Moreover, it is unclear what if any criteria are used to choose police commanders. Criteria for command positions must be based on relevant experience and a record demonstrating honesty, leadership capacity, and respect for human rights. Former members of the Haitian army must submit to an especially rigorous screening process to exclude those who participated in human rights violations and to ensure that they receive extensive training in civilian police practices and respect for human rights.

Haitian human rights organizations began participating in human rights training at the police academy at the end of 1995. The police academy faculty and the International Criminal Investigative, Training and Assistance Program (ICITAP) should intensify their relationships with the Haitian human rights community and request that they participate formally in the human rights portion of the academy's training. Police recruits should establish a dialogue with Haitian human rights advocates: Members of the human rights community need to meet the recruits and observe how they are being trained for the nation's new and perhaps only armed force. Encouraging discussions between these two groups as soon as possible is the most effective way of improving relations between them and of dispelling the pervasive feelings of fear and distrust, stemming from years of brutal police behavior, of the general population.

The government should launch a public education campaign on human rights and justice that would inform people about the steps being undertaken to reform and revitalize justice in Haiti. Improving community-police relations should be a core theme; neither the HNP nor the Haitian population has had any experience with ways in which the police can work effectively and appropriately within the community. All media should be used to help forge these important ties, especially radio. The government should consult and work in close collaboration with Haitian human rights organizations. The UN Human Rights Centre should be called upon to offer its expertise in human rights education. The OAS/UN International Civilian Mission should also contribute its expertise and extensive human rights documentation to all public education campaigns.

Medium-Term Action

Haiti's Commission on Legal Code Reform should begin work as soon as possible to revise and modernize Haitian legal texts. This commission should consult with Haitian jurists, legal scholars, and practitioners from France and other civil-law countries. The commission should eliminate all code articles that conflict with the Haitian constitution and international human rights treaties ratified by Haiti, and issue comprehensive new codes that will reflect current Haitian law and eliminate obsolete provisions. One example involves soldiers who have claimed the defense of "acting under a superior's orders," as defined in article 272 of the Penal Code, when civilians have accused them of committing human right abuses. While this article has been superseded by the 1987 constitution, the Penal Code has not yet reflected this change.[9] The Criminal Procedure Code should be revised to clarify responsibility for criminal investigations and to establish time limits for prosecutors and investigating judges to complete investigations and write their reports. Penalties should be imposed for failing to meet these obligations.

All laws should be translated into Kreyòl, and court proceedings should be conducted in Kreyòl if any of the parties so request.

The government should establish a national system of free legal aid to represent defendants in cases involving serious felonies. This system could also permit people accused of less serious offenses to be represented by paralegals and law students before the justices of the peace.

Codes of professional conduct governing lawyers, judges, and prosecutors should be drafted and adopted; disciplinary procedures with full due process guarantees should be established to determine if someone has violated the code of conduct.

Law schools should be provided with resources. Classrooms are in a deplorable state. Professors must receive an appropriate salary. Uniform standards for graduation and admission to practice need to be established and enforced.

The government must create new judgeships, especially at the level of justice of the peace. Port-au-Prince has only four justice of the peace courts for a population of at least 1 million; other jurisdictions suffer proportionately similar shortages. More investigating judges, who are responsible for investigating serious crimes, are also needed in every jurisdiction.

Criminal court sessions must be held throughout the year, not just twice yearly for brief periods as the law currently prescribes. Under the present system, detainees wait months, sometimes years, before they go to trial.

The Ministry of Justice must create a juvenile court to hear matters involving minors. Homes for juvenile offenders that provide counseling, rehabilitation, and training and education programs should be established.

The government should encourage the creation of alternative dispute resolution mechanisms that avoid the expense and delay of formal litigation. Arbitration, mediation, and counseling services could help resolve many disputes. These services would be appropriate in an impoverished country where most people cannot afford a lawyer and most lawyers work in the cities.

USAID has taken a leading role in judicial reform in Haiti, to the consternation of some observers. The agency has awarded an $18 million administration of justice project to Checchi, a U.S. consulting firm. This six-year project was started in October 1995 and covers virtually every aspect of legal reform: equipment procurement, training, publication of codes, public education, legal services for the poor, case management and administrative improvements in the Justice Ministry and the courts, and mentoring programs for judges and prosecutors. The program was designed to employ an array of subcontractors, mostly from the United States. While the project is comprehensive, many observers are concerned that the vast differences between the U.S. common law system and the Haitian civil law system argue against a U.S.- dominated approach to legal reform. What is required is extensive participation of experts from countries that share Haiti's civil law traditions and jurisprudence, especially French- and Kreyòl- speakers from France, the French Caribbean, and francophone Africa and Canada. For example, the Canadian Ministry of Justice has conducted extensive judicial training in francophone Africa. The Canadians have developed lesson plans and role-playing and group exercises—even videotaped mock trials—for their judges and prosecutor training. African countries also inherited the French legal system and are largely poor and illiterate. Kreyòl-speakers from the French Caribbean share more than just a language with their Haitian peers; they also have close historical and cultural ties and are only an hour away by plane.

Another essential element to any successful legal reform project is close consultation and collaboration with Haitian jurists and human rights organizations, which has not happened. Several leading Haitian lawyers and human rights advocates have complained that the Checchi/USAID project has ignored their advice and recommendations.

Legal reform must also incorporate the views and elicit the participation of Haitian human rights and other non-governmental organizations. A "top-down" approach imposed by self-proclaimed "experts" is doomed to fail.

Another concern is the reluctance of some international donors to fund improvements to the infrastructure of the legal system. The Justice Ministry's appeal in 1995 for money to refurbish courthouses, install telephone lines, obtain essential and inexpensive basic office equipment, and purchase vehicles so that judges and prosecutors can investigate crimes was contemptuously dismissed by some donors as "bricks and mortar." Fortunately, the Canadian government agreed in May 1996 to rehabilitate all fourteen civil court tribunals in the provinces.

Conclusion

The intervention by the U.S.-led multinational armed forces under U.N. Security Council Resolution 940 (July 31, 1994) broke the back of the military's dominance of law enforcement and the administration of justice. The opportunity to effect sweeping changes to a decrepit and despised judicial system was never greater or more necessary. While the reforms recommended above are necessary to erect the rule of law in Haiti, they are not sufficient. Haitians must permanently eradicate outside interference in the courts, the police, and the prisons. Implementing these reforms will help Haitians succeed in their struggle to create the rule of law.

Notes

1. See Working Group on the Haitian Justice System of the OAS/UN International Civilian Mission in Haiti, *Analysis of the Haitian Justice System with Recommendations to Improve the Administration of Justice in Haiti,* March 17, 1994.

2. Aristide supporter Antoine Izmery (September 1993) and priest and human rights advocate Father Jean-Marie Vincent (August 1994) were, along with Minister Malary, among the most prominent of the untold number of Haitians murdered during the military regime.

3. Recent exceptions, which occurred well after the mission's 1994 report, were the convictions in absentia of a Haitian military officer and a sergeant in July and August 1995 for the death of Jean-Claude Museau in 1992 after he was arrested and tortured by the military. The officer had been detained before the trial but mysteriously escaped, thereby reinforcing doubts about the validity of the process. Former police chief Michel François was convicted along with several other police officers in absentia in September 1995 for the September 1993 assassination of Antoine Izmery.

4. For an extensive analysis of the Haitian justice system, which identified many of the same problems highlighted by the OAS/UN Working Group on the Haitian Justice System, see William G. O'Neill and Elliot Schrage, *Paper Laws, Steel Bayonets: The Breakdown of the Justice System in Haiti* (New York, 1990).

5. Under Haitian law, with one limited exception, only an investigating judge has the authority to issue an arrest warrant. Yet according to information provided by the OAS/UN mission, justices of the peace, mayors, and prosecutors continue to issue these warrants. See OAS/UN International Civilian Mission in Haiti, "Communiqué de Presse" (CP/95/12), August 16, 1995.

6 Interviewees, who requested anonymity, reported via a third party to the author.

7. See *International Covenant on Civil and Political Rights,* article 11; *American Convention on Human Rights,* article 7(7).

8. "Haiti's Second Free Elections, Haiti Field Reports," Foreign Service Officers' report for U.S. embassy, Port-au-Prince, spring and summer 1995, at Haiti field reports 1.

9. Article 27-1 of the 1987 constitution states, "officials and employees of the state are directly responsible under the Penal, Administrative and Civil Codes for their acts that violate rights."

CHAPTER TWELVE

Haitian Education under Siege: Democratization, National Development, and Social Reconstruction

Marc E. Prou

HAITI IS the poorest country in the Western Hemisphere and has a history of abject poverty. It has one of the highest rates of infant mortality in the world.[1] It is also a country with a significantly uneven distribution of wealth, with only a few people controlling a vast amount of the country's wealth and resources. These are some of the symptoms that reveal the Haitian elite's severe myopia. As Segal succinctly puts it: "Elite attitudes and behavior, while not uniform, do constitute a significant factor in what is wrong in Haiti. Changing those attitudes will be extremely difficult, although there are precedents from Jamaica, Barbados, and Africa."[2]

The economic and political plight of Haiti has become widely known in the international community during the past decade. With the overthrow of the two Duvalier regimes in 1986, followed by the 1990 election of President Jean Bertrand Aristide, the subsequent military coup d'état in 1991 overthrowing the popularly elected government and its unequivocal restoration in 1994, the UN special mission dealing with the crisis in Haiti brought this home vividly. Unfortunately, however, talk is easier than action. This is also true of educational priorities for democratization and development.

Education occupies a very important place in the national development of most countries, whether they are developed, underdeveloped, or undeveloped. As Giddens reminds us, "the possession of recognized 'skills'—including educational qualifications—is the major factor influencing the market economy."[3] Haiti suffers from high illiteracy (estimated at 75 percent of the total population), which indicates the sociopolitical nature of the limited role of education in the process of democratization. Because of widespread abject poverty in Haiti, education is often regarded as the only mechanism by which economic conditions can be improved. The Haitian elite look upon schooling as the key to social mobility while maintaining the status quo. It is therefore not surprising that one of the most fervently pursued goals of many Haitian families is to enroll their children in European and North American universities in pursuit of higher learning.[4]

In theory, education is accessible to every Haitian, but in practice, educational opportunities are extremely limited for over 70 percent of the population. It is not surprising that under these conditions there exists a wide disparity between rural schooling in Haiti and urban public and private schooling. For instance, in 1980 the Ministry of Education reported that there were 935 public schools and 2,031 private primary schools in Haiti. Private schools represent over 70 percent of that proportion today and, according to the Ministry of Education, 75 percent of primary schools in Haiti are private.[5]

Haiti's educational priorities must be addressed in the context of other pressing national concerns. Many educational priorities influence the process of democratization and national development; however, problems related to population growth, food and agricultural shortages, poor economic growth, and the need for improved economic management are the core of Haiti's crisis. In other words, restructuring Haiti's educational system involves far more than merely reforming its schools; it involves the total environment of society. Development priorities and the role of education within these initiatives must be examined if there is to be any overall economic progress in Haiti. Haiti's problems of deforestation, high population growth, and decline in food production can be tackled only by improving human resource development, establishing educational priorities, and guiding foreign assistance to specific areas.

Haitian Educational System

Education in Haiti, faced with numerous social, political, economic, and technical problems, is dominated by a high illiteracy rate and high rate of attrition. These problems have been attributed to Haiti's economic underdevelopment; its lack of adequate educational facilities, trained professionals, materials, and supplies; and other factors such as language differences, culture, and administrative mismanagement.[6] Haitians lack pedagogical training for both teaching and administrative personnel. Classes are oversubscribed, having an average student-teacher ratio of 80:1. The content of the curriculum as well as the antiquated teaching methodologies are incompatible with the sociocultural realities and the unresolved problems associated with the Kreyòl-French barrier. Haitian education has become a prominent arena for the country's cultural and linguistic power struggle to play out. Education in Haiti also serves as a tool that the elite can use to maintain social stratification.[7] Because of exclusionary practices that the elite intend to maintain at all costs, unless the state government intervenes, few school-age children have access to quality learning, the only road to prosperity.

Two critical developments within the Haitian educational system during the last twenty years include the tremendous growth in the number of children of school age and a significant increase in the number of private schools at all levels. The increase in the migration of poor populations from rural to urban areas has swollen the urban student population in both public and private schools. This increase in school population exacerbates the social and economic cleavages between the poor and the elite in cities, which in turn magnifies similar divisions within urban schools.[8]

Haiti's educational system has always reflected the sociopolitical realities of Haitian life in their starkest forms. The Haitian educational system has long invited searing criticism: De Regt has concluded that

> the stakes are high. Education is crucial for the development of Haiti. Haiti, now in the midst of an economic recession, looks towards the expansion of the industrial sector to promote economic growth. Industry will need workers at the skilled-worker and managerial levels. In agriculture, the largest sector, the workers need to be able to understand simple recommendations on cultivation practices and erosion control.[9]

On the other hand, Locher has observed that "the public school system in Haiti is run by individuals whose personal interest does not lie in expanding and improving that public system but rather in improving their own working conditions within that system."[10]

Haiti's educational system suffers from a lack of both economic support and human capital formation. Human capital formation is a sine qua non for economic growth and expansion of education, yet too many people in Haiti lack the willingness, responsibility, and commitment necessary to bring about badly needed changes.

Both De Regt and Locher accurately reflect crucial concerns facing Haiti's educational system as the country undergoes a transition to democracy. Only through a greatly improved educational system can Haiti strengthen its human capital formation enough to promote economic growth, yet improvements in education depend on significant economic support as well as a strong commitment on the part of many people. Thus education, socioeconomic development, and democratization are inextricably linked.

From a national development perspective, the Haitian educational system presents an alarming picture. It is one in which too much is expected of too little, and in which results are sacrificed to bureaucratic convenience. The facts are simple and irrefutable. Only a massive investment in human capital formation will bring economic and social progress in Haiti. Yet economic growth and industrial expansion rely on education as a key factor for human capital formation. The major dichotomy between the two is that education can influence national development only to the extent that individuals are able to put the interests of the nation ahead of their personal interests.

This chapter focuses on the role of education in Haiti's human capital formation and the problematic relationships between national development and democratization that impede the schooling system. It analyzes the implicit and explicit purpose of the elitist quality of Haitian schooling. It also provides an analytical framework from which an increased understanding of the problems of schooling, national development, and democratization in Haiti can be conceptualized.

Haitian Education under Siege

The Haitian educational system is moribund. It is beyond reformation, renewal, or restructuring. Joseph C. Bernard, former education minister, designated the 1980s as the decade of educational reform; debate continues, however, about the success of educational initiatives during that period.[11] In late 1994 at a colloquium in New York, Charles Tardieu, former minister of education, introduced the Education 2004 Plan, which called for major educational improvements. Although both educational reforms present some radical initiatives such as the decentralization of the system and its management, the use of Kreyòl, and a greater state role in school finance, they are not well received by all segments of the population. The general implementation of these reforms has faced a political battle. Nowhere has the discourse of crisis in the Haitian educational system been more strident than the Presidential Palace and the Ministry of Education in Haiti.

Despite universal agreement that Haiti's educational system is indeed still in a crisis, no consensus on Haitian educational priorities can be easily reached among the various constituents. There are too many conflicting priorities, too many conflicting interests and political decisions, and too many financial limitations to arrive at easy solutions. However, five educational priorities are generally agreed upon by policy-makers in Haiti: expansion of basic education for youths and adults; improvements in the quality of education; expansion of technical and vocational education; improvements in the quality and relevance of university education (public and private); improved management in education. While many Haitians recognize that combating drought, erosion, and deforestation and promoting food and agricultural development may be more important priorities than educational reform, economic priorities and educational priorities need not be different. The essential point is that education plays a major role in all areas of development, and democratization is crucial for social reconstruction.

If the literature on Haitian schooling were simply books and articles or analysis by a few academics on a subject of passing interest, we could afford to discuss them on their technical merits alone. But the most important of the literature on Haitian schooling is not written by academics. Much of the writings are position statements by syndicated columnists that influence both academic and nonacademic thought and in turn affect the thinking of donor countries and foreign countries offering assistance to Haitian education. Sometimes, they give important clues to the kinds of reforms that will be taking place in the Haitian schooling system.

Over the years, foreign governments and international agencies have recommended widespread educational changes. The Haitian societal structure affects not only the nature of education but also that of the institution of schooling. Once solidly entrenched in the society, the educational system is crucial to economic and social formation. Haiti needs to develop a strategy for working within the educational system to help create social and economic change. As Macedo has noted,

> the notion of educational transformation involves the democratization of the pedagogical and educational power so that students, staff, teacher, educational specialists, and parents come together to develop a plan that is grassroots generated, accepting the tension and contradictions that are always present in all participatory efforts, thereby searching for a democratic substantivity.[12]

Haiti's educational structure is deeply rooted in the traditions, values, and political history of the culture.

Schooling, Development, and Democratization

The Haitian educational system has had a significant impact on national development and democratization. In recent years, a sudden profusion of literature has emerged that has attempted to address the relationship between education and national development. De Regt found that the limitations of basic education in Haiti had multiple causes, consequences, and constraints that directly influenced national development.[13] Fleischmann has questioned whether language and literacy had an impact on the social underdevelopment of Haiti.[14] Latortue has suggested that the effects of the language problem are so pernicious in promoting inequity in Haitian society that a symbiosis between schooling and language is a prerequisite for economic and social development.[15] More recently, Pamphile has argued that school policies in Haiti during the U.S. occupation (1915–1934) had little effect on school attainments and economic development, social mobility, and political stability.[16]

One of the latest entries in the debate on the role of education in national development and democratization was Rodrigue Jean, *Haiti: Crise de l'Éducation et Crise du Développement.* Jean furthered the debate about the role of education in national development and democratization in Haiti. Most of his observations and recommendations still hold true. He suggested that Haiti's educational crisis was caused by two conditions. He assumed that because social and economic aspirations were unfulfilled, a higher average education implied a greater propensity for radical change. He also assumed that in general the educational crisis in Haiti was rooted in the country's historic underdevelopment, which had permitted the transformation of the economy, polity, and culture to conform with France's educational standards while negating Haitian realities.

Using inadequate comparative data, Jean attempted to analyze the dichotomy between the role of schooling in democratization and the distinction between democratization and national development. He stated:

> From the above statistical analysis, it appears that, although it has been formally recognized that every Haitian is entitled to compulsory and free education, the Haitian school system provides access only to a minority group composed predominantly of males and urban dwellers. In other words, the school system blocks access to education by discriminating in the selection process and excluding potential applicants.[17]

According to Jean, Haiti underwent rapid demographic, social, political, and economic change after 1946. The educational system also changed rapidly, but not as rapidly as other aspects of Haitian culture. This insufficient change ultimately led to greater disparities between the educational system and the nation's other cultural institutions.

Jean noted four especially important causes of the disparities, which resulted in

—a very high concentration of the school population in the west (31.5 percent of the primary school students and 65 percent of the secondary school population).

—the predominance of the private sector (57 percent of the primary school and 83 percent of the secondary school student population).

—very low school attendance in the rural areas (in 1982, five children out of ten attended school).

—the progressive elimination of women and rural dwellers in successively higher grades in the educational system.[18]

According to Jean's analysis, Haitian schools (public and private) had become significant obstacles to economic mobility and democratic political schooling rather than fulfilling the historical mission of facilitating a process of social mobility. In fact, the schools in Haiti had fallen under the control of the Haitian middle class, which had failed to use them to help others gain access into that class. The middle class might even have used the schools to block further upward mobility within the class structure. If Haiti does not undergo significant changes in both its economy and its educational system, the growing disparity between education and society will inevitably crack the frame of the Haitian educational system and create fissures in the frame of Haitian society.

Mintz (and Jean) believed that "Haiti's current crisis is historical. Even while conceding the very real importance of scanty resources, dilapidated infrastructure, and popular exhaustion, the forces that have helped keep Haiti immobilized (if not immobile) were in place soon after independence."[19]

On the other hand, the country was far from satisfying its future needs for skilled labor; thus an expansion of the Haitian educational system was necessary but not sufficient for a sustained level of economic development. In effect, Mintz warned that "unless there is to be some investment in Haiti's human capital, real change will prove impossible."[20]

Jean suggested that primary consideration should be given to increasing economic output, so that every Haitian eventually could prosper.[21] The impending crisis could be avoided through increasing the economic growth rate, and all schooling initiatives should be aimed toward that objective. He did not believe that Haiti was in trouble because of unequal distribution of income. On the contrary, he ignored the elimination of social inequality as an important social and political objective. This viewpoint was consistent with a belief in linear, evolutionary development. Jean believed, hence, that both at the national and departmental levels improved equal access to resources could and should best be achieved through economic growth and political persuasion and cooperation rather than through radical structural change.

For Jean, the principal problems of Haitian education stemmed from the inefficiency of its management and the inadequacy and irrelevance of its teaching techniques. He determined that the Haitian schooling system was inefficient because the curriculum was not relevant to the reality of the country and the needs of the majority of Haitians. Currently, the curriculum heavily emphasizes the humanities, while more technicians and agronomists are needed. Within this framework, he stressed the importance of the relationships among the rural mass of uneducated Haitians, the labor force, and the educational system. He argued cogently that Haitian civil society had to provide many more resources for schooling than in the past because of its increasing population, increased per pupil expenditures, and increase in levels of schooling demanded by the average Haitian family for its children.[22]

Most of Jean's recommendations regarding educational reforms needed in Haiti are still relevant. His remedies include a combination of technology, informal training aid, and national will so that every Haitian would achieve a level of learning sufficient to enhance the nation's socioeconomic development.[23] Internal reform of the Haitian educational system also has to take place simultaneously. The curriculum must be changed to meet the needs of a changing nation; Haitians need to be educated for jobs that exist or will exist in the near future. Both private and public schools must be run more efficiently; they must employ improved teaching techniques, include more evaluation, and permit more freedom for teachers and students. Other institutions in Haitian society have to change as well. The bureaucracy must be more flexible and willing to receive ideas in order to build consensus among all sectors of Haitian society. The Haitian traditional economy has to be converted to a modern one by encouraging the private sector to fully participate in the formation of new cadres that in turn will be prepared to assist in national development.

The 1805 Haitian constitution stressed education for all citizens. In fact, education according to the constitution has been expected to be "free and compulsory."[24] The Haitian constitution of 1987 also stipulates free and compulsory education for all Haitians. Its implicit assumptions are clear: All school facilities and teacher characteristics are assumed to have equal effects on all students; the distribution of resource inputs at the school levels is independent of student characteristics. But if schooling in Haiti has been considered free and compulsory, more and more privatization of the schooling system at all levels has shattered the spirit of the constitution.

An increasing number of policy planners and decision-makers in Haiti believe that investment in public education by the government has been a waste of time, energy and money. These individuals claim that the Haitian government has too much to say regarding how the schools are run and often cite examples of the lack of autonomy at the national university to support their position. However, too many of these critics refuse to acknowledge the positive role of public education in a democratic society. It provides opportunities, innovations, and information to large segments of the population that the private sector cannot reach. While these policy-makers claim that national examination scores of public school students have stagnated, they fail to realize that no administration of this nation state ever promised higher national exam scores. More recently, under Aristide, the government, through a series of national and international colloquia, promised to increase the opportunities and academic standards necessary to enable the schools to face the challenges of the year 2004 and beyond.

The current discourse in Haitian economic circles tends to use the term *democratization* synonymously with *privatization,* where foreign assistance to the Haitian state for education, health, and the environment will be handed over to the private sector. It is a siren song of easy money to the non-governmental organizations with no string attached. Doing so would prove disastrous in the long run. In fact, democratization cannot and should not be equated with privatization. As Macedo has explained:

> A democratic society that gives up its public responsibility is a democracy in crisis. A society that equates for-profit privatization with democracy is a society with confused priorities. A democratic society that falsely believes, in view of the S&L debacle and the Wall Street scandals, for example, that quality, productivity, honesty and efficiency can be achieved only through for-profit privatization is a society characterized by a bankruptcy of ideas.[25]

In fact, as Cieutat has pointed out, if foreign assistance for education continues to be channeled to the private schools only—effectively depriving the public schools of any resources—the neediest children, whom the government wanted to help in the first place, would become the wretched of the system once again.[26]

Furthermore, Jean made a good case for democratization in Haitian education. The Haitian government may have to offer higher wages to civil servants and provide greater educational opportunities to all of its citizens. Therefore, education equality should be undertaken only as a means of achieving democratization, which is necessary for maintaining political stability. In referring to democratization of the Haitian school system, Jean described the process as follows:

> Democratization first implies the generalization of education (regardless of social environment and location, all Haitians must have access to knowledge and culture); democratization also implies respect for diversity; it excludes elitism, not the existence of an elite. An elite will always be necessary, but it should be recruited on the basis of each person's initial potential. The selection process should be replaced by an orientation process which, as a polyvalent structure allowing for horizontal as well as upward mobility, will allow everyone the opportunity of a second chance, rather than being eliminated from the system, and to participate in society as a competent active citizen.[27]

He was concerned not only with the best and the brightest students; he was concerned with the disadvantaged, the dispossessed, and the discouraged as well. He recognized that all students were critical to Haiti's future. Jean did not reject equality as a secondary objective of Haitian society, but he did not treat it as the possible basis for more efficient schooling practices. His belief was that equity and excellence should be the basic elements of a democratization process.

In fact, equity and excellence are not just educational problems. They are undoubtedly the most serious of all of Haiti's many national problems. Accordingly, the challenge is to rise above partisanship and adopt pragmatic ideas to help all learners. At the very least, the Haitian people, in dire need of a strong education, deserve to know what the policymakers think about education and what they propose to do about it.

Haitian education should go well beyond the status quo. Like the systems that govern it, Haitian education is dynamic but conservative. Despite the many educational reforms that Haiti has undertaken in the past, many changes still need to be made in Haitian schooling. Every school in Haiti (public or private) has different needs, but all schools should provide students with the educational foundation necessary for building a better future for the country. The Haitian government will have to participate in these efforts. At this juncture, it is necessary to examine the limited role of public education in a democratic society, and to provide national leadership and the greatest educational opportunities and innovations possible. However, the basic opportunities, innovations, and information that our students receive may come from various sectors and need to be allocated equally among all school age children from both public and private schools.

Conclusion

A participatory education that allows individuals to discuss issues freely and take appropriate action in order to better their own lives and those of others throughout the world is essential for Haiti. This form of education should emphasize critical, analytical, and creative thinking, humanistic values, and mutual respect between teachers and students that represent a quest for mutual humanization by students and teachers. For change to take place in Haitian education, people must first become aware of themselves and evaluate critically their social environment and

structures. Having raised their consciousness, Haitian learners can initiate actions to transform oppressing social structures. They will move
from passive objects to reflective and active subjects. They then can
"become actors in the reconstruction process of a new society."[28]

Have no doubt about it, the stakes are high in Haitian education. As
Archbishop Bakole Wa Ilunga of Zaire warned over a decade ago:

> The aim of education is not to provide a 'document' that will assure
> its possessor of a certain income and that often becomes a tool for
> getting a hold over others. The primary purpose of education is to
> form men and women capable of living in an increasingly compli-
> cated society and living in it in a worthy manner, capable of doing
> a job in it and providing services that call for ever greater compe-
> tence. An education and system of instruction that forms human
> beings is possible only if educators themselves are liberated.[29]

Because Haitians have had little experience with democracy, they
must create a democratic framework appropriate for their unique economic, social, cultural, and educational needs. Many educators and
policy-makers agree on at least a few principles. Democratization does
not mean privatization; that belief is critical at a time when many
Haitians are vigorously debating the future direction of the country's
educational system for social reconstruction.

The further development of the National Plan—Education 2004 must
include the following considerations:

— Development of a new political culture of democratization in Haiti
must be accompanied simultaneously by efforts to encourage an active
cultural and character education.

— Access to schools in rural areas is extremely limited for many
school-age children in Haiti. The Haitian government must build more
schools, learning facilities, and better roads, and provide free public
transportation and free or inexpensive lunches for school children. Books
and basic supplies such as paper and pencils must be provided to all children, as stipulated by the 1987 constitution.

— The nationwide literacy campaign should be improved and
expanded beyond the teaching of basic reading skills. It should be
designed to encourage Haitian peasants as well as urban dwellers to
become a functioning part of the economic development and democratization process. Literacy on a wide scale among all Haitians would help
ensure effective participation in the national development process.

—It is also important not to import prefabricated educational models. They can constitute deadly forces that may destroy the country, its culture, and its people. Even though a highly educated population is most likely to support vigorously the principles of democracy, in an underdeveloped country such as Haiti where education is for the privileged few, any systematic educational changes can be seen as a destabilizing force to the status quo.

—Haitians must take control of their destiny during this period of reconstruction. Democratization, national development, and education are processes that are not subject to preplanned short-term crisis solutions. Further analysis and a better understanding of these processes are needed in order to outline long-term strategies to ensure Haiti's progress.

Notes

1. Victor J. Cieutat et al., *Evaluation du Secteur de l'éducation et des Resources Humaines d'Haiti* (McLean, VA, 1986), 3–4.

2. Aaron Segal, "What's Wrong with Haiti? Can It Be Fixed?" Paper prepared for the Haitian Studies Association Conference (Boston, 1994), 7.

3. Anthony Giddens, *The Class Structure of the Advanced Societies* (New York, 1973), 103.

4. Cieutat et al., *Evaluation du Secteur,* 4–5.

5. See Uli Locher, "Primary Education in a Predatory State: Private Schools Take over Haiti," unpublished ms. (Boston, 1990), 2–5.

6. For an account of the dynamics among language, development, and schooling, see Rodrigue Jean, *Haiti: Crise de l'Éducation et Crise du Développement* (Port-au-Prince, 1988). See also François Latortue, *Système Educatif et Developpement: Le Problème de la Langue* (Port-au-Prince, 1988), 64–69.

7. See Marie B. Racine, "Adaptation of Haitian Students in American Schools," unpublished ms. (Washington, D.C., 1981), 1–10. See also Yves Déjean, *Dilemme en Haiti: Français en Péril ou Péril en Français* (Port-au-Prince, 1975), 40.

8. For a thorough discussion on the predatory nature of schooling in Haiti, see Locher, "Primary Education," 3–9.

9. Jacomina De Regt, "Basic Education in Haiti," in Albert Valdman and Charles Foster (eds.), *Haiti—Today and Tomorrow: An Interdisciplinary Study* (New York, 1984), 134.

10. See Locher, "Primary Education," 1–7.

11. For a thorough understanding of the strengths and weaknesses of the reforms initiated by Bernard, see Jean, Haiti, 95–107.

12. Donaldo Macedo, *Literacies of Power: What Americans Are Not Allowed to Know* (Boulder, 1994), 168.

13. De Regt, "Basic Education," 134.

14. Ulrich Fleischmann, "Language, Literacy and Underdevelopment," in Valdman and Foster (eds.), *Haiti,* 105–108.

15. Latortue, *Système Educatif et Développement,* 102.

16. See Léon Pamphile, "America's Policy-making in Haitian Education, 1915–1934," *Journal of Negro Education,* LIV (1985), 99–108.

17. Jean, *Haiti,* 19, trans. from the French by Marc Prou.

18. Jean, *Haiti,* 18.

19. Sidney Mintz, "Can Haiti Change?" *Foreign Affairs,* LXXIV (1995), 73.

20. Ibid., 85.

21. Jean, *Haiti,* 126.

22. Ibid., 127.

23. Ibid., 127–128.

24. For an understanding of the legal foundations of education in Haiti, refer to the 1987 constitution, which states:

> Article 32-1:
> Education is a responsibility of the state and the local communities. They must provide free schooling, accessible to all, and oversee the quality of teacher training in both public and private sectors.
> Article 32-2:
> The first responsibility of the state and the local communities is to undertake a massive schooling campaign, the only road toward national development. The state must encourage and facilitate private initiative in this domain. Translated from the French by Marc Prou.

25. Macedo, *Literacies of Power,* 170.

26. Cieutat et al., *Evaluation du Secteur de L'éducation,* 3-4.

27. Jean, *Haiti,* 126.

28. See Paolo Freire and Donaldo Macedo, *Literacy: Reading the World and Reading the Word* (New York, 1987), 159.

29. Bakole Wa Ilunga, *Paths of Liberation* (New York, 1984), 152.

About the Authors

Patrick Bellegarde-Smith is a professor of Africology at the University of Wisconsin-Milwaukee. He has written extensively on Haitian social thought and development. His latest book is *Haiti: The Breached Citadel* (Boulder, 1990).

Anthony V. Catanese is a professor of economics and management at DePauw University. His many publications focus on Haiti's rural poverty. His professional interest in Haiti and Haitians began in the early 1980s with a three-week stay in the rural northwest with DePauw students. Since then he has lived and worked in rural Haiti regularly. His interest in Haitians is now extending to Haitian-Americans' changing demographic characteristics.

Robert Fatton Jr. is a professor and associate chair in the Woodrow Wilson Department of Government and Foreign Affairs at the University of Virginia. He is the author of three books and numerous articles in scholarly journals. Born in Haiti, he is writing a book on the recent political history of the country.

Clive Gray is an institute fellow at the Harvard Institute for International Development (HIID). Since 1970 he has served as a resident director of HIID advisory projects in planning ministries and related agencies in Colombia, Ethiopia, Indonesia, and Morocco. Previously he carried out other resident assignments in Nigeria and Kenya. Gray has advised governments in those and other countries in Asia, Africa, Latin America, and eastern Europe on development policy.

Michel S. Laguerre teaches at the University of California, Berkeley. He is the author of ten books, including, *American Odyssey: Haitians in New York City* (Ithaca, 1984), *The Military and Society in Haiti* (Basingstoke, 1993), and *The Informal City* (Basingstoke, 1994). His new book, *Minoritized Space: An Inquiry into the Spatial Order of Things*, based on a series of lectures delivered at the University of Quebec at Montreal, is forthcoming.

Mats Lundahl has been a professor of development economics at the Stockholm School of Economics since 1987. He has published numerous articles on the Haitian economy and three books: *Peasants and Poverty: A Study of Haiti* (London, 1979); *The Haitian Economy: Man Land and Markets* (London, 1983); and *Politics or Markets? Essays on Haitian Underdevelopment* (London, 1992).

Robert Maguire is the representative for Haiti of the Inter-American Foundation, responsible for a program of grants in support of Haitian efforts for grassroots development. He is also the Haiti program coordinator of the Georgetown University Caribbean Project, and chair of the Advanced Area Studies Seminar on Haiti at the U.S. State Department's Foreign Service Institute. In 1994–1995, he was a visiting scholar at Johns Hopkins University. His publications on Haiti have addressed rural and grassroots development, civil society organizations, civil-military relations, migration, politics, and human social and economic relationships.

Jennifer McCoy is an associate professor of political science at Georgia State University and senior associate at the Carter Center in Atlanta. She has published numerous articles on democratization and economic reform in Latin America and on the role of international actors in processes of democratization. She is editor of and contributor to *Venezuelan Democracy Under Pressure* (New Brunswick, 1995). She was a member of the Carter Center's election observation delegation to Haiti in 1990.

William G. O'Neill is an international lawyer specializing in human rights and refugee law. He served as the director of the Legal Department of the OAS/UN International Civilian Mission in Haiti during 1993–1994 and has been a legal consultant to the UN Human Rights Field Operation in Rwanda and the National Coalition for Haitian Rights. From 1989 to 1993 he was deputy director of the Lawyers Committee for Human Rights in New York. He has written extensively on human rights and international relations.

Robert A. Pastor is a professor of political science at Emory University and director of the Latin American and Caribbean Program at the Carter Center. He advised the Carter-Nunn-Powell delegation to Haiti in September 1994 and observed elections in Haiti in 1990 and 1995. He is the author of ten books and more than two hundred articles on U.S. foreign policy, democratization, and Latin America.

Marc Prou is an assistant professor of bilingual education and Caribbean studies at the University of Massachusetts, Boston. He has extensive teaching and research experience in bilingual education and Haitian immigrant students in U.S. public schools. His areas of specialization include bilingual education, curriculum development, cultural diversity, and sociolinguistics and national development. Prou is a founding member of the Haitian Studies Project and is currently the director of the Haitian Creole Language Institute at the University of Massachusetts.

Robert I. Rotberg is the president of the World Peace Foundation, a research associate at the Harvard Institute for International Development, and a teacher at the Kennedy School of Government. Rotberg was professor of political science and history at the Massachusetts Institute of Technology from 1968 to 1987 and then became academic vice president of Tufts University and president of Lafayette College. He is the author of a number of books and articles on the politics of Africa and Haiti. He wrote *Haiti: The Politics of Squalor* (Boston, 1971).

Donald E. Schulz is a professor of national security affairs at the Strategic Studies Institute, U.S. Army War College. He is the coauthor of *Reconciling the Irreconcilable: The Troubled Outlook for U.S. Policy Toward Haiti* (Carlisle Barracks, PA, 1994).

Michel-Rolph Trouillot is the Krieger-Eisenhower Professor of Anthropology and director of the Institute for Global Studies in Culture, Power, and History at Johns Hopkins University. His books include *Haiti: State Against Nation* (New York, 1990).

The World Peace Foundation

THE WORLD PEACE FOUNDATION was created in 1910 by the imagination and fortune of Edwin Ginn, the Boston publisher, to encourage international peace and cooperation. The Foundation seeks to advance the cause of world peace through study, analysis, and the advocacy of wise action. As an operating, not a grant-giving foundation, it provides financial support only for projects which it has initiated itself.

Edwin Ginn shared the hope of many of his contemporaries that permanent peace could be achieved. That dream was denied by the outbreak of World War I, but the Foundation has continued to attempt to overcome obstacles to international peace and cooperation, drawing for its funding on the endowment bequeathed by the founder. In its early years, the Foundation focused its attention on building the peacekeeping capacity of the League of Nations, and then on the development of world order through the United Nations. The Foundation established and nurtured the premier scholarly journal in its field, *International Organization,* now in its forty-ninth year.

From the 1950s to the early 1990s, mostly a period of bipolar conflict when universal collective security remained unattainable, the Foundation concentrated its activities on improving the working of world order mechanisms, regional security, transnational relations, and the impact of public opinion on American foreign policy. From 1980 to 1993 the Foundation published nineteen books and seven reports on Third World security; on South Africa and other states of southern Africa; on Latin America, the Caribbean, and Puerto Rico; on migration; and on the international aspects of traffic in narcotics. In 1994 and 1995, the Foundation published books on Europe after the Cold War; on the United States, southern Europe, and the countries of the Mediterranean basin; and on reducing the world traffic in conventional arms control.

The Foundation is now focusing its energies and resources on a series of interrelated projects entitled Preventing Intercommunal Conflict and Humanitarian Crises. These projects proceed from the assumption that large-scale human suffering, wherever it occurs, is a serious and continuing threat to the peace of the world, both engendering and resulting from ethnic, religious, and other intrastate and cross-border conflicts. The Foundation is examining how the forces of world order may most effectively engage in preventive diplomacy, create early warning systems leading to early preventive action, achieve regional conflict avoidance, and eradicate the underlying causes of intergroup enmity and warfare.

Index

235